CH01429435

THE TWO ARCTICS

Their Peoples and Their Problems

Professor Eric R McVicar

To my Grandchildren, in the hope that their world becomes better than the one they inherited from my generation.

CONTENTS

TWO ARCTICS, THEIR PEOPLES AND THEIR PROBLEMS.

A teenage girl looks east across the frozen sea to watch the sun rise above the horizon.

It is the first day that the sun has come above the horizon since the previous autumn.

The place is the Inuit town of Uummannaq, on the island of the same name. Positioned 300 miles north of the Arctic Circle, off Greenland's west coast, Uummannaq - which in the Greenlandic Inuit language means 'heart shaped mountain'- is the central hub for the population of around 2200 people who live in the settlements around the fjord.

The girl is not alone. Her name is Pipaluk, and around her are many of the other occupants of the town, turned out - as they have done for many years - to welcome the sun which brings light after the dark long night of the Arctic winter.

But this year is different from the past. The sun has come two days earlier than its traditional appearance day.

The reason is that the icecap on the mainland of Greenland has decreased to such an extent that the sun is able to be seen earlier than in previous years.

Greenland is melting.......

-------It may be in our lifetime, or that of our children, that the glaciers will vanish. Life will go on, species will adapt and evolve. But what of the near future and its effect on the indigenous people of the North? What is likely to happen or is already happening?

PREFACE

Back in the 1970s, Professor James Lovelock came up with his "Gaia" theory. This put forward the view that Planet Earth could be regarded as one large living organism. If it was injured, by say man's inability to control population growth, the overall life form of the planet would find a way to resolve the problem. In the past, plagues, famines and wars all played a part in human control indicating that his theory did in a way stand up to scrutiny.

So, if we view "Gaia" as correct, where in this super-organism does the Arctic fit in and what part does it play?

Looking at animal life-forms, whether fish, reptile, bird or mammal, all have one thing in common. They all have hearts. This is where the Arctic Ocean fits. It is the planet's heart.

If we take a look at the annual cycle in the Arctic Ocean, we see clearly that it is one of two distinct physical changes. First, as the sun moves out of view and winter approaches the Arctic Ocean freezes, then in the spring, when the sun returns, the ice starts to melt. This, of course, is because not only does the Earth rotate around the Sun but it is also rotating daily, but around an axis which is not perpendicular to that of the elliptical orbit it takes around the sun. This means that in winter the North Pole is in total darkness and in summer it has twenty four hours daylight.

This Freezing/Melting cycle is the single, annual heartbeat which helps to drive the deep ocean current known as the "Deep Ocean Conveyor" which encircles the planet and passes through every ocean. It is estimated that if a molecule of water from the summer melt joins this deep current at the northern icecap it will be a millennia before it returns to refreeze in the Arctic Ocean. The planetary heart that is the Arctic Ocean may beat very slowly but like any heart, if it is to remain healthy, we must take care of it and that we are failing to do in a spectacular fashion.

The often gale lashed North Atlantic not only separates Europe from North America, it also creates two very different Arctic climates. The Cold Arctic is the home of the Inuit of Canada and Greenland while the Warm Arctic is the home of the Sami people of Northern Norway, Sweden, Finland and the Kola Peninsula of Russia.

But before we look at these two amazing, resilient peoples we first have to define what we mean by Arctic. We must also look at why there are two Arctics. We also need to look at what causes this difference and why does what happens in this far off remote region have serious implications for every living species on this tiny planet we call home. At this time in the history of our universe Planet Earth is the only planet we have. Unlike in human medicine we cannot have an Arctic Heart Transplant so let us look at what exactly this Arctic Heart is.

The Arctic can be defined in many ways, each of which is correct within its own context and yet can be at great variance with the other accepted definitions of Arctic.

The most easily defined and probably the most generally accepted and understood definition of the Arctic is that of "the area north of the Arctic Circle". It is also the most geometric and geographic definition.

The 'Arctic Circle' is the imaginary geographic line of latitude north at which there is at least one twenty four hour period where the sun does not drop below the horizon during the summer (the summer solstice) and, conversely, there is at least one twenty four hour period during the winter in which the sun does not come above the horizon, (the winter solstice).

Currently the 'Arctic Circle' - the latitude at which the midnight sun, or " Midnatsol", as my Norwegian friends call it, is found - is around 66deg 33min north. This occurs around the 20th of June and on this latitude the twenty four hours of darkness is around the 21st of December.

The second way in which the Arctic is defined relates to permafrost.

Permafrost, by definition, is a "thick subsurface layer of soil that remains below freezing point throughout the year".

This may be a satisfactory and suitable definition of "Arctic Zone" where countries such as Canada, Russia and Greenland are concerned. However parts of Norway and land areas such as the Himalayas in Asia or the frozen regions of the South American Andes have vast areas of permafrost. Located far from either the Arctic or Antarctic, it is only the altitude of both the Himalaya and the Andes that cause them to have permanent zones remaining frozen throughout the year. Norway, however, is a very different case.

Norwegian territories such as the Svalbard Archipelago and the islands of Jan Mayen, in the north west Atlantic, and Bjornoya, or Bear Island, which is situated north of Norway but south of Svalbard, are undoubtedly well within both the Arctic Circle and the areas of permafrost and therefore must be termed Arctic.

Mainland Norway is very different from these territories. For although it has a large landmass which is north of the Arctic Circle, this area has little in the way of permafrost. Indeed, Norway's largest area with permafrost is the Hardangervidda Plateau, in the south west of the country, inland from the famous Fjordland. Another point to note is that the largest glacier, the Saltfjellet- Svartison Glacier, drains into a fjord just a few miles south of the Arctic Circle. Whereas the Svartison Glacier can undoubtedly be regarded as part of Arctic Norway the Hardangervidda Plateau, which is separated by hundreds of miles of permafrost free lands south of the Arctic Circle, cannot.

Yet another definition of Arctic is that of the 10oC Isotherm. This definition is simple. It includes all areas north of a line where the mean July temperature does not exceed 10oC at sea level. This definition manages to remove most of Northern Norway and the southern half of Russia's Kola

Peninsula from the Arctic classification. Basically, it leaves the Varanger area of Finnmarken as the only part of mainland Norway defined as Arctic, while on the western side of the Atlantic it reaches as far south as the Grand Banks off Newfoundland. The Grand Banks are notably on the same latitude as Cornwall and Southern Ireland.

It is also possible to define the Arctic in terms of vegetation using the northern extremity of tree growth as the southern boundary of the Arctic. As can be seen on many of the maps used by students of both geography and botany , this can extend as far south as the entrance to James Bay, the inlet at the southern end of Hudson's Bay in Canada, or as far north as Finnmarken in Norway.

Boundaries are, of course, not only confined to land but also apply to the marine environment. One such natural boundary is where the low salinity cold water flowing south out of the Arctic Ocean interfaces with highly saline warm water heading north. In the case of the North Atlantic, this can be viewed as where the north east flowing remnant of the Gulf Stream, more correctly termed the North Atlantic Drift, interfaces with the cold water coming down the Fram Strait. This equates to 65oN on the Greenland coast and about 80oN west of Svalbard.

It is really up to the individual to decide which of these definitions or combination of definitions to use. But in addition to these climatic and geographic limits can be added political and cultural definitions of Arctic. For the purposes of this book, it is this last measure that will be used. So, our definition of the 'Cold Arctic' is the area of Eastern Canada and Greenland occupied by the indigenous Inuit. Our 'Warm Arctic' is the area of Norway, Sweden, Finland and Russia inhabited by the Sami people.

The reason I have chosen the areas inhabited by two groups of culturally very different indigenous peoples is that they have both survived in this harsh environment for millennia in harmony with what nature has provided. It was only once their way of life was altered by what we often term "civilised people" that they had any adverse impact on their surroundings.

Unfortunately, they are the first victims of "civilisation's excesses".

This book is not meant to be read as a complete history of these people, nor is it a complete record of the problems being faced not only by the Sami and the Inuit, but the planet as a whole. It is merely an insight into their way of life and how modern civilisation, with its excesses of consumerism, population growth and self interest, is impacting on not only their historic cultures but also their very existence.

The Gulf Stream

The main reason that we have two different "Arctic" climates is the ocean current often referred to as the Gulf Stream, but by the time its flow reaches the North Atlantic, east of Nova Scotia, it should be more correctly named the 'North Atlantic Drift'. This ocean current acts as a massive heat source which contributes around forty percent of the energy needed to maintain the thermal differential in winter temperatures between the east coast of the American continent and the much warmer west coast of Northern Europe. Although it officially starts at the point where it leaves the Gulf of Mexico and is joined by north flowing Antilles Current, its origins start much further south. It eventually diffuses well into the Arctic waters to the north west of the Svalbard Archipelago and east towards Franz Josef Land.

The first chapter tries to explain what this current is, how and why it functions and the effects it has on our marine life.

THE GULF STREAM

If I stand in front of a lecture theatre full of intelligent students and ask them if they think that the sun rises in the east and sets in the west it can be guaranteed that, on most occasions, all of them will say yes. So why do I bother asking such a stupid question?

On the surface it may seem to be a stupid question, but in reality it is not.

The fact is that the sun only 'appears' to rise in the east and set in the west. As far as our solar system is concerned the sun is the "constant". It is the centre and is the fixed point about which all our planets circle or orbit. Add to this the fact that the Earth itself rotates about an axis which runs through the planet from the true North Pole to the true South Pole in a west to east direction and we have the illusion that the sun "rises" in the east and "sets" in the west.

It is misunderstandings like this that make life difficult for scientists teaching adult members of the public who have ideas planted in their minds from childhood. Children under the age of ten are much more responsive to new ideas, as we all know. The well-known saying, with regards to computers: "If you can't sort the problem, ask a ten year old!" has more than a grain of truth.

The fact that we rotate around an axis which is offset and that the planet itself is in turn (pardon the pun) rotating around our sun, is the reason we have ocean currents and tides. Added to this rather complicated set of circumstances, we have the added effect of the gravitational effect of our moon. Our moon may be much smaller than the sun but - due to its much closer proximity to the earth - its effects on tidal movements are much greater than that of the sun. It is important at this stage to understand that although tides and currents do in many cases work together, they are very separate entities which operate independently. Before going into the intricacies of ocean currents, we will briefly look at how tides function.

Tides

Tides are the result of the gravitational forces of the moon and sun interacting with the rotation of the earth. As the orbit and distances of both the earth and the moon from the sun are constantly changing the combined gravitational forces of the sun and moon on the earth's surface water is constantly changing. Maximum pull is exerted when the moon and sun are in alignment. This creates the monthly "spring" tides, the greatest of which occur around the spring and autumn equinox when earth's elliptical orbit is closest to the sun. The smallest tidal ranges occur when the moon and sun are at their furthest apart, i.e. the moon is on the opposite side of earth from the sun, and this creates the small "neep" tides. Both "spring" and "neep" tides occur twice every lunar month.

Ocean Currents.

No doubt many of us will have encountered the suicidal drowned insect in our drink. Whether it is coffee, tea, beer or any exotic creation from the bar, they all have one thing in common, other than the base ingredient being water. That common factor is that the damned insect will, in more than 90% of cases, commit suicide on the side next to your mouth. Where I live on the west coast of Scotland, it can be reasonably assumed that in August the insect will be a species with the imposing scientific name of Culicoides impunctatis, better known as the "midgie". But, no matter what the species of insect, they will have one thing in common and that is that, whatever direction you rotate the cup or glass, the said dead insect remains firmly in position directly adjacent to your parched mouth. This happens because as you turn the cup or glass the gravity induced inertia of the fluid tends to hold all but the outermost layers of molecules exactly where they are. The molecules of liquid in contact with the glass are, however, different from the glass and therefore have a different coefficient of friction which enables them to rotate like ball bearings and move along with the glass (or cup if you are, like me, a non-beer drinker.).

The fact remains, the dead insect is still there. Result, either do the "macho man" thing and swallow the added protein or remove the insect.

What this has to do with ocean currents is relatively easy to explain and hopefully understand.

Let us try to envisage planet earth as a beer-glass. This time, however, the beer is on the outside, conveniently held on by gravity. If we then rotate the glass from west to east the beer will remain exactly where it is. But, to a bacterium lodged on the inside of our dirty beer glass, the beer will appear to be flowing east to west. Same as you lot thinking the sun rises in the east and sets in the west. Easy mistake to make!

So what happens when there is, very inconveniently, a great land mass in the way is that things start to get very complicated.

At the Equator - north and south of it, that is - parallel currents flow in what appears to be (but we now know that in reality they don't) an East to West direction. These currents are warmed by the sun which is directly overhead as the equator is the nearest part of our planet to the sun at midday – but, due to the great depth of the ocean, it does not get excessively warm. What happens next, in the case of the Atlantic Ocean, is that these equatorial currents crash into South America.

Where the South Equatorial current crashes into Brazil, just like the bows of a ship, it splits the oncoming flow into two divergent currents, one flowing northwest, the other flowing southwest towards the Argentinean coast.

The north-west flowing leg of this soon joins the North Equatorial current. Not only does this increase the overall mass of the flow, it also increases its total enthalpy, which is its total heat content. (See definition of enthalpy).

The north-west flow, with this much increased volume, flows towards the relatively shallower waters of the Caribbean Sea. But, such is the volume and surface width of this flow that it cannot all enter the island restricted southern approach of the Caribbean basin. The northerly portion of the flow is diverted to the east of these barrier islands to become the Antilles Current.

Once inside the Caribbean and Gulf of Mexico, the heat of the sun raises the temperature and it expands. Since it can only expand in an upward direction, with the exception to the strait between the Florida Peninsula and the island of Cuba, this is where the rapidly increasing flow goes. This, now east flowing, current flows outwards into the Atlantic Ocean. Once there it is again joined by the north flowing remnant of the Antilles Current near the Bahamas. From here on it is known as the Gulf Stream and - now assisted by the south westerly trade winds - it heads north east, holding in its fifty mile width the heat that controls the climate all the way to Arctic Norway and beyond.

Logic tells us that with this vast ocean ahead it should diffuse and slow down. But it doesn't! To understand why this is not the case we start by looking back at our drowned fly, the water wants to stay where it is. But where it is the seabed is moving at great speed in an easterly direction. This in turn tries to squeeze the clockwise North Atlantic Surface Gyre over to the west. This has the effect of squeezing the north flowing Gulf Stream into a narrow corridor along the eastern seaboard of the USA. As water is to most intents and purposes incompressible, the only way it can cope with the incoming volume from the south is increase the velocity. Simple physics! The faster it travels, the more volume gets through the restriction in a given time (a bit like queues at the New Year sales!).

The speed at which it runs north along the coast of Carolina is often in excess of ten knots. This 'sling-shot' effect gives it enough momentum to reach the other side of the Atlantic. However, before it reaches the other side many things happen. First of all, when it reaches a position south-east of Newfoundland and at a longitude directly between St John in Newfoundland and Cape Farewell on Greenland, it meets the very cold south-flowing Labrador Current which originates away to the north in the area between Greenland and Baffin Island, beyond the Arctic Circle. This current is fed constantly by the icebergs which calf from some of the world's largest glaciers in area of North West Greenland and Ellesmere Island. This is supplemented by the south flowing current to the east of Greenland which curls round to the south of Cape Farewell to enter Baffin Bay via the east side of the Davis Strait. By the time it travels anti-clockwise around Baffin Bay to spill south as the Labrador Current along the eastern coast of Canada it annually carries many thousands of icebergs. The area off Labrador and Newfoundland it is aptly named Iceberg Alley. It was in this area that the 'Titanic' met its fate back in 1912.

Now, common sense tells us that when very cold water meets warm water the temperature of the warm water will drop significantly. But that is not what happens here. Despite being less salty, which if both currents were the same temperature would make it less dense, this cold water is much denser than the warm water of the Gulf Stream and so it sinks beneath it to continue into the depths of the North Atlantic. From here, this cold water joins the Deep Ocean Conveyer which continually circumnavigates all the world's oceans. According to one source, for a complete circuit of this system to travel all the oceans takes a thousand years.

One effect of the meeting of these two currents is to create what is termed the 'front' where banks of dense fog occur, caused by the warm moisture in the air above the cold water condensing.

It was in this area that the ill-fated Titanic hit an iceberg during its maiden voyage. The chances of this being repeated are constantly decreasing due to a combination of improved navigational aids such as radar and the fact that, due to climate change, sea temperatures are rising. Most icebergs have melted before they reach south of Newfoundland Banks.

Just how sharp the change in surface temperatures is was clearly demonstrated by the US Coast Guard Frigate Tampa. During a patrol of the 'front', or as it is also termed the 'cold wall', scientists aboard recorded temperature readings from both bow and stern as the captain carefully positioned the vessel to straddle the line of the 'cold wall'. At the bow the recorded temperature was 33oF (1oC) while at the stern the recorded temperature was 56oF (12oC). Such differences over the length of a relatively small naval vessel clearly indicate just how immiscible the waters of the two currents are due to density differentials. At 1oC a human will only survive a few minutes before hypothermia sets in. At 12oC survival time is greatly enhanced. So if you do become a MOB, i.e. man overboard in this vicinity just make sure you choose the right end of the ship to fall off. As already stated it is this phenomena that causes the Grand banks to be one of the worlds foggiest places with air temperature differentials of up to 50oF being recorded at points only five miles apart. The warm air from the south condenses just like steam coming off a bath when it collides with the frigid air of the Labrador Current.

The next thing that has an effect on what now should be termed the North Atlantic Drift, or NAD as oceanographers tend to call it, is that parts of its southern side flow peel off to join the North Atlantic Gyre. What is left then continues east and north towards Europe.

Somewhere between south of Iceland and Great Britain, the driving force of the Gulf Stream begins to lessen but the current still carries on to the north-east, all the way to the Arctic Ocean. What actually keeps this massive body of relatively warm water flowing toward Northern Europe is the fact that the sea ice of the Arctic Ocean forms then melts on an annual cycle.

When sea water ice forms, it leaves out salts - a process known as brine exclusion. When this process is allied to the process of evaporative cooling, where the salinity is increased and the result is the formation of water that is still liquid at a temperature where it would normally freeze. This colder, denser water then sinks to join the deep ocean conveyor. (This process is similar to the convective action of a lava lamp.)

This sinking flow, known as cold water chimneys, creates a suction effect which then "draws" the warmer surface waters north. If one thinks of a waterfall where the surface water downstream is drawn toward the fall and you get an idea of what is happening, but on an immensely larger scale. Hence the North Atlantic Drift continues all the way north to the Barents Sea and Western Svalbard, 80oN.

This is why temperatures on the European side of the Atlantic are much higher, at any given latitude, than those on the American side. Hence the Sami of North Troms and parts of Finnmark can keep livestock and grow a limited variety of crops. The Inuit of Eastern Canada and Greenland, on the same latitude, cannot grow food and would be totally dependant on a "hunter – gatherer" existence if it were not for the "white-man's" economy based influence.

This is why we have two Arctics: The cold Arctic of the Inuit and the warm Arctic of the Sami. But for those of us who come from a modern, industrialised society to understand these indigenous people and understand the detrimental impact that modern industrialised society is having upon them we have to ask ourselves the following questions.

1)   Who are the Sami?

2)   Sami Issues in Modern Times - how were they resolved?

3)   What effect is climate change having on their

lives and their environment?

      4)   Who are the Inuit?

      5)   What effect is climate change having on their lives and their environment?

      6)   Is there one single root cause of what is happening in our two Arctics?

      7)   If there is a root cause, what can we do to sort it?

The primary objective of this book is to inform and, educate those who are genuinely concerned about our planet and what type of future our grandchildren will face. Hopefully the following chapters can address and give answers to these questions and also give some insight into the problem that these people have faced over past millennia. More recent problems, often politically motivated, are also discussed and possible solutions given.

Note: - Enthalpy—A thermodynamic quantity equivalent to the total heat content of a system. It is equal to the internal energy of the system plus the product of pressure and volume.

WHO ARE THE SAMI?

The modern Sami people are thought to be direct descendants of the Komsa people who first inhabited the Arctic regions of what are now known as Norway, Sweden, Finland and the Kola Peninsula in Russia. Archaeological discoveries indicate that they first reached the North Coast as far back as eight or ten thousand years ago in the wake of the retreating ice age. This indicates that the modern Sami can view themselves as one of the oldest surviving cultures on the planet. Their isolation on the edge of the then known world in some way helped preserve their way of life which pre-dates many better known cultures such as the ancient Egyptians or Assyrians.

Initially, these people were undoubtedly hunter-gatherers but indications that they soon became involved in small-scale farming activities are evident. As all the materials used by the earliest of these Arctic dwellers were biodegradable, there is little in terms of archaeological remains. What do remain are the remnants of 'pitfall' traps and drive lane systems for diverting herds of reindeer into the traps, or in some cases over cliffs. Although this latter type of hunting would undoubtedly have caused suffering among the deer which fell victim, it meant that an even cull of adults and juveniles was taken. In some cases rows of cairns stretched for miles to funnel the deer toward the killing area. Elsewhere petroglyphs, drawings on the rock structure, are found in modern day Finland as well as along the north coast of Norway. The largest and most impressive collection of rock art in Europe is undoubtedly at Alta in the Finnmark Province of Arctic Norway. The Alta drawings clearly illustrate a way of life involving activities such as hunting reindeer and fishing using boats which would eventually evolve into the renowned Viking longships. The position of these drawings relative to where sea level was in post glacial times has helped date their origin to circa 5000 BC. The oldest drawings are at the highest level and predate the lowest drawings by around three thousand years. The reason for this is that as the weight of the glacial ice reduced Scandanavia began to rise out of the sea faster than the sea level rose from the melt water. This classic example of what scientists term "tectonic rebound" is also noticeable on the west coast of Scotland and the Isles of the Hebrides. In the Scottish case it is in the form of raised beaches. The carvings at Alta Fjord were only discovered in 1973 and are now classified as a UNESCO World Heritage Site.

What I find very difficult to grasp is the fact that many Norwegians that I have spoken to insist that the Sami Culture is less than two thousand years old. On one occasion I was buying a book on Sami Origins in a bookshop in Tromso when the shop owner told me, quite seriously, that the book was complete nonsense and nothing but Sami propaganda. What I found even more astonishing was that the proprietor of this particular bookshop appeared to be of Italian origin. Maybe the thought of the Sami Culture being not only much older than that of the Romans but that unlike the Roman Culture it had endured much longer.

Dilution of the original culture occurred and

assimilation with other later arrivals over millennia continued right through to well within historic times.

Wild reindeer in the interior, fish in abundance in the rivers, lakes and coastal waters, shellfish in the tidal zones. From the land, berries such as cloudberries and blueberries were plentiful and a valuable source of vitamin C. These were the main food sources and so it remained for thousands of years. Even the design of the traditional Sami "Gamme" house made out birch boughs and covered in turf survived well into the twentieth century with surviving examples now being used as tourist attractions.

In around 100AD, the famous Roman writer and historian, Tacitus, described the people he called the "Fenni". These "primitive people", he stated, "dressed in animal skins and slept on the ground". They may have appeared "primitive" to Tacitus, who was more accustomed to toga-wearing Romans, but these people were perfectly equipped to survive in their natural northerly environment.

They are also mentioned in writings from the earliest decades of the eighth century. In these texts, it is obvious that they are wearing what are clearly skis, as they are noted to be hunting over snow covered ground while wearing curved pieces of wood strapped to their feet, even older evidence of skiing are indicated on rock drawings. It is obvious from these texts that the Sami we know today have been around the Arctic since, in effect, before the dawn of modern civilisation.

The Sami never created a state system but, nevertheless, they did have a much organised society based on a social unit system known as the Siida.

The Siida was an area of land alongside a river, fjord or lake large enough to support a group of up to around a dozen families, which were usually related. This was a communal area where each family had different living zones dependant on the season of the year. The Siida council decided how these resources would be assigned for harvesting throughout the seasons so as to retain the sustainability of these resources. This applied to all the assets, whether grazing, berry harvests, fish or wildlife.

Towards the end of the middle ages, the stocks of wild reindeer - and probably other wildlife resources - started to decline. The reason for the decline was not due to Sami hunting but due to the impact of southern races using the deerskins as a source of leather for clothing. All the southern races which are now the dominant races in the area by then were setting up settlements and trading posts in the Sami territories. It was around this time that some of the inland siidas started to semi-domesticate the reindeer in small herds. As the herds grew in size, more grazing land was needed to sustain them and this led to changes in the Sami social system. The divergence of the Sami into groups which either "owned" reindeer herds, or not, led eventually to the establishment of the system we have today.

More grazing land was needed to sustain the increase in grazing pressure, meaning that no single Siida had enough grazing. From this, the semi-nomadic practice of moving the herds from the inland plains to the coast and back was born. This annual movement, based on the reindeer's breeding cycle, meant that herds had to cross many siidas. This led initially to the decline in the siida system of old but, in its place, a new social structure emerged. This new structure was one which was mutually beneficial to all groups of Sami peoples. Firstly it enabled the nomadic reindeer herders to seek shelter with settled groups during the migrations. It also meant that trade on a barter system thrived. Reindeer products such as meat, skins and bone, all of which the other groups used, were exchanged. In return, the herders would receive dried or smoked fish and woollen products from the coastal or Sea- Sami who, by this time, were small-scale farmers. The Sami groups living along river valleys such as the Tana, (or Deatnu, in Sami-) or Alta-Kautokeino - which were highly prolific salmon rivers - traded cured fish and berries. This barter system also allowed the various Sami groups to inter-marry which, in turn, prevented the problems faced by many indigenous peoples regarding genetic diversity.

Another reason that the siida system declined was external pressure from other cultures colonising what previously had been exclusively Sami land.

Norwegians, Swedes, Finns and Russians all contributed to the decline. Even as late as the 18th century incomers impacted on the Sami land and culture. However the Kvens, an ethnic group from the Gulf of Bothnia area of the Baltic, very much integrated with the Sami. This group, who migrated north because of a prolonged period of famine in the 18th century, have similar origins to that of the Sami. The Kven culture is still very much in evidence in the north east of Finnmark, in the Varanger Peninsula towns of Vardo and Vadso. The Kvens were the last people to settle Sapmi in any meaningful numbers but, unlike the Norwegians and Swedes, they settled as neighbours as opposed to overlords and governors.

One further barter trade that functioned from as early as the 13th century was that of dried fish for grain. Although a limited variety of vegetables can be grown in the fertile areas, such as the Manndalen and Storfjord areas of North Troms where it is possible to grow both potatoes and carrots, it is not possible to grow grain crops. In the most northerly areas only very resilient vegetables or berries can give a viable crop.

Dried fish were traded for grain as part of the Hanseatic League trading which saw large quantities of dried cod heading south to Bergen from northern areas such as Lofoten Islands and Troms from around 1400 to 1800. This trade was dominated by German-speaking merchants who dominated trade in both the Baltic and North Sea areas at that time.

The drying racks shown in the picture are at Svolvaer on the Lofoten Islands, with today's dried fish trade being mainly to Spain and Africa.

Later on, in the 18th and 19th centuries, the most northerly areas of Sapmi, Finnmark and North Troms established a trade with Russian merchants known as the Pomora.

This Pomor trade was based mainly on fish and dried meat for barley or rye, known as 'Russian Flour',

But, where possible, coffee, sugar and salt were also traded as 'luxury goods'.

SAMI BELIEFS

From around 1700 the Sami culture - across the whole of what was Sapmi - was under intense pressure, nowhere more so than in Norway, where a programme of "Norwegianisation" was being introduced. Attempts to remove the Sami culture using the church, education and the law were being rigorously implemented.

The Sami religion, like those of many other indigenous Arctic races, was that of Animistic Shamanism. The word Shaman is a Tungus term which found its way into other European languages via Russian. Many Sami communities still retain remnants of this culture by having members of their communities who act as 'pain takers'. As I have had first hand experience of this practice when I suffered toothache while staying with Sami friends in a remote area of North Troms, I would certainly not discount the practice lightly.

The Sami religion contains many gods who steer the powers of nature in many different ways. The manner in which the gods were working was interpreted by the Shamans, who were known as Noaids. This was totally contrary to Christian beliefs and, on the arrival of Christian missionaries; an edict was issued that a man's consciousness could only be ruled by one god. That god, needless to say, was Jesus Christ.

Before the arrival of Christianity, the Sami religion had evolved from the hunter's relationship to his prey and the natural world surrounding both hunter and prey. A similar situation existed among both the North American Inuit and the First Nations People of the Pacific coast of Canada.

The wind god, Bieggaalmaj, sent warming or chilling

winds to help the Sami and was given sacrifices of appeasement. Other gods gave different elements to daily life. The most important of these gods was the Sun god, which brought heat to melt the snow and ice. Its light and warmth brought life to nature. The Thunder god was the mightiest. It could light up the night sky or set fire to the forest, but also brought rain, without which nothing would grow. Every aspect of Sami life had a designated god to whom the Noaids could turn to for intervention or help.

In daily life the Noaids were ordinary members of the community. However, if hunger or illness entered the community, the Noaid would - with the aid of the sacred drum - work himself, or herself, into a state of trance. Once in this state of entrancement, the Noaid took on the spirit of an animal being freed from time and space. From this position the Noaid became the intermediary of the gods. The sacred drum carried by the shaman was also used to lead the singing of the Sami folk song known as jojking.

The 'Jojk' is a singing style where the melody and verse are of equal importance. Improvised while being sung, it expresses the feelings of the singer, whether love or sorrow or even hate. By singing Jojk, the singer identifies himself with someone or something. So close is the song to the spirit of the person or object that the singer does not sing 'about' the subject but is deemed to be Jojking the subject. Many young men will Jojk their dearest who, in turn, will say they have been 'Joiked'.

The fact that the Noaid sang Jojk and drummed himself into a trance to reach religious ecstasy did not go down well with the higher echelons of either government or church. This led to Jojking being branded as the 'Song of the Devil' and, subsequently, it was banned and remained banned until into the second half of the twentieth century.

Today, thankfully, things have changed and both Sami radio and TV channels regularly broadcast Jojking competitions. Many of the younger participants are accompanied by modern instruments such as guitars, the music being influenced by modern western music. Many of the Sami people who now entertain tourists who arrive in coaches at modern Sami Lavvu attractions will demonstrate the Jojk.

Suppression of Sami shamanism in Norway was brutal and, from 1691 when Sami Shaman Lars Nillson was burned at the stake in Sweden, many Sami were executed for witchcraft. The area around Alta was notorious for its burning of Sami Shaman and ill treatment of the Sami population in general. It was only in the 1840s, when a Swedish Lutheran pastor named Lars Levi Laestadeus, who was himself part Sami, worked in a sympathetic manner with the Sami people that Christianity was accepted by the Sami. Despite this apparent conversion, many communities have, as already stated, retained Shamanistic traditions as part of their local culture.

Laestadeus preached in Northern Sweden and the Finnmarken district of Norway in the years between 1825 and 1861. There are still many communities in Northern Norway, Finland and Sweden where Laestadian congregations worship. The Laestadian movement reached North America in the 1860s when immigrants from Finland, including those of Sami extraction, settled in the areas around the Great Lakes. The first formalised congregations were established in Cokato, Minnesota, in 1872, followed soon after at Calumet, Michigan, in 1873. In 2009 there were 29 registered Laestadian Lutheran Church in the United States and Canada, served by nearly 70 registered lay preachers.

In some ways, these were very similar to the Scottish Free Church which is regarded as ultra conservative. Strict Laestadeans disapprove of such things as birth control, make up and dancing, which are viewed as conduct unbecoming of children of God. Thankfully, this religious persecution and attempted eradication of the Sami culture is a thing of the past and within the last few decades a much more multicultural Norway has emerged.

WHAT'S IN A NAME?

Lapps, Finns or Sami?

In English the word 'Finn' means someone from Finland. However, in earlier times it meant coming from Finnmark, or Finnmarken, the area which now forms the most northerly district of modern Norway. The term Lapp was the name applied to the indigenous people of Lapland, or Lappmarken, which is the northern area of present day Finland.

For many centuries these indigenous people were regarded as "primitive, barely human," according to their political masters and were treated very much as second class citizens. During these centuries of what would now be termed oppression, the term Lapp or Finn was used in a disparaging manner and it is only in recent times that the term Sami, derived from their own word Samit, has replaced the older names which, until very recently, still carried a stigma.

To give a better idea of how badly these indigenous people were treated and how little worth was placed on their lives and culture, one has only got to look back at the 17th century. Silver deposits were discovered in the area of Nasafjall, on the Swedish-Norwegian border in what is now Nordland, which at the time was under Swedish control. The Swedish administration of the time enslaved the local Sami population as forced labour to mine the ore. Not only did they use the people, they also took their domesticated reindeer to transport the silver bearing ore, the deer being used as one would have used draught or pit ponies elsewhere. Those Sami who refused to co-operate were keel hauled under the ice as an example.

That was just the beginning of the Swedish state's systematic claim to the forests, rivers and mineral rights in the regions where the Sami people had lived in harmony with nature for millennia.

The Sami are Northern Scandinavia's indigenous people. When Sapmi was colonised by the Swedes, Norwegians, Finns and Russians, much of the old established reindeer grazing lands were lost. With the loss of these lands, went much of the Sami history and cultural inheritance. The damage caused to the Sami through taxation, racism, and ruthless exploitation will take a long time to heal. We must, therefore, try to remember and acknowledge the fact that the history of Scandinavia started many millennia before the arrival of the Vikings.

THE SAMI AND THE VIKINGS

Whenever Vikings are mentioned, the first thing people envisage are fierce warriors who terrorised the inhabitants of whichever country they decided to visit during their summer holidays from their farms in the fjords.

The image endures of sleek longboats with figureheads of dragons, with blood red sails and multitudes of muscle-bound men with long red or blond beards, wearing helmets with horns. At least that is what the film makers of the 20th century would have us believe.

How much of this is true?

Not a lot!

First of all, Viking helmets never did have horns. Horn was too valuable a material to waste as a decoration. It was much better to use a horn as an instrument of communication or as a drinking vessel. Viking women used horn for making buckles and other small household items.

As for the sleek longboat, it was only used as a military vessel when required to sneak up estuaries or go up river on raiding voyages. The most common Viking vessel was a much more practical ship for trading and was based on the much larger and more sea worthy Nordland boat of the Arctic.

What is probably more surprising is that, in many cases, it was not the Vikings who built these vessels.

To go back to the origins of the Nordland boat one has to go back in time to around 5000 BC when the Komsa people settled the coastal land of what is now Northern Norway. The petroglyphs at Alta clearly show fishing and hunting scenes with boats which have raised stems and sterns.

Later drawings show these boats to be of 'Clinker' built design, some with the characteristic square sail and multiple oars associated with the Viking ships. Now it all starts to look familiar! Archaeological finds from across modern Scandinavia reveal that these vessels were indeed 'clinker built', but without the use of the metal fastenings which were to be found in later Viking ships. These ancient vessels were held together by reindeer sinews and pliable roots from plants such as willow, which was plentiful in the northern marshlands and tundra. Sewing dry planks together then soaking them until they expanded to form a sealed joint was the technique developed by these ancient people who were the forefathers of our modern Sami.

One drawing from 1555 shows Sámi boat builders building a boat for a Norwegian owner. Close examination reveals a building in background which is clearly not the type of house inhabited by Sami. It is not a turf constructed, single level Gamme as lived in by Sámi. It is a two level wooden house, the home of a Norwegian.

In one saga, written around the 10th century, it states the following: 'These sleek, light and extremely fast boats could outpace any other vessel in the world. But how such an innovative, beautiful yet fearsome thing could a century earlier have been built by such unschooled people was a mystery. These ships caused fear and panic from the Hebrides to Phoenicia and the Baltic to the Mediterranean. They had developed from similar high prowed ships which had planks sewn together with hide.'

The "unschooled people" clearly referred to the "primitive Sami" who traditionally had built clinker boats without metal fastenings using sinew, strips of hide or pliable roots to sew the planking together.

The vessels being described were, of course, the Viking

longboats - lighter, longer, faster and held together with iron nails. Perhaps the use of saws enabled thinner planks to be cut. Older boat remains in what later became known as Viking territory indicated that the earliest Norsemen used vessels more akin to dugout canoes with paddles. This gives us a clue as to where the technology of the Viking ship originated.

As can be seen from both the Nordland Coat of Arms and the pictures of typical Nordland boats of today, the design has hardly changed from the pre-Viking era to the present day. Nowadays these vessels are used either as pleasure craft or heritage vessels which are raced in the fjords. Up until well into the 20th century they were still being used as coastal trading vessels carrying cargoes of timber or fish. It was vessels similar to these that carried cargoes of dried cod or stockfish from the northern fisheries of Lofoten and beyond which sustained the Hanseatic traders of Bergen throughout the 16th and 17th centuries.

The Nordland coat of arms illustrates the fact that this design of vessel has survived across the centuries and still embodies the spirit of those who developed it as a means of both transport and trade. The Nordland boat has a very long history and although it is first recorded in writing around 940 AD, at the height of the Viking era, it had evolved long before then as the basis for the longship design.

However, there were differences between the earlier Sami built vessels and the Norse built vessels of the later period (or vessels built for Norse owners by the Sami). Iron was not readily available to the Sami, hence the "sewn planks". The Norse used iron rivets. One feature that was shared was that of disposable ballast, usually rounded beach stones. The reasoning behind this idea was that if the boat capsized the ballast fell out but the boat, being made of wood, remained afloat.

Although the indigenous Sami of the coastal areas were

primarily fishermen and small scale farmers, their ability as boat builders was not lost on their Norse neighbours. Their ability to adapt meant that they were soon building riveted vessels for their Viking neighbours or overlords. However, the famous Icelandic historian Snorri Sturluson records the sale of two 24 oared sewn vessels to Icelandic King Sigurd Slemdadiaekien when he visited Northern Norway. This is the same Snorri Sturluson who recorded many of the sagas which had previously been handed down verbally. Written sources from the 15th century onward regularly refer to Sami building vessels for Norwegian clients. The vessels mentioned by Snorri were stated to be about 18 metres in length, which is about 60ft.

Another picture showing Sami fishermen off the Lofoten Islands in a typical Sami fishing boat of the 18th century clearly demonstrates its origins. With the exception of the stern hung rudder, it might well be a small vessel of the 10th century during the Viking era.

Another Viking legend of Hollywood origin that is quite easily slain is that of large 'Viking Longships' being dragged across Europe to sail down rivers like the Volga.

A well known drawing of Sami men carrying a newly built boat demonstrates how light these vessels were and clearly shows the clinker construction. Many of the famous overland journeys to the east and down into the Black Sea were most likely carried out using small vessels of the type shown in the drawing rather than the "Viking Longships" portrayed in Hollywood films. These vessels were between five and six metres in length. When in the water these lightly built, shallow draft vessels could easily carry around eight fully equipped men. This was ideal for the descent of major rivers or for portage on rivers of less stature. When long overland portages were required it was quite easy to turn the vessel over and, by pushing the oars through the rowing ports, use the oars as an easy way of lifting the boat. So it was much easier for a large number of men to carry a number of small light boats between river catchments than try to drag a single, large ungainly ship. The story of two hundred Viking longships crossing from Sweden down into the Black Sea does not hold water (pardon the pun!). Apart from the physical improbability, how would you feed two hundred fully crewed longships companies while crossing 10th century Northern Europe? Two hundred fully crewed longships is somewhere between twelve and sixteen thousand men. Mission impossible! However two hundred eight man vessels are one thousand six hundred men. The latter is possible not only because of food logistics but also because they could also travel a lot faster.

Strange though it may seem the drawing of the Sami carrying a boat, as previously mentioned, has the Sami boatmen carrying the vessel the right way up.

A clinker built vessel of twenty three metres in length was excavated from the Nydam Bog in Jutland, Denmark. It is the oldest preserved vessel of its kind being dendrodated at circa 320AD. It is iron fastened and was accompanied by iron swords and spears. It was made of oak and powered by thirty oars. It was this type of vessel that carried the Jutes to England in the 4th century AD. The fact it was made from oak indicates that it was not built by Sami craftsmen in Northern Norway as Northern Scandinavia is devoid of oak. However, at that time the Sami people were to be found as far south as the Oslo Fjord where oak did grow.

Another possibility is that Sami craftsmen could have been taken south as either workers or slaves. Although it is the oldest riveted hull it is almost a century younger than the Vaderoy Boat, dated at circa 245 AD, which is a sewn construction.

One of the secrets of the Sami boat builders that made their boats so light yet strong was the method they used to cut planking. Unlike other boat builders, who cut or sawed planks that had parallel sides, the Sami used a form of "Radial Cutting". This method of splitting a log lengthwise to give planks which had a cross section in the form of a wedge was unique to Sami built vessels of antiquity. If one thinks of cutting a large round cake into triangular portions, this would be the equivalent except lengthwise along a log. This not only gave the plank a grain structure which was stronger and less likely to crack, it also meant one edge was thicker than the other. This may seem to be a problem but it is not. It can be of benefit when forming the bottom or side of the boat where the hull form curves.

This has another advantage. If the vessel is grounded, the thickest part of the plank is in contact with the ground. Where iron rivets were used, it allowed the outside end to be sunk deeper into the plank as an additional protection. This was of particular use where longships, or even smaller vessels, were dragged overland on rollers.

In 2014 I was visiting Canada and had the good fortune to visit L'Anse Aux Meadows, the site of a Viking settlement in Newfoundland. It is assumed that this was the site used by Lief Eriksson, son of Erik the Red, and later by his half sister Freydis Eriksdottir. The sagas and historic writings tell us that Freydis sank two longships there on one of her infamous bloodstained voyages, circa 1010AD. I was discussing the construction of Viking vessels with one of the guides who had been a youngster at the time Helge and Anne Ingstad were excavating the site in the 1960s. He told me that, on an unusually low tide, he found a piece of old wooden wreckage which had tapered planking. He took this to one of the archaeologists who immediately dismissed it as being of no importance. Could it have been a piece of one of the Freydis vessels? The fact that the planking was tapered should have been noted and modern dendrodating and carbon dating would have revealed the truth one way or the other. The fact that the planks were tapered would also indicate that Sami craftsmen were likely to have been involved in the vessel's construction. Unfortunately we shall never know for certain. Incidentally, in my travels I have seen a few "replica Viking ships", none of which had tapered planking, but these vessels were not built by Sami. Genuine Viking burial ships, as displayed in Oslo, have tapered planking!

Footnote: - Two places where Viking Longships were probably dragged overland were both to be found in what is now Scotland. The first being at a narrow isthmus on the Shetland Islands, which at the time was under Viking rule. This enabled ships to cross from the East to West of these island without sailing a considerable distance North or South to continue their voyages to and from the New World.

The second site is the narrow pass between the village of Arrochar, at the head of Loch Long, and the village of Tarbet on Loch Lomond. (Tarbet or Tarbert derives from the Gaelic "An Tairbeart" meaning a narrow strip of land.) This was the site where in 1236 a Viking raid led by King Haakon of Norway dragged their longships over the one and a half mile isthmus to avoid the Scots defences at Dumbarton. This enabled them to carry out an unopposed voyage of plundering and carnage unequalled anywhere in the history of Viking raiding in Scotland. The indiscriminate killing of women and children, including nuns on an island convent, had an impact for many years on the rural life of the communities surrounding the loch. After three days of pillaging the Vikings exited the loch via the River Leven to re-enter the Firth of Clyde at Dumbarton. From there they rejoined the main Viking fleet in Rothesay Bay only to be cut to pieces, a few days later, by the forces of Alexander III, King of the Scots, when they were driven ashore by a south westerly gale. This battle, known as "The Battle of Largs" in effect ended the Viking rule in mainland Scotland.

THE KAUTOKEINO REBELLION

The Sami revolt in Kautokeino (Guovdageaidnu in the Northern Sami language.) in the autumn of 1852 was the ultimate result of the local Norwegian administration's exploitation of local Sami reindeer herders. It ended with the conviction of more than thirty Sami men and women, five of whom were given death sentences. Two of these death sentences were carried out. Eight Sami were sentenced to life imprisonment and another three to twelve years in prison. Whereas the men were imprisoned in the Akerhaus Jail in Oslo, the women were imprisoned in Trondheim.

Although all the death sentences were appealed, the Supreme Court of Norway upheld two of these. The two men who were beheaded in public at Alta in 1854 were deemed to have been the ringleaders of what is now known as the "Kautokeino Opporet" or Kautokeino Uprising. The severed heads of Mons Somby and Aslak Haetta were sent to Oslo and placed in the anthropological skull collection as the authorities at the time wished to demonstrate that the Sami had smaller skulls, hence less brain capacity than "normal humans" such as Norwegians and Swedes. Their headless bodies were then buried outside the church grounds at Kafjord church as the state church regarded them as heathens unworthy of a resting place in consecrated ground. The reasoning of the Supreme Court just about sums up what the attitude of the authorities in both Norway and Sweden in the 1850s was toward the Sami people:

'The crimes which (....) by (....) the lowest class of society spread widely across a major part of the civilised world a desire to apply force and violence in order to break down all natural boundaries between themselves and the upper echelon, and thus enforce a similarity which would destroy all civilisation.'

Were the Sami really that big a threat to civilisation?

So what caused this "uprising" that left, for many years, the area around Kautokeino to be described as a "spiritually burned land"?

By the 1850s, the Sami reindeer herders relied on trading with Norwegian and Swedish merchants who operated trading stores across the north of Scandinavia. These merchants and their local allies within the Norwegian state church systematically exploited their monopoly over the Sami people. Flour, salt and coffee were seen as essentials to the Sami, but could only be purchased from the local merchant. Those who went outwith the area to bring in supplies would be refused future trade with the local merchant in Kautokeino, even when it was an emergency.

The main causes of the uprising were not the fact that the merchant was exploiting the Sami by undervaluing their produce but, firstly, that he was supplying alcohol to which the Sami people, like other indigenous Arctic people, have little tolerance. Both the legal and illegal liquor trade being operated by both trader and priests had an unparalleled effect on both the Sami economy and social behaviour. Once dependent on alcohol, the local herders became easy targets for the unscrupulous merchant.

The second trigger point for major dissent was that of religion. For centuries the Sami had been shamanists and had only recently taken on the brand of Christianity preached by the part-Sami Swedish preacher, Lars Levi Laestadius.

Once Laestadius became involved, things changed dramatically. The only church that the Norwegian authorities allowed was the state church. Sami converts to Laestadian teachings sought the moral high ground and caused disruption during state church services. Using Laestadius's ideologies as a guide, they set out to achieve a change in the social standing within Norwegian society and so saw their grievance against both church and merchant exploitation as just - which it undoubtedly was.

On the 8th of November 1852 the whole thing came to a head when a group of reindeer Sami from the Kautokeino area attacked the authorities and merchant's premises. In the resulting battle, both the local merchant and sheriff were killed, the merchant's house burned down and the local priest and his family whipped (the exception to the whipping being the priest's pregnant wife).

The 35 or so Sami were led by Mons Somby (27 years old), Aslak Haetta (28),

Ellen Skum (25), Lars Haetta (18) and Henrick Skum (20). All five of whom were subsequently sentenced to death at the trial which followed. The latter three had their sentences reduced to life imprisonment with hard labour alongside another eight (four men and four women). Another 15 were given sentences ranging from a few days to twelve years. Three others died before or during the trial of injuries sustained in the conflict and four were acquitted.

At the trial it became clear that the Sami, although inspired by Laestadian teachings, had also their own beliefs and considered themselves as people without sin who had acted on God's behalf against evil, unrepentant and sinful people. In their trial statements they referred to themselves as "God's Children".

Other local Sami, who had also been influenced by Laestadius's teaching, believed that the group led by Somby and Haetta had gone too far in their interpretation of these religious teachings.

Even today there is still an underlying feeling that the Sami people involved were badly treated and many relatives of those concerned still live in the area. The names Somby and

Haetta are very much alive and present in today's Sami politics and at the Sami parliament (Samidiggi) in Karlsjok, east of Kautokeino.

The treatment of Mons Somby and Aslak Haetta had a deep and lasting psychological effect on the Sami people of Finmark and Troms. So much so that in a letter to the Department of Anatomy in 1985, Niilas Somby requested the skull of his grandfather's brother be returned to the family for burial. The Department of Anatomy refused this request and a prolonged legal battle ensued. It was not until 1997, when the grandchildren of Aslak Haetta joined the legal battle by demanding the return of their grandfather's skull, that the case was resolved.

Initially, the Department of Anatomy refused to surrender the skulls. However, after a legal debate between the Sami parliament, the University of Oslo, and Ministry of Church Affairs, Education and Research, the university administration finally ordered the Department of Anatomy to return both skulls for burial. The burial took place in November 1997, one hundred and forty five years after the event.

One other outcome of the uprising was that Lars Haetta, who was eighteen at the time of the incident, spent his time in prison translating the Bible into the Sami language.

The teaching of what is essentially "alien beliefs"and conversion to such religions has more than once been the cause of conflict. The religious wars of the sixteenth century are a classic example. Even in the more enlightened times of the twentieth and twenty first centuries, religious differences among sects of the same religion were rife, for example in Northern Ireland among Christians of Roman Catholic and Protestant faiths, or in the Middle East between Sunni and Shiite Muslims. However in indigenous people whose original beliefs were very different from the beliefs thrust upon them by Christian missionaries the fall out is often more severe as was seen in Kautokeino and more recently with the Inuit of the

Belcher Islands in Canada's Hudson Bay.

TRADITIONAL SAMI BUILDINGS

The Sami people, like many indigenous people, lived in harmony with their environment. Materials for building their homes were taken from the environment, but they were also returned to that same environment.

Reaching back in time to the Komsa people, the Lavvu, as shown above - which was still extensively used by those Sami in the Reindeer Herding communities - was similar to the Tepee of the Plains Indians of North America and the summer tent or Tupik of the Inuit. Using poles of birch from the

Tundra covered in reindeer skins, it left a sufficient open area at the apex to enable smoke from the centrally located fire to escape. Regarding themselves as part of nature, it was the Sami philosophy that no permanent trace of their presence should be left on the landscape. By only leaving the scorch mark of their fire, nature soon hid all traces of their presence.

Those Sami who lived in semi permanent settlement along the coastline and river valleys built houses using a frame of birch wood covered with turf. Right up until the Second World War, this type of dwelling was common in both North Troms and Finnmark. The retreating German Army recorded burning many "turf houses" between Alta in Finnmark and Manndalen in North Troms. Most of the Gamme in existence today were built as tourist attractions or as museum examples, although a few are still used as holiday homes and transit accommodation for the reindeer herders.

Like the Lavvu of the Reindeer Sami, the Gamme will naturally biodegrade leaving little more than another lump amidst what is a naturally lumpy landscape.

Since these forms of dwelling were very low impact and the materials used from a sustainable source, it is difficult for archaeologists to locate ancient Sami settlements using the remains of dwellings. It is from other sources such as shell dumps and petroglyphs, such as those at Alta, that the Sami past has been revealed.

Both the Lavvu and the Gamme were traditionally built on a round base with a central fireplace above which a hole let the smoke out. The inside layout of both dwelling types was very much based on the concept of 'a place for everything and everything in its place'. The firewood was always placed just inside the door, pots and cooking utensils were behind the fire. In the case of the Lavvu an additional flap at the rear was regarded as a sacred entrance through which - after a successful bear hunt - the bear carcass would enter. All the occupants had their own dedicated sleeping place and an area was reserved for visitors.

Living and working with nature came naturally to the traditional Sami people right up to the 20th century.

In areas where the process of Norwegianisation had greatest influence, the local Sami population had adopted the Norwegian standard of housing. Wooden houses with modern facilities such as plumbing and electricity are now the norm, but even after WW2 some wooden houses belonging to Sami people did not have these basic facilities.

A true story I heard about the house pictured here in Lockvol in the Manndalen Valley clearly demonstrates how trusting, even if somewhat naïve, many older Sami were at that time. The story starts after the resettlement of the population of the areas which had been subject to the "scorched earth" policy of the retreating German army.

A salesman from a Norwegian company arrived in the Manndalen area selling stainless steel sink units complete with both hot and cold taps. On reaching a very small wooden house near Lockvol he found the only person home was an elderly Sami lady. The house belonged to her son, a fisherman, who was out in his boat fishing in the fjord. Undaunted, the salesman made his pitch. 'Wonderful stuff stainless steel. Doesn't rust. Two taps, one supplying cold water, the other supplying hot water.' The elderly lady was duly impressed and bought the unit after being assured that this was the modern way - hot and cold water. It was only when her son came home that she was informed that to have running water, either hot or cold, you first need to be connected to a water pipe.

The house that the government had supplied this Sami fisherman with to replace the one that the Germans had destroyed did not have that luxury.

SAMI LANGUAGE

The Sami languages, for there are different dialects which vary sufficiently enough to be classified as of individual standing, have roots common to those of ancient Magyar tribes. Languages with these roots are classed as Finno-Ugric. Other languages within this group include modern languages of Hungarian, Mordovinian, Finnish, Zyrian and Estonian. From this it can be assumed that when the forbearers of our modern Sami - the Komsa people of the post ice age - moved north as the glaciers retreated, they either went overland to the sea around Alta, via the eastern shore of the Baltic and Gulf of Bothnia or across the Skaggerak and then along the west coast of modern Norway. The fact that the archaeological remains, in the form of petroglyphs, are most prevalent around Alta Fjord would suggest that the overland route, following migrating reindeer herds, was the route taken by these hunter gatherers.

By taking the route along the eastern Baltic then north to either the Altavidda or to the valley of the Tana they would have left settled enclaves in their wake. These enclaves would be the source of the other Finno-Ugric languages in later times.

As it now stands, the Sami languages and their related languages were isolated from each other due to geographic features to such an extent that they are now mutually unintelligible. The Northern Sami language or dialect has survived in Northern Norway and is the most spoken of all the Sami languages as well as being the one used in both Sami literature and education.

HOW MANY SAMI?

This is a very difficult question to answer in Norway. First, how do you define "Sami"?

The official definition in Norway is that of having a parent or grandparent who spoke the Sami language. This definition allows a person to register as a voter in the elections for the Samidiggi, or Sami Parliament. However, it does not really take into consideration the detrimental effect that the policy of "Norwegianisation" had on generations of Sami people in areas such as Finmark and Troms.

If you wanted to own a house or land you had to prove that you were Norwegian by being able to speak Norwegian. Because of this, many families where the natural language would have been Sami stopped using the language of their birth so as not to disadvantage their offspring. By speaking Norwegian, it was hoped that these children would be accepted as social equals among their neighbouring Norwegian communities. After a few generations many, otherwise Sami, communities had totally lost their native language and with it their Sami identity. A similar situation arose in the Highlands and Islands region of Scotland right up to the mid 20th century. Speaking Gaelic in school was punishable and highly discouraged. I was reprimanded more than once for referring to my Grandmother as 'an Caillach'. Few, if any, school teachers (other than my Great Aunt Christina) were Gaelic speakers and probably even fewer tried to learn the language. It was only a few years ago, just before my own father died, that I found out he was a natural Gaelic speaker. His elder sister was also a Gaelic speaker but neither his younger sister nor younger brother "had the Gaelic", as they say in the Highlands, despite the fact that my grandmother was from a prominent family on the Island of Lewis. (Strange though it may seem, they were of partly Norwegian descent and I still have relatives in Norway.)

As my mother was a lowland Scot, she was not a Gaelic speaker. As a result, neither my brother nor I learned Gaelic as a natural language. Does that mean I am any less a Gael?

So how many people are either full Sami or part Sami due to the effects of assimilation?

That question is now impossible to answer, even with modern technology such as DNA sequencing. There are at least 30,000 Sami in the recognised Sami areas of Norway but twice that number is not an unrealistic number. It is reckoned that there are more people of Sami origin living in the area around Oslo than actually beyond the Arctic Circle. The smallest population of ethnic Sami is that of the Kola Peninsula in Russia where the Sami population numbers around 2,000.

A classic example of how skewed the statistical account may actually be is that of those declaring Sami ethnicity in the Porsangerfjorden district of Finmark in the 20th century.

At the beginning of the century, the vast majority of the population declared to be of Sami origin. After the Second World War, the number of people declaring Sami ethnicity had declined into single figure percentage. It was assumed by most that declaring Sami ethnicity - in the wake of the Nazi scorched earth policy that left the area from the Russian border of Finmark west to the communities of Samuelsberg and Manndalen in North Troms totally devastated - might leave them disadvantaged. At this time, the Norwegian government at the far off Storting in Oslo were replacing, at government cost, the homes destroyed during the retreat of the German army. Public belief in both Troms and Finmark was that those of Sami ethnicity would receive much inferior homes to those declaring themselves Norwegian. So the much reduced number of Sami in the area concerned is highly questionable.

It is not only the Arctic environment that threatens the Sami culture.

SAMI NAMES

Since the establishment of the Samidiggi in the last two decades of the 20th century there has been a resurgence of the Sami culture across the board. From music and handicrafts right down to the now fashionable hobby of genealogy, interest levels have risen dramatically. However, due to the suppression of the Sami people from the 17th century onward, it is very difficult to trace and ascertain Sami lineage.

Few Sami names have actually survived into the 21st century.

Looking at the few names that have survived, it becomes obvious that the Sami relationship with nature was a strong one.

Many of the coastal Sami in Norway, in areas where Norwegian influence was strongest, tend to have more or less similar names to their Norwegian neighbours.

However, this does not apply to such an extent among those Sami who live in the more remote and inland areas where both first names and surnames of Sami origin are more likely to be encountered.

In the far north, names such as Somby, Magga, Turi and Haetta have survived as family names passed down through the generations from origins lost in time. The origins of some names are, however, more obvious. An example of this is the surname Solhaug, meaning literally "sun high". This family name is, I have been assured, derived from the location of this family's home. Reputedly, the place where they built their home was where the first rays of the sun struck the valley floor after the long winter night. This example clearly demonstrates the Sami connection and understanding of nature.

Among the "South Sami", of the area around the Trondelag district, many have surnames ending in "Fjell". The word "fjell", of course, means mountain in Norse languages. So such names as Kappfjell, Knitfjell and Dunfjell give a fair indication as to where a family's origin lay.

A parallel can be drawn with Scottish names such as Sutherland, Nairn and Crawford, all of which are surnames and geographical locations. In all four countries where the Sami live, the patterns of naming have long been influenced by the surrounding races. In the Kola Peninsula of Russia, the local Sami have Russian sounding names - indeed very Russian sounding names. From the earliest Tsarist era right up until recent years - particularly under the communist regime - standing out as a minority group left you exposed as a potential scapegoat when things were going wrong. Think, Jews in Germany in the 1930s or Shiites in Syria and Iraq in the 21st century. However, in Finland, Sweden and Norway it is often quite easy for locals to recognise a name as Sami.

Until recent years, Norwegians who were trying to trace their ancestry would conveniently come to a dead end if a branch of the family tree proved to be, or even hinted at being Sami. Things now are, thankfully, changing and will hopefully continue to do so. I have a 'Norwegian' friend whose family suddenly came into money toward the end of the 19th century. An ancestor who was a ghillie/ attendant to a branch of the Swedish royal family was given land in Finnmark and a significant amount of wealth in return for marrying a young Sami lady who had become the focus of attention of a young royal male. At that time, it would have been unthinkable for a royal to have a liaison with someone of Sami blood. *It has to be remembered that at the time concerned was still being ruled by Sweden, hence the land in Finnmark, as far away from Stockholm as they could get.* The Sami lady dutifully produced a family for the Norwegian courtier and the family still prospers to this day, but it is only now they admit the Sami connection. I am certainly not in a position to criticise as, like many families, my own has a similar skeleton in its cupboard. My surname is McVicar, a name prevalent on the very much Presbyterian island of North Uist in the Hebridean Islands of Scotland's north-west coast.

My great, great grandmother was an Irish Catholic who was widowed around the time of the Irish Potato Famine in the mid 19th century. She was left with little choice but to immigrate to Scotland with her two very young children. She was fortunate to find employment with a Scottish gentleman from Uist, living in Glasgow, as a housekeeper to him and his invalid wife. After his wife died, leaving two children, he married my great-great–grandmother. My great grandfather and his sister adopted the name McVicar, thus disguising their Irish Catholic origins in an era when "mixed" marriages were socially unacceptable and those involved ostracised.

Thankfully, in a much more liberal and secular era, behaviour of this nature has now greatly declined in many of the more civilised societies.

SO WHAT DO SAMI LOOK LIKE?

A hundred years ago it would have been much easier to recognise someone of Sami origin. Like all Arctic races they were, in most cases, small in stature. Hair colouring was usually dark. Eyes would be slightly slanted to cope with the low sun. Skin colour would be darker than the neighbouring Nordic races. Races such as the Mongols of Eastern Siberia and Mongolia and the Inuit races - from the Chucki or Chukota of the far north east of the former USSR to the Inuit of Eastern Canada and the Kalaalit Inuit of Greenland - have all retained these characteristics. The Sami of Northern Europe are much less likely to have retained these features as the process of assimilation has eroded the genetic structure of the race, this being most obvious in areas where the process of Norwegianisation was most rigorously enforced. My Norwegian friend, whose great-great-grandmother was Sami, is a tall blond lady who shows no traces of her Sami heritage as she now only carries one sixteenth of her Sami DNA. So it is with many of today's Sea Sami in arctic Norway. Where the reindeer Sami are more likely to have kept within their own ethnic circle, a throwback to the Siida system, the accepted image of the Sami is more obvious but is less so where marriage out with that circle occurred.

So a modern Sami could easily be blond, blue eyed and tall or short, dark haired and swarthy-skinned or any variation in between. But one thing is certain; they will be proud of their ancient heritage and, dependent on which area they come from, may be distinguished from their Norwegian countrymen by their dress.

SAMI DRESS
AND CRAFTS

To Norwegians and tourists to the area of Sapmi, the traditional brightly coloured clothing of the indigenous people is often referred to as the Kofta. My Sami friends in both the area of Kaafjord Commune in North Troms and in the settlement of Maze in the Alta-Kautokeino river catchment in Finmark refer to their traditional dress as Ghakti. A couple of years ago I was acting as an escort to a busload of tourists from a cruise ship who were visiting a Sami settlement at Maze up on the Altavidda. The young Sami lady who was the proprietor of the Lavvu visitor attraction referred to her Sami dress as 'Kofta'. When I asked her why she referred to it as such and not as "Ghakti" she was very surprised as well as delighted that someone who was not Sami actually knew the term. She then explained to the tourists that it was Norwegians who called it Kofta, while the Sami themselves called it Ghakti. A bit like the English calling a kilt a skirt.

No matter which of these two terms one decides to use, the fact remains that the traditional dress of the Sami people, both male and female, is always impressive. The work involved in producing such intricate and colourful garments demonstrates the skill and dexterity of the craftsmen and women of the north.

Nowadays, traditional clothing and footwear are no longer the everyday clothing. Modern Sami wear modern clothes. Just as most Scotsmen only wear their kilts on formal occasions, so it is with the Sami. Even within the Reindeer Sami communities one rarely sees the traditional double skinned reindeer skin jacket or sealskin or reindeer skin boots with upturned toes. However, on formal occasions or at the Sami tourist attractions, the full range of Sami clothing and craftwork adornments are displayed with real pride.

The traditional Sami dress had its origins in being functional in an Arctic climate. As my friends tell me: "There is no bad weather - just bad clothes."

The principal behind the design was to use the materials that nature had provided for making warm clothes.

The Sami reindeer skin jacket, or pesk as it is known, took the hides of up to six deer to make. The women examined the hides to decide how to best utilise them, the shape of the hides dictating the shape of the finished product. The pesk has two layers; the inner layer has the fur to the inside while the outer has the fur open to the elements. It was this design of jacket that allowed Amundsen to reach the South Pole ahead of Scott. As loss of body heat meant that fewer calories were burned than when wearing the waterproofed canvas jackets that the British explorers wore, less food needed to be carried. Less food meant less weight and faster travel. The woman's pesk was a little longer than the male version.

Trousers for winter wear were either deer or sealskin as were boots.

The modern Sami national costume is a much more recent part of Sami culture and is made from a woven woollen cloth, the design being based on the shape of the outer layer of the traditional pesk. Again, a parallel can be drawn with the modern pleated kilt worn on formal occasions by the Scots. This garment "evolved" from the "Feileadh mhor" or great plaid, the modern garment being developed in the 18th and 19th centuries into what we know today.

As with the tartans of Scotland, the Sami clothing and head-dress vary considerably from district to district - in parallel to Sami dialects. Some local variations, such as those in the Kola Peninsula, are influenced by the other neighbouring races. Hats also vary widely, the star-shaped hat of eastern Finnmark with its four upturned points being just one example. The women of the northern districts wear red bonnets with ribbons tied under their chin while in areas where the more conservative influences of the Laestadean church are prevalent; the designs are much less flamboyant.

In the area of Lyngenfjord around Manndalen, the traditional design of footwear -which had upturned toes, (apparently to aid ski bindings) - resulted in the local name of "komager" being applied to the inhabitants of the district.

One of the most colourful and familiar examples of the traditional dress is the Kautokeino Kofta. Elaborately decorated in a multitude of different coloured fabrics and ribbons, it is held in place with clasps made from either antler or silver. Depending on whether the owner is Reindeer or Sea Sami, the leather belt worn by the men will have either bone or silver buttons. The woman's belt can be either woven fabric or leather with bone or silver buttons. Where square buttons signify that the wearer is married, round ones indicate that the wearer is single. The highly decorated silk shawl worn outside the female kofta is held in place with an equally elaborately decorated silver brooch or buckle.

Although termed the Kautokeino Kofta, it is also widely worn among the Sami of both Sweden and Finland.

The folk art of the Sami people is termed Duodji and

covers many craft forms from wood carving to textiles and jewellery. Duodji is a traditional form of handicrafts dating back to the times when many Sami settlements were isolated from the rest of Scandinavian society. In many cases this applied well into the twentieth century.

Tools, often made from bone, antler or wood, are still produced. Often these items - for example, sewing kits from antlers or net repairing needles - were adorned with artistic carvings. Wooden items such as the birch-wood drinking cups were made from selected burr wood so as to give them a patterned finish as well as being practical. Many other Duodji items are functional, e.g. knives, sheaths to hold them, ladies bags and traditional clothing.

Whereas the craftwork of the men tends to include mainly items made from wood, antlers and other reindeer bones, the women use skins to make leather goods and wool from their arctic sheep to produce elaborate patterned knitting and felt-work. The traditional Sami colours of red, green, blue and yellow were originally produced from natural plant dyes but nowadays are frequently produced using synthetic dyes.

The practicality of this artwork stems from the people's need for - in the case of the Sea Sami - good boats and fishing equipment. While the reindeer herders up on the tundra areas such as the Finnmark Vidda, where temperatures can reach minus 50oC, required good warm clothing to avoid freezing to death, the Sea Sami obviously needed clothing that was waterproof as well as warm.

In recent years there has been an increase in those wanting to produce these craft forms and, because of this, there are now people dedicated to teaching the required skills to the younger generations at schools and colleges throughout the north.

SAMI ISSUES IN
MODERN TIMES

The seeds of a new era in Sami history were sown in the 1970's when the Sami people stood up against the Norwegian authorities in the Alta-Kautokeino region of Finnmark. This initial protest followed by other notable Sami led examples of what Mahatma Ghandi would have described as 'peaceful civil disobedience' led eventually to the foundation of the Sami Parliament at Karlsjok in Finnmark on the 24th February 1989 followed by its official opening on the 9th October that same year. Following are the stories of a few events which contributed to the formation of this institution which gives reason for optimism among the Sami in this the 21st century.

The Alta Case.

Not since the Sami uprising at Kautokeino in 1852 had the Norwegian authorities been as upset with their indigenous people from the north as they were when they decided to create a hydroelectric scheme on the Alta-Kautokeino Catchment in Sami dominated territory in Finnmark in the late 1970s. But before going into the details of the Alta Case itself, let us look at the overall situation in Norway regarding the production of electricity.

Norway's Hydroelectric Story – Not all it appears to be!

Norway is a country in which the population only reached 5 million in the early years of the 21st Century. It is well known for its fjords and waterfalls, and it is these geographical features that have created and sustained its world famous tourism industry. These same waterfalls have also produced the power for its inhabitants for many hundreds of years. Waterwheels powered the grain mills and sawmills since Viking times. Now in the 21st century they are used to produce electricity. Indeed, more electricity than this modern Scandinavian country actually uses. So why does this country, which is blessed with all this natural, clean and renewable energy, buy electricity from countries such as the Netherlands and Germany - generated by less clean technology?

Let us look at some facts and figures.

From this information, it is not wrong to assume that this country will have lots of fast flowing rivers descending from the mountain tops to the fjords. Rivers which, if harnessed, will produce copious amounts of "clean and renewable" energy. A real way forward in a time when global warming created by man's dependence on fossil fuels threatens the way of life of every creature on the planet. So why are the Norwegians buying in "dirty energy"?

With the average electrical use by Norwegians, including the Sami, much greater than the average use by members of EU states, there is still a considerable surplus of electricity being generated. In 2007 there were 1166 hydroelectric schemes generating more than 98% of the country's power requirements. These were the major power schemes and do not include the many small private schemes which are prevalent in rural districts. So where is this surplus going?

Why are the Norwegians buying electricity from the EU?

Why does the average Norwegian citizen use nearly four times as much electricity as his counterpart in the EU states?

Without doubt, Norway has a climate that is, on average, colder than that of most EU states. Although this is a contributory factor, it is not really all that significant as the insulation standard of Norwegian houses is very high. Allied to this, many - possibly the majority - of households use highly efficient energy saving technology such as air or ground source heat pumps to heat their homes. The long winter nights mean higher usage of lights, but this is countered by less use during the longer summer days. Energy saving light-bulbs and very frugal LED systems are also now the norm.

The really significant factor is that the amount of electricity used by Norwegian industry. Industries such as aluminium smelting have massive power requirements. This consumption averaged over such a small population may give the impression of a race of people whose homes are crammed with power hungry gadgets left on 24/7 along with the lights. Unlike the USA, this is certainly not the case.

How does this come about?

Norway has no fossil fuel power stations. It does have coal mines in Svalbard but they only produce electricity for the 2000 or so inhabitants of Longyearbyen and that power station is being used to develop carbon capture technology. So why does 42.2% of its electricity come from fossil fuels?

Norway has no nuclear power stations, yet more than a fifth of its consumption is from nuclear generation. Why?

The simple explanation is that electricity is a commodity and, like any other commodity, can be traded. The price varies according to demand and this is the key to the conundrum. Demand at night is lower than that of normal daytime consumption. We are all familiar with the term "Off Peak" electricity. Well, Norway is definitely king where "off peak" is concerned. The cost of producing hydro power is constant, so if you can buy "off peak" cheaper than you can produce hydro, why generate?

That is exactly what Norway does. Whereas you can switch a hydro scheme on and off at will, that is not the case with either fossil fired or nuclear powered generating systems.

So, during the night - that is, night-time in the EU - the Norwegians are using power from Germany and the Netherlands and during the day are selling Hydro power to these same countries cheaper than they can generate from their own fossil or nuclear plants. By buying in this "clean energy" it also enables the German and Dutch governments to declare that X % of their energy use is from renewable sources. Cunning!!!

Not only that, the Norwegians use the "Dirty Energy" to pump water uphill to "pump storage hydro schemes". This enables them, in effect, to store energy which is then sold back to the EU at a profit.

So, as is normal, there are Lies, Damned Lies and Statistics!

THE ALTA CASE

Norway's amazing expansion in the field of hydroelectric generation has not been without hiccups. In fact, it has been and still is something contentious and the cause of conflict between the Norwegian Government at the Storting in Oslo and the indigenous populations of Sami peoples in the far north.

40 kilometres upstream from the city of Alta, capital of Finnmark, the river is dammed with what, at the time of its build, was the most controversial hydro scheme in Norway. This 150MW generation plant actually led to a complete rethink in the philosophy and manner in which hydro schemes were developed. It also involved changes in both the law and the manner in which the wishes of indigenous peoples were assessed.

In 1978 the Storting (Norwegian Parliament) adopted a bill for the construction of a 110 metre high dam on the Altaselva, upstream of the city of Alta. This was a much smaller power plant than had originally been planned in 1970. Also, unlike the original plan, it did not involve submerging the Sami village of Maze north of Kautokeino.

Even this revised plan met strong opposition from civil society, particularly from the Sami community. The first demonstrations against the development were organised that same year in Maze. In the years that followed, the opponents organised demonstrations and campaigns. Various environmental movements tried to get the Storting decision to build the dam reversed. Sami groups held hunger strikes outside the Storting. Their objections were based on ecological and environmental concerns. The Altaselva was one of the world's most famous salmon rivers. Its giant salmon were legendary in international angling circles and these iconic fish were worth more than their market value as food. Foreign anglers brought money to these remote areas; they employed local people as fishing guides and accommodation providers. Damming the river would affect this, predominantly Norwegian controlled, enterprise. The "Sami Rights" aspect of the opposition was based on traditional Sami land and water rights claims. One major negative impact it would have was on the centuries old semi-nomadic reindeer herding communities that used the grazing land along the river valley during their seasonal migrations.

The opposition culminated in the largest civil disobedience incident seen in Norway since the end of the Second World War. In January 1981, some 600 policemen had to forcibly remove the demonstrators from the project site. From there, the conflict moved into the legal realm of the Norwegian Supreme Court which ruled in favour of the development project. The power plant and dam were eventually finished in 1987.

This was not the end of the matter, for such was the strength of the opposition that in 1980 and 1981 a number of meetings were held to conduct future negotiations between the Oslo Government and a delegation of representatives appointed by the Norwegian Sami Association, the Sami Reindeer Herders Association of Norway and the Sami Council's Norwegian Section. The result was that the Government appointed two committees to discuss Sami cultural issues and Sami legal relations. This latter committee was called the Sami Rights Committee and *prioritised towards a democratically elected body for the Sami people*. Ultimately, this resulted in the Sami Act of 1987 which, in turn, was the foundation for the establishment of the Samidiggi (Sami Parliament) in Norway. This opened for the first time on

October 9th 1989. The other concrete achievements of the Sami Rights Committee are the 1988 amendment of the Norwegian Constitution and the adoption of the Finnmark Act in 2005. This act transferred ninety five percent, around forty six thousand sq. Km, of land to the mainly Sami inhabitants of the Finnmark area. It is managed by a committee of six people of whom three are members of the Sami Parliament in Karlsjok.

The Kaafjord Case is another example of the Hydro electric industry falling foul of the rights of indigenous Sami. In this case it was due to the manner in which the large hydro scheme at the top of the Kaafjordalen Valley operates. The natural flow of north Norwegian rivers is that they are very low in winter as the water is frozen on the mountains. In spring the snow-melt fills the lakes and increases the flow down the rivers. This melt flow continues right through to the autumn and allows migratory fish such as salmon, sea-trout and arctic char to reach their spawning grounds. In the case of the Kaafjord hydro scheme flow throughout the summer was restricted so that water stored in the hydro dam could generate electricity when demand peaked in the winter months. This created a very un-natural situation in the fjord. As the less dense freshwater floated above the salt water of the fjord it froze. This in turn meant that local fishermen were denied access to their local fishing grounds at the peak of the cod fishing season when they normally would harvest enough cod to feed the communities for the year. Much of this catch would be hung up to dry on the many drying racks which are visible from the E6 coastal road between Samuelsberg and Olderdalen. What was not used by the local community was sold to passing trade, giving a boost to the local economy. The hydro company agreed to compensate the local fishermen but the number of compensation claims was well in excess of the number of boats "actively fishing". The reason given was that it was the right of every family to catch cod to feed themselves and that right had been denied by the hydro company. The result was that the company had to compensate all concerned. The recent warmer winters have reduced the surface ice problem.

OVER-FISHING AND ASKILL TROLLVIK'S LETTER

Back in the 1980s the Norwegian salmon farming industry was expanding rapidly. Not only was this expansion rapid, it was to a great extent unregulated - with little regard given to the ecological impact it was having on the marine environment. *One aspect of this impact was that of what was being fed to the caged mutants that were being passed off as salmon.* Processed capelin - a small oily fish related to salmon, prolific in the Barents Sea - was the food of choice. Unfortunately, this same little fish is a vital link in the food chain of the Arctic waters and for all the species which dwell within. Within a few years of over-fishing, the stocks of fish such as cod and haddock were in severe trouble. Adult cod were feeding on juvenile cod and haddock. Disruption of year class structure was one worrying feature of the famous Barents Sea fish stocks. The cod stocks, the mainstay of the North Norway fishing and fish processing industry, collapsed.

The outcome of this disaster was that the Norwegian government, The Storting, in far off Oslo declared a moratorium on all fishing in the Barents Sea. This put a severe financial strain not only on the full time commercial fishermen in the districts of both Troms and Finnmark but also on the whole local economy of the north.

Those with registered commercial fishing vessels were

paid not to fish, while those who had small, unregistered vessels were not. This impacted mainly on the Sami communities where the traditional low impact methods of fishing were employed.

Fishing methods such as static nets, long lines and the juksa - a hand line with a large lure on the end - do not damage the sea bed and are very selective about the size of fish caught as they avoid catching and damaging juvenile stock.

To enforce this moratorium, the Norwegian Navy set up patrols in the northern waters. This went to plan until one day the patrol entered Kaafjord, which joins the much larger Lyngen Fjord, south east of Olderdalen in the Commune of Manndalen.

What they encountered was a Sami fisherman out exercising his indigenous right to catch fish as a way to help feed his family as the Sami of the area had done since before Viking times. That Sami fisherman was Askel Trollvik. On being challenged, he refused to stop fishing and from this incident on he challenged the authority of the Norwegian Government's claim over what he saw as the waters and fish stocks rightfully owned by the Sami.

The following is a translation of a letter he sent to the Storting in Oslo.

Askill Trollvik's Letter.

"Firstly. You do not have any *juridical* basis for making a decision on how the inhabitants in coastal Sami areas should manage their resources. Both in Norwegian and international legal practice Sami rights to land and water *as* fastened as a principle. International law and legal practice regarding minorities and indigenous rights are crystal clear. When it comes to resource management, we in the Sami areas have to resort to ancient rights and the local formal rules – until the Sami Parliament has started to exercise its legal authority.

Secondly. I would like to state that the authorities you represent, the Norwegian, have shown neither ability, will, nor competence in managing resources in the North. The current crisis along the coast and in all the fjords and which might turn into a catastrophe is not caused by coast and fjord fishers with nets and other passive gear. The crisis, which could turn into a catastrophe, we who practice fjord fishing in the Lyngen Fjord have long predicted. Already in 1935 the Lyngen local court sent a request that seine and trawl should be banned. Since then so many requests from local organisations and unions have been sent on this issue, that I cannot count them all. No concern from the authorities You represent has ever been taken regarding our local knowledge and our local judgments. Many of the requests regarding reasonable resource management we have sent, through almost 60 years, have not even been answered. Enough injustice has been committed against us. For my part I will not resign my right to fish. There is no reason that I and others in the coastal Sami fjords shall suffer because Norwegian capital and modern high technology has committed senseless resource plundering in the Barents Sea and at the richest fishing grounds along our coast. By allowing trawl and seine in the fjords, Norwegian authorities, whom You represent, have also destroyed to a considerable degree the basis of life for us who live here. These fjords are a Sami area.

Thirdly. I will deal with Your letter, as the Norwegian authorities have done with letters from us who live in the fjords. Fail to take their contents seriously.

I intend to continue to fish as before with my nets, if that is what suits me. Or fish with a line or juksa, if that is what suits me. I will fish for my own use, for cutting into fillets or for hanging to dry. The fish I do not use I will give away or sell.

This is for your information."

Not only did he carry on fishing, the law was changed to permit small scale subsistence fishing. Once the Sami Parliament - the Samidiggi - became functional, many inshore areas became prohibited to trawling and the fisheries have returned to their previous prolific levels. Now the Sami have the modern vessels as shown below.

STRIP FARMING AND THE MANNDALEN CASE

The traditional form of farming in the Sami settlements of areas such as Troms was identical to the strip farming system that was found throughout many European countries right into the 20th century. It is still practiced in areas such as the rural districts around Stuttgart in communities like Echterdingen in Southern Germany. The general system involves the division of individual fields into strips so that when the children of the "farmer" inherit the land, each has an equal portion of both good and poorer land. Eventually after a few generations a "farmer" can own a "farm" which consists of a number of small unconnected strips of land, often quite a distance apart. This is of course highly inefficient in terms of both time and production. Usually when or before it reaches this state a tidy up occurs. This involves the owners trading strips of land with each other to return their fields to a viable working size. In the 1990s "fields" around Echterdingen were often no more than four or five metres wide and did not have fences otherwise they could not be ploughed. A few rows of cabbages would be growing next to a few rows of beetroot or kohl rabbi. Each crop would belong to a different farmer. This was similar to the situation in the Manndalen Commune in North Troms at the end of WW2. The following is a translation of the notice at the pier in Samuelsberg describing what happened when the Norwegian Government wanted to change a system that, in the case of the Sea Sami, had its origins in the "siida" system of ancient times.

"Manndalen is one of few communities in Norway where traditional strip farming is still common.

Farms each have three or more strips of land scattered across the valley. The original idea was that everyone should have access to different types of land to meet their various needs. Through inheritance, the properties have been divided into ever narrower strips over time. Property wise the landscape in Manndalen is highly complex and varied.

In 1947, the government tried to persuade the local population to farm their land to Norwegian standards. The rebuilding process after WW2 was a golden opportunity to replace the old strip farming system. Consequently, a surveyor was sent to the community to regulate the properties in the valley but the locals were having none of it. They met the surveyor with knives drawn and threatened to take his life.

The surveyor was then escorted to Samuelsberg, where a boat was waiting for him. The boat took him to

Lyngenseidet, and he had to pay his own fare. The surveyor was not discouraged, however, and later returned to the community with police protection. His efforts came to a halt when his superior issued new regulations pursuant to which only properties where the owners gave permission could be surveyed. Few landowners gave their permission and the attempts were thwarted. Strip farming was allowed to continue."

To this day the Sami farmers of Manndalen still carry on their traditional farming culture. They keep the very hardy local breed of sheep and grow a locally developed variety of potatoes. The main crop is grass which at one time would have been made into hay, but nowadays is made into polythene wrapped bales of silage using modern farm equipment.

RIDDU RIDDU

On New Year's Eve, back in 1991, a group of young Sami at Olmmaivaggi in the Gaivuotna commune in North Troms launched Riddu Riddu. This, now annual, festival of Sami music and culture soon expanded to include the cultures of other indigenous peoples from across the world.

Olmmaivaggi in Gaivuotna is known in Norwegian as Manndalen in Kaafjord. The same place that the locals retained the right to strip farm.

A decade on from the time that the revitalisation of the Sami culture started, young Sami were asking "Why did the Norwegians try to remove both the Sami language and culture?" They also wanted to know why they should not be proud of their ancient Sami heritage. It was from these questions and the need these young people felt to reassert their culture and heritage that Riddu Riddu, which means "small storm on the coast" was born.

At the time it was launched the majority of the local population, who previously would have deemed themselves "Sami", were officially registered as Norwegian. The main reasons for this being the process of "Norwegianisation" instigated over many years by the Norwegian Parliament or "Storting" and also by anti-Sami sentiment in the area. During the 1990's Sami road-signs were regularly defaced and in many cases peppered with gunshot holes.

Now backed by the Sami parliament and other official bodies, it has a permanent home on the banks of the Manndalen River and has seen performers from many cultures across the world take part.

One performer, of international repute, to have made an impact at Riddu Riddu is Mari Boine. Born in 1956 near Karasjok in Finnmark, Mari's parents were River Sami who made a living from salmon fishing and farming. From a young age she fought against the racism then being faced by the Sami people. (See note:- Mari Boine.)

The five day festival, held in July, has grown from humble beginnings to become one of the most significant international festivals of indigenous music and culture in Europe. It has a wide and varied programme covering activities for children, youths and adults. Music, films, seminars and workshops, art, literature and theatre are all represented. It is also one of the best places to see the Sami in their regional variations of national dress.

The examples that we have presented were representative of the issues that have shaped the present day outlook and philosophy of the modern Sami, not just of Norway but across the whole of Scandinavia and the Kola Peninsula of Russia.

What the future will bring can only be speculated upon but one thing is sure and that is that climate change will impact upon both humanity and wildlife. This impact will initially be most noticeable in the marine environment due to the alterations that are already evident in the temperature and flow of the North Atlantic Drift.

Note: - Mari Boine objected to the attitude of Norwegian society in her formative years. She intensely disliked being referred to as "Lappish", which at that time inferred a degree of inferiority to that of being Norwegian. When asked to perform at the 1994 Winter Olympics being held in Lillehammer she refused. The reason being that she viewed the invitation as merely a token attempt at including the Sami minority in Norway at the opening ceremonies. Since then she has performed in many different countries and has received many awards. In 2003 she was awarded the Nordic Council Music

Prize. In 2009 was knighted as a Knight First Class of the Royal Norwegian Order of St. Olav. 2012 saw her become "Statsstipendiat" as an artist with state funding, the highest accolade that any Norwegian artist can receive.

EFFECTS OF CLIMATE CHANGE ON THE SAMI AND THEIR ENVIRONMENT

The Reindeer Sami account for less than ten percent of the Sami population in Norway but it is this group who are already experiencing difficulties related to climate change. However, before we look at the problems that can be directly placed under the heading of climate change, we must first look at two other problems facing reindeer herders. These problems are encroachment on their traditional pastures and predation, both of which have contributory elements brought on by climate change.

Loss of pastures.

By the very nature of the Arctic climate and tundra, the grazing area required by a herd of reindeer is vast. It may be possible in places like Scotland to support eight ewes on an acre of fertile cultivated grass in east coast Strathmore or the Mearns. Even on Scotland's west coast, in what are collectively known as the Highlands and Islands, it is possible to keep large numbers of livestock. Cattle, sheep and even farmed deer can thrive on the lush grazing of the hill ground where grasses, sedges and a vast variety of wild flowers thrive in the moist Atlantic climate. However, it takes a lot more land to feed one reindeer in any of the areas designated as Sami Deer Herding Areas.

Reindeer need undisturbed grazing areas throughout the year which can be given time to regenerate by constantly moving the herds on a centuries old migration pattern. For many years the Sami herders have had to contend with ever more demands on their traditional grazing lands from outside their own community. Wind power development requires access tracks and during construction phases causes disturbance to the herds. Hydro stations cause alterations to migration routes as well as permanent pasture loss. Mining of the North's rich mineral resources changes the environment for ever. All of these have caused problems to the herders but the very popular Norwegian culture of owning a cabin or hut as a wild retreat for family weekends and holidays is also having an impact.

Since Norway's oil industry came on stream, a great deal of money has been spent on road improvement in the North. Roads such as the E6 enable town and city dwellers to reach areas previously only accessible by boat or a long hike over the tundra. Now every lakeside that is near a road or track appears to have a colony of huts or cabins. (Hytte in Norwegian.) They may be a great thing to keep the Norwegian population fit and connected to nature but the presence of humans, their children, dogs and vehicles such as quad bikes and snow scooters all add to the disturbance of grazing deer. In most areas where these activities are present, the grazing has in effect been permanently lost. Milder winters and longer periods of weather which allows access to both mountains and tundra will no doubt increase the presence of humans in these areas. Humans other than the indigenous Sami Herders!

Predators.

According to figures from the Reindeer Husbandry Administration, the greatest losses to reindeer herds are caused by predation by the "Big Five" natural predators found in Norway. In 2006/2007, this accounted for just over 80% of reindeer fatalities.

In numerical terms, this equates to more than 50,000 animals. Of the "Big Five"- which are wolverine, eagle, wolf, lynx and bear, it is the wolverine (Gulo gulo) and the golden eagle (Aquila chrysaetos) that have the greatest impact.

In the case of the lynx (Lynx lynx), it is very difficult to give an accurate figure of the number of deer killed and/or eaten by either male or female of this species. The naturally secretive nature of the lynx means that often its kills can go unnoticed if the prey is killed in a secluded place or dragged there to be eaten. NINA, the Norwegian Institute for Nature Research, puts the predation levels at 22.5 reindeer killed and eaten per month by male lynx and 8 per month by females. However, lynx have been known to kill as many as twenty reindeer in one night.

The actual numbers of the "big five" predators in Norway may not appear to be large but the cumulative damage on the reindeer herds attributed to them is considerable. Estimated numbers given by the Predators Portal (Rovviltportalen) in 2008 are as follows:

Wolverine 320 – 400, with estimated 300 in Sami herding areas;

Golden Eagles 850 - 1,200 (no estimate given for Sami areas);

Lynx 430 – 450, with an estimated 220 in Sami herding areas;

Bears 128, with an estimated 90+ in Sami herding areas;

Wolves 12 – 18, mainly found along Swedish border.

It can be deduced from these figures that the wolf is no longer the problem it once was to deer herders due to its almost extirpation from Norway in the second half of the twentieth century.

Predation Compensation.

In 1976, an agreement with the Norwegian Government in the Storting set out what is known as the 'Reindeer Husbandry Agreement' with the purpose of preserving and developing traditional reindeer herding practices in the Sami areas of the north.

Through this system a compensation payment is made for every reindeer proven to be lost to any of the listed predators. The reindeer owner is entitled to full compensation for the loss. The herder applies for this payment on an annual basis through the production unit, siida, to which he or she belongs. The figure is calculated on the basis of the average weight of a carcass over the past three years and the current slaughterhouse price.

Predator Committees are politically selected to control each management area and have overall control for predators within that region. This, in theory, helps prevent wildlife crime as the "big five" are subject to wildlife protection laws and can only be culled under strict legal supervision.

Effects of Climate Change on the Reindeer Sami.
Although such problems as loss of grazing to modern technology, such as hydro-electric, and human intervention, such as roads and holiday chalets, are undoubtedly a serious issue they are soon to be overshadowed by the issue of climate change.

The Arctic Climate Impact Assessment of 2005 (ACIA 2005), which was commissioned by the Arctic Council, clearly indicated that temperatures in the Arctic are rising faster than anywhere else on the planet.

This study, which took into account the findings of more than 250 scientists and researchers, also indicated that this will affect both the environment and those who live in Arctic communities. Obviously, the Reindeer Sami are going to be one of the first groups to be affected.

Overall increases in temperature will lead to shorter and

milder winters. This will enable the chalet owners to lengthen their season, causing added disturbance to grazing deer. But that is merely adding to an existing problem.

Herding reindeer has evolved in a manner that works totally in harmony with nature and the climate of the tundra. So any change in that climate will require changes in herding practices to ensure that the deer's welfare is not compromised.

How much the climate will alter and how the herds will respond is at present, at best, a guess. However, the indigenous people of the Arctic have generations of experience and knowledge of their environment and changes have not gone unnoticed.

More changeable weather has led to autumn weather in some areas alternating from freezing to raining. This often creates a layer of hard ice on the ground which prevented the deer reaching the lichens upon which they depend. In some years this has led to increased losses in many herds. Less snow has also exposed other grazing areas which allowed herds to strip them to the extent of permanent damage. One of the most important food sources of reindeer are the ground lichens known as 'Reindeer Mosses'. These are most commonly found on relatively dry areas which may become saturated due to increased rainfall. If this causes a decrease in lichen growth to any great extent, herd sizes may be affected to allow for a degree of sustainability.

The effect of shorter winters will also lead to an altered programme for the annual migrations to the coastal grazing used in summer, much of which is on islands just off the coast. The reason for islands being the favoured location for summer grazing is that they are mainly predator free. This meant that the survival rate for newborn calves was greatly improved. However, if the shorter winters lead to more "open grazing" and snowmelt causes rivers and lakes - which when frozen formed part of the migration route - to thaw, the migration journey will take much longer. In recent winters, this has actually happened to herders moving their herds from

PROFERICROBERTMCVICARFRGS

Kautokeino in Southern Finnmark to the island of Arnoya near Skjervoy in North Troms.

A further issue to be faced by herders is the possibility that increased survival rate among predators - due to increasingly more available food sources, from arctic hares to the sheep of the coastal dwelling Sea Sami - will cause losses of stock. Most at risk would be pregnant females during the migration.

There is already conflict between reindeer herding families who are contesting who has the right to graze their animals on pastures in Finnmark. In some cases this has erupted into violent clashes between rival families. Also aggravating the situation is the fact that the Norwegian Government is trying to limit the size of individual herds and how many head of reindeer each member of a herding family can own. The reason behind this legislation is to prevent the overgrazing of the lichen on which the deer feed. This has led to legal actions being taken in North Troms where herders maintain that the size of the herds and number of animals they are permitted to keep is insufficient for them to earn a living wage. Some of these Reindeer Sami have come up with a solution to this problem by setting up tourist attractions with lavvus and gamme turf houses to entertain tourists. Reindeer sleigh rides in winter in traditional boat shaped sleds, tales of the Sami culture around a fire in the lavvu accompanied by jojking or selling Sami craftwork made from reindeer hides and antlers to tourists arriving in ports such as Honningsvag on Megaroya (North Cape Island), are all regarded as honest ways of increasing the family income of herders.

Mental Health Issues among young Sami Reindeer Herders. The whole idea of herding reindeer on the northern tundra of Arctic Norway may seem like an idyllic and romantic way of life to urbanised Europeans. The reality is
actually very different, as was clearly stated by one young

Sami herder at the Circumpolar Mental Wellness Symposium, which was held in Iqaluit, Baffin Island, in March 2015.

Per Jonas Partapouli, a young Scandinavian reindeer herder who is with the Sami Youth Association laid bare the problems being faced by young Reindeer Sami.

These problems are having a financial impact on the young Sami. But of even greater concern is the fact that they are also affecting their traditional culture and mental wellbeing.

According to Partapouli, traditional reindeer grazing land has been appropriated by the state for both resource development and sustainable energy projects such as wind farms. And these projects get the go ahead without the Sami people being brought into the consultations.

The effect of these problems has had a life changing impact, particularly on the younger generation of herders. It is estimated that one in three of reindeer herders between the ages of 18 and 29 has considered suicide. There is no mental health support available specifically for the Sami. Even if there was it is highly likely that many of those affected would not come forward. The reason is these people have traditionally projected an image of strong independence and self sufficiency.

As Partapouli emphasised, the Sami's attachment to the tundra is not merely financial. The emotional impact of losing access to the land which their ancestor's reindeer herds had for centuries grazed was leading to young herders feeling that they were being unjustly deprived of their cultural inheritance. He then highlighted the importance of indigenous people to have a self determination over matters concerning their traditional lands. The fact that being able to say "NO" to a project is very different from actually doing so. From this it is able to deduce that the Sami community would not necessarily reject all development in Sapmi.

Surely it would be only just and fair to allow the Sami herders the choice in such matters, particularly if it helped reduce the risks of suicide among their younger generation?

The Reindeer Sami and the "little blue pill".

You won't find many Sami reindeer herders that have anything good to say about the "little blue pill", better known as "Viagra". The reason for this is simple; it cut off a once lucrative source of cash for Sami herders. Prior to the invention and introduction of Viagra those practitioners of Chinese alternative medicine recommended a concoction made from powdered reindeer antler that was still in velvet as the best remedy for erectile dysfunction. The best source of the raw materials was of course the reindeer herds of the Sami. Many thousands of deer were annually de-horned when still in velvet and their antlers sent to China. This trade totally dried up after Viagra became widely available. The price being paid for the "velvet" from the antlers was as high as $120 per kilogram. So the loss of this market had a significant impact on the herders.

The "velvet" wasn't the only product that was exported to China for use in their "traditional medicine" trade. The reindeer penis was also regarded as a source of high grade aphrodisiac. Dried penis, tails and leg tendons were all valuable by-products which added to the viability of reindeer herding. The antlers are used to treat calcium deficiencies, tendons as a health tonic and the dried penises, not surprisingly, to enhance virility. The loss of this market was undoubtedly a blow to the herders, but interestingly sources in Australia indicate that many Chinese men are now returning to the deer based remedies in preference to the "little blue pill". Australian deer farming is very different from the herding practices. The deer bred in Australia are the fallow deer (Dama dama) and the red deer (Cervus elaphus). However it would appear that the Chinese market does not have a species preference. Initially when Viagra became available on the Chinese market the Australians, like the Sami, could not give away these products but in 2016 things started to change as the return to traditional medicine became more prevalent.

Most of the Australian produced antler a penises are not currently exported to China, but sold to the resident ethnic Chinese population in Australia. This hopefully will leave the door open for the Sami to resume trading with the Chinese homeland population should they also return to their culture of traditional medicine.

THE SEA SAMI

By far the largest group of indigenous Sami people are the Sea Sami whose ancestors were the builders of the Viking ships of Norse folklore. The descendants of these famous boat-building people might no longer build Viking ships, or even many small fishing boats, but they are still very dependent on the seas around them.

For many Sami, from the southern Sami around the Trondelag area to the most northern reaches of Finnmark right across to the Kola Peninsula in Russia, the sea is the mainstay of their existence.

Before we go into the intricacies of the effects of climate change on the marine environment we should examine the importance of the fishing industry to the Norwegian economy.

As already clearly shown in Askill Trollvik's letter and the case of the Sami fishermen in Kaafjord, the Sami take their rights to catch fish very seriously. Many are full time fishermen with a great deal of money invested in boats and equipment. Others catch fish as a supplement to both household diet and as an additional source of income, either as fish sold for money or as barter traded with other local producers, although the latter practice has decreased greatly in recent years.

Fish exports account for 5.7% of Norway's total exports and are therefore vitally important to the country as a whole, but nowhere more so than the areas of Nordland, Troms and Finnmark.

These areas are sparsely populated and so the importance of each job in terms of employment statistic percentage points is greatly increased. Oil and petrochemical industries may be Norway's main economic factor but it is not a renewable source.

Fish should be a renewable source if properly managed. However, to manage climate change is beyond the reach of either local or national governments.

So what is the government currently doing about this problem?

Without sustainable fish stocks, places like the smaller islands in the Lofoten group could become uneconomic as functioning social entities. They could end up like the St Kilda group off Scotland's west coast which had to be evacuated in the 1930s after more than a thousand years of human habitation. For this reason and others the Norwegian Government and institutions such as the University of Tromso, UNIS (University Centre in Svalbard and the world's oldest marine institute, the Scottish Association for Marine Science, (SAMS), are spending a great deal of time and money on monitoring ocean temperatures and changes in ocean currents in the Arctic region.

It may be in our lifetime, or that of our children, that the glaciers will vanish. Life will go on, species will adapt and evolve. But what of the near future and its effect on the indigenous people of the North? What is likely to happen or is already happening?

Back at the start, we looked at the reason why we have the two Arctic climates, the governing factor being the remnant of the Gulf Stream known to scientists as the North Atlantic Drift. This crucial factor in the Arctic equation is changing... and changing in different ways.

Slowing down of the North Atlantic Drift can be attributed to the fact that less ice in the Polar Region means less ice available to melt in the summer. This in turn will slow down the northerly flow as the "draw" effect of the dense cold water sinking will be reduced. At the moment we know that the current has slowed down considerably since records began. It would be logical to think that this would mean the northern ocean and areas such as the Barents Sea would cool down. But this is not happening, because the north flowing current is warmer - to the extent that, despite the lower flow, the overall heat content, or "enthalpy", is actually greater. So the temperature of the northern waters is increasing.

Ultimately, if the total polar icecap went, the northward flow would cease. This could then trigger another ice age just like it has done in past geological times. That scenario is, hopefully, still a long way off.

So what are the future scenarios likely to be and what is currently happening?

In recent years, over less than a decade, species such as mackerel have appeared in areas such as Lyngenfjord. Previously unknown in the area, they are moving north to feed on the increasing food available there. Species such as capelin, now recovered from the over fishing in the 1980s, have also moved their "species range" north.

If the capelin moved too far north, this would have a "trophic cascade" effect on other species. Cod stocks feed heavily on capelin so they would also move north. If they moved to the Barents Sea and ceased their spring migration to the Lofoten Islands and Vestafjord it would be disastrous for the Lofoten Fishery which currently produces around 60,000 tonnes of cod in a sustainable manner from its spring fishery alone.

In the past, many Sami fishermen from the far north travelled hundreds of miles under sail and oar to take part in this fishery. Nowadays modern technology enables as many fish to be caught but with less manpower. Fishermen such as Eilif Helgesen still sail south each spring from Troms to take part in the Lofoten Fishery. His 11m vessel is equipped with gill net hauling equipment but, like many Sami fishermen, he prefers to use a "Juksa'"during the Lofoten Cod Fishery. Using the traditional "Juksa", hand line method, he only catches quality fish. This selective method avoids damaging either juvenile stock or the seabed. Nowadays his juksas are automated, electronic controlled units. This enables one man to operate as many as four lines at any one time, thus reducing the need for additional crew.

Despite the fact that modern technology has reduced the number of men directly employed in the catching sector, without reducing the catch tonnage, it has not significantly reduced the number of people employed in the processing sector.

Whereas fishing communities elsewhere - such as found in Iceland - export frozen or filleted fish, those in the Sami regions of Norway tend to export air dried fish. This fish, known in places like Spain and Portugal as Bacalao or Bacalhau, is still produced in the same manner as it was in the days of the hanseatic trade of the 17th century.

The fish are gutted, the tails are tied together in pairs and the fish are hung up on drying frames to air dry in the cold Arctic air which is of low moisture content. Even the heads are dried separately and get exported to places like Nigeria as low cost protein. A further product is that of the Norwegian and

Sami delicacy of cod tongues. Traditionally, during the spring cod season, the school children would cut the tongues out of the heads. Watching a ten year old with a large razor sharp knife swiftly carving cod tongues from the heads of giant cod is not a pastime for those who are of a fragile disposition. Nor is it a spectacle to be witnessed by anyone involved in either childcare or health and safety. Nevertheless, generations of Arctic dwelling youngsters have earned good pocket money in this manner. (As a youngster I earned pocket money breaking the heads off haddock and scrubbing the gut cavity clean to make what are known as Arbroath Smokies. This kept me out of the way during school holidays spent in the fishing village of Gourdon, where my great aunt owned a fish business. However I was never allowed a razor sharp knife.)

As has been well documented, this spring cod fishery employs a large percentage of the population, from school age to pensioners, and it is the revenue from this that underpins all other aspects of the local economy - from boat repairs and chandlers to local cafes, grocers and hoteliers. In recent years sea angling enthusiasts have congregated each spring at Svolvaer to compete in the World Cod fishing Championships. Every March since 1991 Svolvaer's hotels and self catering facilities have been filled to capacity with anglers hoping to catch their "cod of a lifetime" with many cod of over twenty kilos being brought to the weigh in.

Without the cod and other fish such as haddock and halibut, the economy of the north would suffer severely. The fact that stocks are moving north has not gone unnoticed by all concerned, whether they are scientists, politicians or on the front line as fishermen.

Another factor that could entice fish stocks to move further north is the production of plankton. In all marine food chains or webs, the bottom of the chain is microscopic phytoplankton. It is to the sea what grass is to the grazing animals of both field and savannah. Areas without marine planktons are devoid of all life except marine creatures in transit from one feeding or breeding territory to another. The most classic example of this is the area of the Pacific Ocean that lies between South America and Polynesia. As soon as one clears the coastal zones the water is clear and lifeless making it the planet's largest marine dessert, the last place on earth mariners want to be cast adrift.

Where ocean upwelling carries cold, nutrient rich waters from the dark depths up into the sunlit surface waters, the sunlight sets in motion one of the most spectacular events in the natural world - the plankton bloom.

Over the years, since 2002, the Envisat Earth Monitoring Satellite has captured images of a crescent shaped string of plankton in the North Sea weaving through the Scandinavian region. Norway and Sweden are clearly shown as is Denmark. The emerald green lake seen in Sweden is Vanern, the largest Swedish lake, appearing green due to the algae and freshwater vegetation. The green water around Denmark is due to sediments being transported in the water. Also clearly visible is Norway's second largest fjord, Hardangerfjord.

Envisat's MERIS satellite has also acquired exceptionally clear images such as one taken on 10th June 2006 and again on May 3rd 2010 at a resolution of 300m.

MERIS (Medium Resolution Imaging Spectrometer) – is an instrument optimised to detect ocean colour. The 'Milky' areas of dense plankton blooms are often covering an area larger than countries the size of Greece.

Further north, in the Barents Sea, the plankton blooms in recent years have been greater than ever recorded before. The reason is not only because of the increase in surface temperatures due to climate change but also due to the increased area of open water. This additional area can be compared to a farmer who normally had 100 acres of wheat suddenly having 1000 acres. Of course he will be able to produce more grain. However, in this case, the grain is not wheat but plankton. Not only does the extra acreage increase the ability to produce but this production isn't just proportional to the increased area. The fact that the winds, which mix the surface layers enabling the plankton to bloom, are no longer fettered by the presence of sea ice, means the ability to mix is much greater. This increase does not only extend across the surface, but to a greater depth. Unlike food production on land, which is purely two dimensional, marine production has the capability to do so in three dimensions. One Envisat image captures a plankton bloom covering an area stretching across the Barents Sea off the tip of

Northern Europe. Envisat captured this image on 19th August 2009 with its MERIS instruments which, although primarily designed to provide quantitative ocean colour measurements, have enough working flexibility of their sensors to serve applications in atmospherics and land surface science as well.

Another MERIS image of a large plankton bloom is easily identified as Ireland, it shows clearly the mixing zone just where the deep ocean currents hit the continental shelf, triggering the plankton bloom.

The large aquamarine coloured plankton bloom is shown stretching across the length of Ireland in the North Atlantic. This image was taken on 6 June 2006.

According to the Arctic Climate Impact Assessment (ACIA) and the Norwegian Polar Institute (NPI), species such as capelin and cod will emigrate north in the Barents Sea as the sea gradually warms. This not only affects the creatures that feed on these species, such as seals and cetaceans, but also the fishermen who rely upon them for their livelihood. If the major stocks of these species and others - such as saithe (coalfish), haddock and halibut - move far enough north, it could condemn the Lofoten fishery to a history. On the plus side for the Sami fishermen of Troms and Finnmark, their fishery may experience a boom during the years in which the fish stocks move north.

So what effect does this increased food source at the

bottom of the food chain have on all the other life forms above it?

The minke whale is not the largest cetacean in the Arctic waters but is one of the most prolific. Unlike the giant baleen whales which feed on the plankton and smaller creatures such as the shrimp, Pandalus borealis, the minke whale (Baleanoptera acutorostrata) also feeds on small fish species such as capelin, sandeel and herring. Studies in the North Atlantic, Barents Sea and Norwegian Sea showed that in the northern area krill was the dominant factor in their diet. In other areas this was replaced by herring or capelin, depending on what was most abundant that year. When herring and capelin are scarce, as they were in the late 80s due to feeding salmon farms, cod and other gadoids are found in their diet. In the North Sea, the principal food of the minke is the sandeel, as is also the case off Iceland, whereas the minke whales of Newfoundland during the period 1966/72 contained mainly capelin. So any increase in plankton biomass will benefit all the species across the whole spectrum of the food web. It will come as no surprise that stocks of these prey fish species have indeed increased in recent years. In May 2011, I estimated a shoal of immature herring covered a distance of more than five kilometres in length by nearly a kilometre wide in a North Troms fjord. Our sounding equipment could not tell us how far down the shoal went as the screen just showed solid fish.

A few months later, there were two incidents on the Norwegian coast of herring shoals being so large that they used up all the available oxygen in the water and were driven ashore by wind and tide. One at Reisafjord, near Alta - not far from where I measured the massive shoal - left the beach totally covered with herring – at places a foot deep! - Over an area of several square kilometres. Further south, down near Stavanger, the locals filled their freezers by wandering in with landing nets and baskets when a shoal became anoxic.

From findings such as these, it can be assumed that even if the cod move north the Sami fishermen will do what their ancestors did as the ice retreated—they will follow the food. Processing can still be carried out at places such as Svolvaer, although the fish will need to be brought south from the Barents Sea, but that will not be for quite a few years yet. Overall, the scenario envisaged in the immediate future is of a positive nature and a fishing industry that is thriving and profitable.

There are, however, other factors which may not be as positive for the Sami communities on the coast.

Sami farming activities include the keeping of small flocks of hardy sheep which are usually kept indoors during the winter months. If warmer weather enables these sheep to be kept outdoors for a prolonged period, which then means they are out during longer periods of darkness, it will expose them to greater levels of predation - particularly from wolverines. Other problems such as increased parasitic exposure and disease risks are also likely and it will take time to adjust to the new conditions.

Crops which are currently limited in variety may increase but diseases like potato blight could become more common if the climate becomes more moist. Hopefully, the heritage of a people who have adjusted to millennia of changes with great resilience will continues for centuries to come.

THE SALMON'S TALE

One fish which has a long association with the Sami people, especially those who lived in the river valleys of the great rivers of the north is the salmon. Groups known as the River Sami built a way of life in places like the Tana Valley (Deatnu in Northern Sami) in the eastern area of Finnmark, around this iconic species.

The Tana or Deatnu is often hailed as the world's greatest salmon river. Its remote Arctic valley is home to around 7000 people, the vast majority of them Sami. The everyday language of the locals is Northern Sami. Even the name of the river, Deatnu, means Great River in Sami. The complete catchment area of the river covers three Sami districts - Deatnu/Tana and Karasjohka/Karasjok, both in Norway and Ohcejohka/Utsjok in neighbouring Finland. In cultural terms, it forms the largest predominantly Sami settlement in the world.

The catchment has more than 1000 km of salmon bearing waters, including at least 35 spawning tributaries. Unlike most Norwegian Arctic rivers on the west coast which have fast tumbling waterfalls and rapids, the Deatnu is wide and fast like the large continental rivers of Europe.

It is around its salmon that the local culture is based. Fishing rights are based on hereditary farming rights. If a farmer cuts more than two tonnes of hay he is entitled to fish with either a drift/seine net or a fixed trap system known as a salmon weir, the design of which is lost in prehistory. The basis of this tradition is now enshrined in both the common law of the Sami people and the law of the Norwegian legislature.

How will climate change affect this unique culture which has developed to depend on the harvest of one species?

To understand the ability nature has to adapt to change, there could not be a better species to study than salmon (or Salmo salar, the leaper, as the Romans named it).

To start at the beginning of a salmon's life cycle we need to go to the headwaters of a river system where cold, clean, oxygen rich water percolates through gravel the size of a man's fist. For it is from these remote places, that the king of all fish will emerge to carry on the fight for survival that has faced its kind in the cold northern waters since the last ice age.

If the water temperatures do not fall below 6.5oC during the winter months, it will have a detrimental effect on the spawning of salmon.

Unlike mammals and birds, which have fairly well fixed gestation periods or incubation periods, the incubation of salmon ova is measured in degree days. Degree days are calculated as the average temperature of each day measured in degrees centigrade above Zero degrees. It takes approximately 400 degree days for the ova to develop into alevins (miniature fish still carrying a yolk sack), ready to hatch. Currently, in northern Norway, the salmon spawn before the winter freeze-up in November with the alevins hatching around the end of May. This, in real time, equals 180 to 200 days, which means that the average temperature of the water was approximately 2oC. As we all know, or should know, fresh water starts to freeze at 4oC so, for much of this time, the eggs are just sitting in a state of limbo in the iced up riverbed.

So, what would happen if the average water temperature were to rise to say 8oC?

What would happen to the developing ova?

Firstly, the 400 degree days would only span 50 days in real time. This does not give sufficient time for the ova to develop fully enough to survive outside the egg. This would lead to successful spawning being restricted to those ova deposited in the furthest upstream tributaries at higher and colder altitudes. This has already happened in the salmon's most southerly range where the few remaining salmon in Spain are restricted to a few northern rivers which are cooled by ice melt from the mountains.

At the same time as the southern range of the salmon is slowly retreating north so too is its northerly range advancing.

Fifty years ago the glaciers of Svalbard seldom permitted enough melt water to flow long enough for rivers to be viable biological units. By 2010 the flow from the glaciers in the Longyearbyen area was sustaining enough river flow in the summer months to enable the establishment of invertebrate life which now in turn supports populations of migratory Arctic Char. Local fishermen were also catching stray salmon in the Isafjord/ Adventfjord area. At this time it was the accepted wisdom that the northerly limit of the salmon's feeding range was territory to the south of Bjornoya, or Bear Island as it is known in English. The discovery of not just feeding salmon in the fjords of Spitsbergen but also the fact that they were now being sighted in the estuary areas of melt flow rivers, would indicate that it is only going to be a matter of time before salmon will be colonising these rivers.

This clearly demonstrates that species can and will shift their historic territories if the environmental factors permit. Although this shift north of Atlantic Salmon may benefit such Arctic regions as Svalbard and maybe even Canada's Baffin Island and Greenland, it will be at the expense of the few remaining salmon rivers of Spain and France.

To understand how a species such as Salmon can, if given sufficient time, we can look at a map of the Mediterranean. Why the Mediterranean?

Well, believe it or not, at one time there were salmon in the Mediterranean.

Thousands of years ago, before the icecap and glaciers retreated north; Earth was going through one of its cooler periods. The only remaining evidence of the salmon that once would have inhabited the rivers on the north shore of the

Mediterranean is to be found right up at the top of the Adriatic Sea. The rivers which flow into the Adriatic from Slovenia and Croatia are born in the cold alpine regions and it is there that the evolved remnant stock of what are now called Adriatic Salmon are found.

As the Mediterranean warmed up, these fish were reduced in their range to the slightly cooler waters at the head of the Adriatic. The waters were cooler due to the cooling effect of the snowmelt-rivers draining down from the Alps. Rivers, including Italy's River Po, flowed cold enough for a long time as the glaciers slowly melted. This gradual warming was much slower than the Mediterranean, giving the salmon of the Adriatic's enclosed and slower circulating system time to adapt, or evolve, to suit the changing climatic conditions.

Now, thousands of years later, they are still a salmon, but with sufficient differences in both size and habitat requirement to be classified by scientists as a distinct species. The Atlantic salmon of the Alta and Deatnu can reach a length of over a metre whereas the Adriatic salmon barely grows to half that length.

Unfortunately, their current range and small population numbers of Adriatic Salmon mean that as a species they are now classified as highly vulnerable. Whether they can continue to cope with the current, much faster, climate warming is not known. Due to feeding restrictions, the Adriatic has much lower food availability than the cold North Atlantic; the Adriatic Salmon grows to a maximum of 40 to 50 cm, whereas the record Atlantic Salmon from the Deatnu was treble that length.

Will the salmon of the mighty Deatnu adapt to warmer water? Or will they die out?

Even at the increased rate of climate change, it will be many years before we will be able to answer these questions. The fact that there were once salmon in the Mediterranean and that they still exist today in a different geographical location does give us hope that they, by adaptation, will survive as a species and that the River Sami of the Deatnu will survive in parallel with them.

WHO ARE THE INUIT?

When I was a child in the 1950s, I knew the race of people from the frozen wastes of Canada and Greenland as the Eskimo. So how come we now call them Inuit? Well, this is probably the first thing to note of the similarities between the Sami and The Inuit. Just as the Sami were previously known by the derogatory term Lapps, the Inuit were known by what many anthropologists thought was the Algonquin Indian word meaning "eaters of raw flesh" or Eskimo. However, more recent linguistic research indicates that this might not be the case. It may actually be that rather than coming from the Algonquin language it may have come from the Montagnais word for "snowshoe trapper". This description has less negative connotations.

But the use of the word "Inuit" which is the Inuktitut word for "people" has itself led to problems among the indigenous people of the north, For not all of those people that we once called Eskimos can be termed Inuit as they don't all speak Inuktitut. Most of their languages do however have common roots and just like Gaelic speakers from the Scottish Hebridean Islands who can understand Irish Gaelic the same applies to different Inuit people. Many of the indigenous minority in Alaska and Siberia speak the Yupik language. The closely related inhabitants of the Aleutian Islands call themselves Aleuts and speak the Aleut language. Those indigenous people of Alaska's north coast refer to themselves as the Inupiat while the Inuit of Greenland prefer to be termed Kalaalit. But for the purpose of avoiding confusion I will refer to both the inhabitants of Canada's Eastern Arctic and Greenland as Inuit.

The first white traders and trappers had heard of the Eskimo long before actually meeting them. What they had been told one can only guess, but it was obviously negative in nature and led to the traders of the Hudson Bay Company keeping a distance from the Inuit for many years before an amicable trading relationship was established.

Before going into the problems that are being encountered by the various groups of Inuit in modern times we must understand the traditional ways of the Inuit. The sustainable and sharing manner which enabled their communities to survive in such a hostile environment where the white man perished is certainly worthy of study. When we look into their family life, where devotion to the survival of the group was put ahead of personal survival, we find a truly altruistic ethos seldom seen among what we often term "civilisation". The following pages look into some of the aspects of Inuit life before the coming of the white man with his laws, beliefs and bureaucracy. Much of what is described has now gone as the nomadic ways of these children of the ice have been taken from them in the misconceived ideal that it would improve both their physical and spiritual wellbeing.

If one looks at a map of North America the main area inhabited by the Algonquin speaking tribes lay along the border between modern day Canada and the USA. From their furthest west lands in what is now Alberta right through to the Labrador Peninsula in the east the language of the native people was that of the dominant Algonquin culture. Theirs was a settled culture with permanent villages and like farmers of today they regarded all the lands on which they hunted and fished to be their property and theirs alone. On the other hand the Inuit were nomadic and followed their quarry throughout the year. In the case of the Ihalmiut of the Denbigh culture and the Inuit of the further east Dorset culture this meant that in winter they followed the caribou south on to lands which were hunted on by the Algonquin. The northern limits of the Algonquin was the area of Hudson Bay south of present day Churchill in Manitoba, east round the southern shore of Hudson Bay to the point where the tree line meets the coast north of the Nastapoka River. From there it followed the tree line across to Ungava Bay, The area to the north of the tree line now lie within the semi autonomous Inuit region of Nunavik, the principal town and administrative capital of which is Kuujjuak. The population of the region is approximately twelve thousand, most of whom are Inuit. The coastal region of present day Labrador from the Torngat Mountains in the north all the way south, almost to the Belle Isle Straits, was never regarded as Algonquin land and was permanently occupied by the semi nomadic Inuit. Nowadays it is known as Nunatsiavut with its twin capitals being Nain and Hopedale. With a population of fewer than two thousand two hundred in 2006 it is one of the smallest semi autonomous regions in Canada.

It was in the area around Hudson Bay and on the Ungava Peninsula that friction between the two cultures was greatest. In the case of the Ihalmiut to the east of Hudson Bay there is archaeological evidence that this constant conflict pushed them north to the area around the Foxe Basin.

Recent archaeological evidence from this area indicates a cultural change from a dependency upon the caribou to one more dependent on ice hunting for marine mammals such as seals and small whales such as beluga and narwhal.

Contact between the two peoples was rare, usually hostile, and it was only after the setting up of trading posts by the Hudson Bay Company (HBC) in the James Bay area in the 1750s that contact was finally made between the white man and the Inuit. Initially the white men from the Hudson Bay Company were afraid of the Inuit. Again, this was due to the influence and stories told about these "eaters of raw meat" by the Algonquin. Another factor which greatly influenced the early HBC employees was the tragic episode which led to the death of 14 year old Matthew Warden, who was the Duke of Richmond. He was killed by Inuit hunters in February 1755 while based at the HBC trading base at Little Whale River on the east side of Hudson Bay. However, once an amicable relationship was established and the animosity between Algonquin and Inuit overcome - the 'ice broken' might be a very apt way of putting it - trade between the HBC and the Inuit soon developed into friendship and respect between the two parties.

The map of the Arctic shows the areas which surround the Arctic Ocean. The lands that border the Arctic Ocean can, as previously explained, be divided into two zones, the warm zone and the cold zone. It may sound strange to describe part of the Arctic as a "warm zone" but, in relation to the rest of the area, the parts affected by the North Atlantic Drift are much warmer than the rest of the Arctic Zone. It is this variation that has led to the Arctic being populated by two dominant peoples. The "Warm Zone" is dominated by the Sami peoples and, farther east, the closely related Nenets. Interestingly the Nenets were at one time known as the Samoyed, a name that sounds remarkably like Sami. The name Samoyed is now only used in relation to the dogs of that breed which had their origins as the Nenets sled dogs.

The much larger "Cold Zone" is the domain of the Inuit. Whereas the Sami were originally hunter gatherers who evolved into fishermen, small scale farmers and reindeer herders, the Inuit of the "Cold Zone" had little opportunity to do so.

Instead the Inuit became the Arctic's super predators, top of the biotic pyramid - even higher than the polar bear, which frequently is referred to as the Apex Predator.

As nomadic hunters, seeking prey species in a frozen land meant that large distances were often travelled to find that quarry. A very large area was needed to support a small number of these hunters and their families and this led to the Inuit migrating from the west - from the Chuckchi area of north east Siberia and the Wrangle Islands, off Siberia's north coast - as far as the east coast of Greenland. Their north to south range extended from the North West corner of Greenland to the James Bay area at the south end of Hudson Bay. Even covering such a massive area, their numbers were never great. The population of a small country like Scotland has, in all probability, always outnumbered the Inuit. In places like Europe, languages vary dramatically over a short distance. For example, French, Flemish, Dutch, German and Danish are all spoken along a coastline of less than a thousand miles. The Inuit language, although it has many different written forms, has not been influenced by outside cultures and is spread across a distance of approximately five thousand miles. A Chuckchi Inuit from the west side of the Bering Strait has a natural language very similar to a Kalaalit Inuit from Quaquartoc in Southern Greenland. Unlike the Sami of the "Warm Arctic", the white man has not actively tried to wipe out either their culture or their language.

The original Inuit, which in the Inuit language means "the people", were from around what is now known as the Chuckchi area of Eastern Siberia around six thousand years ago. Tool remains, as well as the modern day Inuit mythology, suggest that these nomads were originally an inland culture which, at that time, had not adopted the coastal culture of the modern race. By around 3000 BC, the Bering Strait had been crossed and the Aleutian Islands colonised. This was not the first human migration across the Bering Straits. The ancestors of the Plains Indians had crossed around 10,000 years earlier and continued to travel south as far as Terra del Fuego at the southern tip of South America.

Once established in the Aleutian Islands, further migration eastwards continued but, at this point, the migrating groups split to form two fairly distinct groups. Those who remained on the coast and colonised the area from the Aleutian Islands to the east Bering Sea became a society dependent on sea mammals and, to a lesser degree, fish.

The Ihalmiut

Those who migrated inland became dependent on caribou and their descendants became known as Ihalmiut, which means "the other people" in the Inuit language.

The relationship between the Plains Indians of the south, principally the Algonquin tribes and the Ihalmiut was always contentious. It meant that the numbers of Ihalmiut were never very great and, although estimated at around 7,000 in 1886, this had diminished to only 30 in 1950 (although other unregistered groups possibly augmented this number.)

The first encounter with the white man, whom the Ihalmiut called Qaplunaat in the Inuktitut language, was during the Barren Lands Expeditions of 1893 and 1894 led by Joseph Tyrell. From then on, the decline of the Ihalmiut culture was dramatic. They relied on the herds of caribou for food and furs but the fur trade with companies such as HBC led to over exploitation of the herds - not by the Ihalmiut but by white hunters. Introduction of alien foods into their diet (foods such as flour and sugar) caused sickness and introduced disease, probably diphtheria, rapidly reducing the Ihalmiut numbers. A further problem that the remaining population faced was that of sled dog sickness, thought to be either rabies or distemper.

By the mid 20th century, the Canadian Government was aware of the situation and tried relocating the few remaining families from the Ennadai Lake to Nueltin Lake. This was unsuccessful and the people returned to Ennadai Lake.

Those claiming Ihalmiut cultural status now number around 3,000. Most of these are located in the Chesterfield Inlet, Rankin Inlet, Whale Cove, Eskimo Point and Baker Lake in the Nunavut Region.

Those Ihalmiut who had been pushed to the Arctic coast by the earlier established "Indian'"races were thought to have settled in the area of the Foxe Basin. Archaeological evidence from this area indicated a cultural change to that of ice hunting. Their earlier predecessors had been termed 'Denbigh' or 'Arctic Small Tool' culture but the later ice hunting people were known as the 'Dorset Culture'.

By around 1000AD the Dorset Culture had vanished but another culture, the Thule, appeared in the coastal areas. These groups had settlements of 200 to 300 people who were dependant on marine hunting. Whether they evolved from the Inuit from along the Arctic coast of the Bering Sea or from Ihalmiut from inland is difficult to establish.

The Thule Culture itself vanished around the 18th century to be replaced by the Inuit society we know today. What caused the collapse of the Thule Culture is not fully understood but it could have been the arrival of the European whalers allied to the "Little Ice Age" that occurred around that time. (Glacial expansion theoretically started around 1550, ending in late 19th century.)

Note:- The word Caribou is most likely to have been derived from the Micmaw word Xalibu with the meaning of "animal which paws through the snow for its food". The Micmaw people are the First Nation People of Canada's Maritime Provinces and the Gaspe Peninsula of Quebec.

THE INUIT AND
THE VIKING

Strange as it may seem, the first North Americans to meet up with Europeans were the Inuit. Norsemen, led by Norse outlaw Erik the Red, colonised southern Greenland. He doubtless met local Inuit of the Dorset period in the area around Qaqortoq (see note). The remnants of his own settlement lie across the fjord from Narsarsuaq at Qassiarsuk. Now a destination for tourists from cruise ships Qassiarsuk is reached by small boats leaving from Narsarsuaq then a short hike of around 2 ½ kilometres to the ruins. Thankfully on reaching there one finds a small cafe and toilet facilities. Eric the Red's son, Leif Eriksson, went as far as establishing a settlement in what is now known as L'Anse aux Meadows at the very northerly point of Newfoundland. This was five centuries before Columbus reached the Caribbean. Any relationship that they might have had with the local Inuit was destroyed by Leif's brother, Thorvald, who murdered eight of the first group of Inuit he came across.

The Norsemen called the Inuit "Skraellings", the best, or most polite, translation of which is "primitive ones". Further attempts by Leif's half sister, Freydis Eriksdottir, were equally disastrous and ended in massacres of the Norsemen. Not by the Skraelings but by those under the command of the rather unstable and bloodthirsty Freydis.

So, apart from establishing themselves in Inuit folklore, the Vikings had minimal impact on Inuit culture.

Note: - Qaqortoq was formerly known by the Danish

name of Julianehab and is located in the south western municipality of Kujalleq, near the very Viking sounding Cape Thorvaldson. Thorvald being son of Erik the Red and brother of Leif Eriksson

INUIT DWELLINGS

The best known of all Inuit dwellings is, as every school child should know, the Igloo. However, the type of dwelling this conjures up - the dome-shaped ice house - is the preserve only of the Eastern Inuit. Even at that, it is only a seasonal dwelling used in the worst of the winter months. The Inuit word "Igloo" means "house" and covers all types of dwelling used by these people. One photograph from 1930 shows a Hudson Bay Inuit putting in a window made of clear ice. Where ice windows were used, they were always positioned facing the side from which the sun shone, that is facing south. Often a sloping shelf of snow was built to enhance the reflection of the weak rays of the winter sun. This is probably one of the earliest known forms of using solar energy as it increased both light and heat within the dwelling. Large igloos, big enough to house a complete Inuit family, were built to last the whole winter and were only abandoned when the warmth of the sun started to melt them on the inside. Depending on the location of the winter camp, this could be any time from early May to late June.

Much smaller ice houses were built by Inuit hunters when they went off to find game or go ice fishing. These smaller ice dwellings often had an internal dimension of around six feet. In Alex Ritchie's story of how he crossed Baffin Island in the winter of 1909 he described sleeping in one of these tiny igloos with Inuit hunters. As he was much taller, he was allowed to sleep across the middle. His Inuit companions slept either side of him. I have vague recollections of his brother, Edward, saying that Alex's feet were sticking into the tunnel that formed the door.

Another interesting feature of the ice igloo was the manner in which it was built. Unlike brick houses which are built one course on top of the other, the Igloo was built in a continuous spiral finishing with a block at the top acting as an effective keystone.

Heating of an igloo is an art, only perfected by Inuit women using a lamp made from soapstone and fuelled with whale or seal blubber. Keeping this lamp trimmed so that it gave heat and light without either melting the home or choking the occupants with acrid smoke took years of practice. Inuit children learned skills like this from a very young age (prior to white man's influence taking over). If the heat started melting the inner walls a hole was cut through to let cold air in to quickly reduce the temperature. This stopped bedding and clothing from getting wet for, once wet, it could not be dried until the next summer. Once the temperature stabilised, just around freezing, the hole would be plugged with snow which soon became part of the original structure.

Another famous illustration, part of the Smithsonian Institution collection, shows the sealskin tent of a western Inuit on a hunting expedition. His kayak and sled are seen on the left of the picture. Very unusual is the fact that this tent, or Tupik, as it is called in the Inuit language, is covered in sealskins. Even for those Inuit who lived on the coastal regions, the normal covering would have been made from caribou skins.

The Tupik of the Inuit has a lot in common with both the Lavvu of the Sami and the Teepee of the Plains Indians – a classic example of different people coming up with the same solution to a communal problem. In this case, the problem was to devise an easily transported and erected dwelling suitable for a nomadic people. The fact that timber for structural support was nearly impossible to source meant that when an Inuit group found timber washed up on the shore it was regarded as highly as white men would buried treasure. In some areas, which were isolated even from other Inuit groups, the people believed that trees grew on the ocean floor. This was a logical conclusion when one understands that Inuit such as those in the north of Greenland or Ellesmere Island in the north of Nunavut had never seen a tree.

This shortage of timber did not go unnoticed by the companies who traded with the Inuit settlements north of the tree line. One company in particular, the Revillon Freres, sent sloops to their many trading posts in the eastern Arctic region of Canada. These sloops always carried larch poles as deck cargo. Larch is light, tough and is naturally rot resistance - ideal for tent poles.

In 1899, a Frenchman, Victor Revillon opened up a wholesale warehouse in Edmonton, Alberta, and in less than five years had 23 stores across Canada. Within a few years this had expanded to include a network of fur trading posts across the north, in direct competition to the Hudson Bay Company. Revillon Freres' Arctic operation was split into two divisions: the western division covered the northern areas of Manitoba, west to the North West territories; the eastern division covered the James Bay and Ungava Bay areas of Northern Quebec using the company's own fleet of vessels based in Montreal, where Revillon Freres had both their major distribution base and their headquarters.

These vessels were mainly schooners bought specifically for working in the Arctic waters. One Revillon vessel, the Jean Revillon, was renamed the Fort James; it was the first vessel to circumnavigate the North American Continent in 1928/29.

By 1909 Revillon Freres had 48 stores in its eastern division while the Hudson Bay Company had 52. Many of the Inuit villages in modern Nunavut are situated on the sites of Revillon trading posts from the early 1900s.

In 1926 the Hudson Bay Company bought a 54% share of Revillon's fur trade operation and by 1936 owned 100%. The resulting fur trade operations were renamed 'Rupert's Land Trading Company' in 1938.

Robert Flaherty's famous 1922 film 'Nanook of the North' was filmed near a Revillon trading post at Inukjuak on the north east of Hudson Bay. The film is said to be Canada's first documentary film and was financed by Revillon Freres.

Sod Houses

The most common type of house of the western dwelling Inuit people, particularly those of Alaska, was the sod or turf house. Another photograph which was taken at Nushagak in Alaska in 1887 is part of a collection from the Smithsonian Institute in Washington is probably one of the best photograph showing a turf igloo of the period. At the time this was taken this was the most common type of dwelling of the Western Inuit.

Its semi-subterranean construction kept the profile low and less affected by wind exposure. It also made the most economic use of available materials. The inner walls were usually of rubble with the turfs placed around the outside. Light and heat were provided by the traditional Inuit blubber fuelled lamp.

As timber was a valued and scarce commodity, the roof supports were often made from the jawbones and rib bones of whales. The more permanent nature of this type of dwelling, which the Inuit referred to as an Igloo, clearly indicates that the hunting of large sea mammals along the coast of the Bering Sea and Pacific coasts was more dependable than elsewhere. This enabled these Inuit to lead a more settled than those of the Eastern Arctic who were, at that time, almost totally nomadic.

The similarity to the "gamme" the type of turf house used by the Sami of Arctic Norway and built on the Tundra clearly demonstrates, once again, how two different cultures - thousands of miles apart - can come up with similar answers to a common problem. There is an example of this type of turf shelter at the Sami Cultural Centre at Manndalen in North Troms, Norway. Nearby stands the bare frame of a Sami Lavvu, similar in many ways to both the frame of the Inuit Tupik and Plains Indian Teepee.

The design of this turf building has regularly been used in temperatures below minus 40oC without detrimental effects on those sheltering inside.

The main differences between the Sami structure and that of the Inuit is the use of timber. The internal construction of the "gamme" is of birch branches covered with sods and further layers of skins. Unlike the Inuit sod igloo, the Sami gamme has a central roof vent to allow smoke from the wood fire to escape. Whereas the Sami have access to firewood this is not the case for the Inuit, particularly those in the Eastern Arctic where wood is too valuable to burn. The only source of wood available to areas such as Greenland, Baffin Island and Ellesmere Island was driftwood, supplemented by wreckage from the whaling ships crushed in the ice or wrecked on the shoreline from the 18th century onward.

POLAR INUIT

Following the collapse of the Thule Culture, which was a sedentary system based in settled communities of two to three hundred people, the Inuit returned to a nomadic existence. Living in small highly mobile groups scattered widely across the barren wastelands from Alaska, through northern Canada all the way to Eastern Greenland,

These groups had their own favourite fishing and hunting areas that were used on a seasonal migration basis. There were few permanent bases in the post Thule era. This started to change once the Inuit began their long relationship with the whaling ships, particularly those of the Dundee whaling fleet from Scotland.

One group of Inuit from Northwest Greenland, forefathers of the Etah Inuit, went into relative isolation. At this time they were the furthest north of any people on the planet.

Their prolonged isolation was so complete that they assumed that the whole planet was frozen and that they were the only people on Earth. They also believed that the trees that washed up on their shores had broken free from the seabed where they believed that trees grew. In reality, these trees had most likely grown in the Taiga and had floated down the great rivers of the north flowing into the Arctic Ocean. Some of these trees may have taken many years to reach Greenland.

It was only in 1818 that the expedition led by Sir John Ross discovered this group of Inuit, who at that time numbered 200 to 300 individuals. Their amazement on seeing a fully rigged British naval vessel must have been worth seeing!

One very interesting point revealed by this encounter was that the Inuit accompanying Ross as translators were able to communicate with these Polar Inuit. This clearly illustrates the fact that lack of outside influence across the Arctic for millennia has enabled the Inuit languages to remain close to their original form.

INUIT WOMEN

Prior to modern times, the Inuit woman was indispensable to the economic life of both the family and the group as a whole. Although, if she had an able bodied husband, she would neither hunt nor fish, (the exception being she would fish for tomcod) her skills lay in the ability to skin animals and birds from which she would make all forms of clothing. Her ability to manufacture clothes from pelts - which she had dressed in such a manner that they were soft and yet weatherproof and warm - was unsurpassed. She could produce hats, jackets, trousers and boots - indeed every item of clothing required by her family to survive comfortably in the harsh climate of even the worst Arctic winter.

Her culinary skills were a whole different matter. As the word "Eskimo" clearly implies, her chances of attaining a Michelin star were minimal. Restaurants specialising in Inuit Cuisine I have yet to find, but I admit I have not gone out of my way to find one. Most Inuit have little objection to eating raw meat or fish. When birds eggs are happened upon, they are often eaten on the spot just as a European would eat a ripe plum from a tree. If freshly killed game, for example seal or narwhal, is still warm this is often shared out among villagers and eaten straight off before it can get cold.

Before commerce was established with the white traders, the only cooking utensils owned by the Inuit were heavy stone pots or buckets made of walrus skin. These "utensils" did not really encourage the development of "haute cuisine". Indeed, the nearest the Inuit wife came to even "hot cuisine" was achieved by dropping a series of hot stones into a stew which eventually gave a semblance of being cooked. (In the case of meat from the polar bear it was essential to cook it to prevent trichinosis.) Nowadays, the Inuit in townships have electric cookers and kettles. They cook and bake just like Canadians or Europeans but still enjoy their "natural" food raw.

Inuit husbands are still much more likely to praise their

wife's sewing and clothes-making abilities than her cooking. In the Arctic it was, and still is, essential for clothing to be warm and well-fitting and for boots to be watertight.

A good wife was essential for an Inuit hunter! The ultimate test was her ability to cover his kayak. His life depended upon her skill, both in preparing the skins and in sewing them securely to the kayak frame.

The prepared skins were stretched over the frame and, using animal sinews as thread, were lock stitched together. Once wet, both the sinews and the skins shrink and become taut like a drum skin.

An essential implement for any Inuit woman was, and in many areas still is, the unusual shaped "woman's knife" known as the "ulu". Before the white man brought metal tools to these Arctic people their tools were fashioned from natural materials such as stone or bone. Artefacts of the earliest Canadian Inuit led to them being termed the "small tool people". Among these "small tools" of the Denbigh Culture were knives made of hard stone and needles made from bone. Once the white man came these tools were soon replaced by metal equivalents and the ulu in its present form came into being. Today's ulu is a crescent shaped blade perfectly shaped for flensing skins to clean off all remains of fat and muscle tissue. Flint scrapers of a similar shape have been unearthed by archaeologists researching Stone Age sites in Scandinavia. These flint predecessors of today's ulus did not have handles but must have had to be held in some form of glove to protect the user's hand. As rock was replaced by metal a wooden handle was added which enabled the user to have more control over the blade. At one time Inuit women would use their ulu to cut walrus hide into a long spiral strip to use as harpoon lines. Narrower strips, known as "babiche" were used to make nets to trap seals under the ice. Different regions of Greenland developed their own particular style of ulu. Three distinct designs are 1) those in the North, the Thule District, which have a single stem splitting into two stems joining the handle to a rounded blade. 2) West Greenland, where a single stem joins the handle to an oval bade which has points either end of the cutting edge. 3) East Greenland Ulu, also known as the tsakkeq, where the blade is more of an oblong shape and is attached to the handle by two stems, one either end of the handle. Although it is the men who make the ulu it is normally the woman that uses it. I say normally because while in Greenland in 2015 I took a photograph of a hunter cleaning a fresh seal skin using his wife's ulu. This just proves that the emancipation of women is far reaching.

INUIT CHILDREN

Traditionally, the Inuit had small families. One of the main reasons for this was the fact that the diet of the adult Inuit was made up entirely of high fat and difficult to digest staples such as seal or whale blubber. This type of food is totally unsuitable for small babies and took a long time to introduce safely into their diet. For this reason, it was the norm for Inuit mothers to continue breast-feeding until the child was at least three years old. Breast-feeding mothers have a lower fertility level due to hormonal changes which act as a natural barrier to conception - leading to a wider gap between pregnancies. European mothers will rarely breast-feed beyond the child's first birthday, resulting in them being able to become pregnant a lot sooner after the birth of a child than their Inuit counterparts. This extended period of breast feeding led to the hormone level of the mother being severely affected. Even after breast feeding ceased it took a considerable period of time before conception was possible. This had the overall effect of keeping Inuit families small with a space of six or seven years between children not being uncommon.

No baby clothes were ever made as, until the baby could walk - or try to walk, they were carried in the overlarge hood of their mother's "amaat". The "amaat" is the female equivalent of the men's anorak. Its uniquely large hood and wide shoulders form a cradle for the child as well as a useful rucksack and - its primary purpose - a warm weatherproof outer garment for the mother. By lying in the hood up against his mother's back, the baby received not just warmth but the vital comfort of the closeness of the mother. This garment was a well thought out and practical garment for a nomadic people. When a newborn or very young child was being carried in the amaat nappies of either caribou skin or reindeer moss were used. Feeding the baby was easily achieved by pulling the wide shoulders round so that the child had access to the breast without being exposed to the cold. The large hood also enabled older babies to peek out over the mother's shoulders. It also allowed air to circulate if the baby was sleeping deep inside the hood. A strap which is attached and fastened to the front of the amaat goes around the back, preventing the collar from constricting the mother's throat and enabling the baby to remain upright. The practicality of having a baby that is constantly content due to the mother's movements may be part of the reason that Inuit children are so happy and close to their parents. Where an older sister is present, she will often wear an amaat to carry the younger sibling. Inuit mothers would normally carry a child in this manner until they were two or three years old.

Inuit parents are very affectionate to their offspring and

children are never punished harshly. To hear an Inuit child utter the words Atata, father, or Anana, mother, one senses both affection and respect.

Once the child was able to walk, the mother made clothes - identical to those of the adult, right down to the miniature sealskin boots. Traditionally, the first toy that an Inuit toddler was given was a miniature sled. Since, in most of the areas inhabited by Inuit, sledging was possible for nine months of the year, the child had ample chance to use his sled. One of the first games the child would learn was to hitch his sled to the nearest unsuspecting Malamute pup that wandered near the igloo. Any Inuit child brought up with Malamute dogs as their guardians soon became friends. They played and bonded with the malamute pups to the extent that by the time they were about twelve years of age they were able to take their own dogs hunting small game such as arctic hare and ptarmigan. Assuming that is, that the encampment was in an area free from predators such as wolves and bears.

Just how endearing Inuit children can be was clearly demonstrated a few years ago when I was visiting Nanortalik in South West Greenland. I was lecturing on board a cruise ship which was visiting this one time trading port, which has an amazing living museum of old houses and settlement buildings dating from the whaling days. On arrival the ship sent a shore party ahead to set up a reception area for the tenders to disembark the passengers. With them, the crew took flasks of coffee, sandwiches and a box of fruit, consisting of bananas and apples. Within a very short time two smiling Inuit children, accompanied by a very large dog appeared on the pier next to the unloading pontoon. Practicing their skills with the English language, which consisted mainly of the word "Hi!", this pair launched their well rehearsed charm offensive of smiles. It didn't take long for the hardened seamen to succumb. The first crewman offered a sandwich to the two little charmers. One of whom promptly accepted and then fed the sandwich to the dog. The crewman then indicated that he meant the sandwiches were for them, not the dog, and then again offered them a sandwich. The pair then pointed to the bananas and apples. This request was promptly granted and each child received a banana and an apple. While the child with the dog remained on the pier the other child ran off toward the village. A few minutes later the pier was invaded by, what appeared to be, every kid under ten years of age in Nanortalik. Needless to say, a quick radio call to the ship saw a load of sandwiches; bananas and apples arrive on a subsequent tender.

UNIQUE INUIT HUNTING AND FISHING METHODS

The methods of hunting described in the following section are not those used by the Inuit of the 21st century. In some cases the techniques described will be totally unknown to the younger generations of today as these methods died out with their great grandparents' generation. However it is important for these hunting methods to be documented and explained to both the Inuit of today as well as those whose interest in the Arctic is either as academic and tourists. By recording these for others to read I hope to encourage a respect for these brave people and the way in which they embraced and in many ways protected the frozen environment that was their home.

SEAL HUNTING

The most important quarry of the numerous Inuit people across the frozen wastes of the Arctic has always been the seal. Over the millennia they have been the most reliable source of not only food but also of blubber to fuel their lamps and hides for clothing, dog harnesses and harpoon lines. Added to these items are boots and a host of other ancillary items that the white man would never contemplate. Whereas the skin of the small ringed seal made fine supple clothing once processed by the industrious Inuit wife, the tough hide of the huge bearded seal was ideal for situations requiring a stronger and more durable material. Such items as the soles of boots, kayak and umiak covers needed to be strong yet pliable when in contact with the Arctic ice but the most important item manufactured from both bearded seal and walrus hides was that of harpoon lines. As previously described, in the section on Inuit woman, the hide was staked out after tanning and a hole cut in the centre. (The leather from the hole was never discarded but used for boot soles or other small items.) From this central hole the Inuit wife would, using her "ulu", cut a single continuous spiral of amazingly uniform width until the edge of the skin was reached. Once cut this line, known as "babiche", was then stretched and dried to be used as a harpoon line of remarkable strength. Despite the great importance of the bearded seal's hide it is the more common ringed seal that is the most abundant and as it is present throughout the year it was the mainstay of the Inuit food economy.

Hunting seals on the winter ice had sustained the Inuit since the earliest of times and prior to the coming of the white man and his rifles was carried out using two notable traits of the Inuit people, stealth and patience.

Seals are mammals and therefore, despite living and feeding beneath the Arctic ice, they have to come up to the surface to breathe. It is this feature that the Inuit exploited. To ensure that they did not get trapped beneath the ice and drown the seals maintained a series of breathing holes which they kept clear by continuous scrapping away of any surface ice as it formed. Using this predictable factor the Inuit hunter would maintain a patient vigil, sometimes for days, over a breathing hole in the knowledge that a seal would eventually surface.

As the ice formed with the approaching winter the seals used their sharp claws to scrape a hole from the underside of the ice. Before the onset of the current climate change this ice would frequently reach a thickness of two metres. This thickness would have been impossible for a seal to claw through so established breathing holes had to be constantly kept clear of ice every time the seal came up to breath. As each seal had a number of such breathing holes it could be a considerable time between visits to any given hole. This problem was somewhat eased by the fact that any series of breathing holes were not the unique property of any individual seal but were communally used by a number of individuals. This increased the opportunities given to the hunter. Even so it takes determination and resolve to stand out in the icy Arctic wind for endless hours clutching a harpoon while waiting to hear the scratching sound of breaking ice then the deep breathing of a surfaced seal.

Despite the fact that openings in the ice, termed leads, were frequently available for the seals to use for breathing the breathing holes were always maintained as the seals seem aware that such openings will inevitably close as the ice pack shifts.

The Inuit locate the breathing holes using their dogs to sniff out their location. Sometimes they are easier to spot than others, even without the use of a dog, as each hole is surrounded by a characteristic mound which resembles a miniature volcano. These "mini volcanoes" are formed from the water which splashes out when the seal comes up into the void and also from the condensation from the seals breath. On newly formed ice that is windswept and has no build up of snow the holes are easily spotted, but once the ice has a snow covering location is nigh impossible without the canine aid. In late winter, as the breeding season approaches, it is possible for the hunter to locate holes that are being used by the bull seal as the smell of the musk produced at this time is unmistakeably pungent. The female unfortunately leaves no scent and is therefore much more difficult to locate.

When a seal visited its breathing hole, the waiting hunter would thrust his harpoon into the centre of the hole without aiming. Hopefully this blind thrust would impale the quarry somewhere around the head in an area with skin tough enough to give the harpoon's toggle head a secure hold. The knowledge that the Inuit have accrued over many generations regarding the manner in which different seal species construct their breathing holes enabled the traditional hunter to gauge the angle of the thrust to increase the chance of a successful hunt. Most seal species in the Arctic do not excavate their breathing holes vertically from bottom to top. The most usual form of cavity was excavated at an angle from the underside of the ice that then formed a ledge on to which the seal could haul out before reaching the actual breathing hole. Knowing which way this platform was orientated was crucial if the single harpoon thrust was to connect. Each hole, on discovery, was probed using the butt end of the harpoon to determine this orientation so that the hunter knew exactly from which direction the seal would approach the hole.

Despite all this knowledge and preparation, breathing hole hunting was still an arduous occupation requiring tremendous patience and endurance. Although it was possible that a seal might appear after a few minutes, the more common scenario was that of a prolonged wait in absolute silence. Even the slightest sound of a foot movement on the surface of the ice was sufficient to alert the seal and the wary creature would then move off to a neighbouring hole.

The manner in which the hunter positioned himself at the hole was also crucial to the outcome of the hunt. He had to be downwind of the hole to prevent his scent drifting into the path of the seal. He would try to make his stance as comfortable as possible. Avoiding facing into the wind was almost essential. Despite the warmth of his parka's fur rimmed hood facing into a sub-zero Arctic breeze over a long period could easily induce facial paralysis or frostbite.

Occasionally, if snow conditions permitted, a shelter screen would be built to reduce the effects of the wind. The penetrating cold also affected the hunter's feet. The snow which covers sea ice is permanently wet as the salinity of the sea water lowers the point at which the snow remains frozen. To combat this, the Inuit hunter would, under most circumstances, avoid standing directly on the ice. At the very least he would spread a hide on the surface of the ice. This not only gave an additional layer of insulation but also helped muffle any unintentional noise when the hunter changed stance. A more common method keeping the hunter's feet dry and warm was the use of a small, three legged stool. This method was also thought to reduce the shadow of the hunter's feet which may have been visible from beneath the ice.

While, either standing on a hide or perched on his stool, the hunter would slide one arm inside his caribou parka. This helped retain body heat in the event of a long wait.

During the long wait the harpoon was either held in the free hand or supported on stilts stuck in the snow as was the large knife which would be used to enlarge the hole once a seal had been harpooned.

The importance of staying downwind of the breathing hole was crucial as the first thing a seal does on arriving at the hole is sniff the air for potential predators. Another thing it does, particularly in daylight hours, is to see that there are no inexplicable shadows or shapes visible from above the translucent ice cover.

Only once the wary seal has satisfied itself that there is no imminent danger will it haul itself onto the ice shelf beneath the breathing hole. At this point it will then use its claws to scratch away any ice which has formed around the vent before finally taking several deep and audible breaths. This is the point at which the hunter strikes.

Plunging his harpoon through with maximum force he hopefully impales the seal. If the strike is successful and the seal is engaged one of two events will happen. Either the harpoon shaft will disengage and fall onto the ice or it will be pulled into the hole where it will prevent the seal's escape from the ice shelf. In either case the hunter will now jump down from his stool and stand on the harpoon line. At the same time he will pick up the large ice knife and start to enlarge the hole to a size where he can withdraw the struggling seal. It was very seldom that the initial harpoon strike would prove fatal, on most occasions it was a live and violently struggling creature that was hauled from its icy cavern onto the sea's frozen surface. Agile as they are while in their aquatic environment, seals are awkward and nearly helpless on land. Even more so on ice that offers little in the way of traction. Once the seal was on the ice the hunter swiftly rolled the hapless creature on to its back before lifting its head and upper body clear of the ice, all the time avoiding its teeth filled snapping jaws.

Then, using the full weight of his body, the hunter then forced the animal's neck down onto its chest. A loud cracking noise signalled that the vertebrae in the neck had been disarticulated and the spinal cord broken. This swiftly ended the seal's struggle. Once dead a thong with a handle, usually made from either bone or ivory carved to resemble a seal, was attached to the carcass to enable the hunter to drag the trophy back to camp or to a small sled built for the purpose.

Tradition demanded that, unlike whales and walrus, the skinning and butchering of seals was the domain of the Inuit wife. Unlike the larger creatures seals were processed inside the igloo, whether it was the ice house of the eastern Inuit or the semi-subterranean sod house of the Inuit who lived in the west. This process was not carried out without its taboos and rituals. After laying the seal on a layer of fresh snow and before skinning commenced, fresh water was poured into the mouth of the dead seal. The reasoning behind this was that the Inuit believe that as the seals live in salt water they must be continually thirsty. By showing respect the seal's spirit would be appeased and speak favourably of those who treated it in an honourable manner. (Strangely, it is also a custom among Highland deerstalkers in Scotland to place fresh grass into the mouth of a newly shot stag, again this is to show respect to the animal.)

Another part of the ritual processing of the seal carcass is that of observing the strict taboo of not to mix the spirits of land creatures with those of sea. No Inuit wife would work on the seal carcass if she had worked on a land animal that same day and vice versa. Nor would she ever cook the meat of both at the same time in one pot.

Late in the winter the breathing holes are easily spotted as most of the snow has gone from the sea ice. When these conditions prevail the opportunity to hunt seals using a different technique comes into play. First all the holes in a given area are located and marked. If enough people are available, women and children as well as the adult males, then one are stationed at each hole. Far from being silent they create noise at each hole. This ensures that the seals will avoid surfacing at these holes. Only one hole will be left undisturbed and that is where the hunter will be waiting, but unlike the others he will be waiting, silent and downwind with harpoon at the ready. By making sure that all the other holes are unavailable the chance of the seal arriving at the hunter's hole within a short time are vastly increased. Often, if insufficient people are available to cover all the vents, a hunter, or his wife, will urinate down the uncovered vents. The scent will ensure that the seal will venture elsewhere before coming up for a breathing rest.

It is knowledge such as this that has enabled the Inuit, from the Chukota of Eastern Siberia to the Kalaalit of Greenland to survive for millennia in the inhospitable environment of the Arctic winters.

Although "breathing hole" hunting was the most widespread method of seal hunting among all Inuit people there were other methods of seal hunting.

In Alaska, where strong ocean currents occurred, the ice would break forming open leads. This enabled the Inupiat to capture seals using nets made from "babiche", the strong leather ropes made from mainly walrus hide. By hanging the nets along the edge of a lead to form a curtain seals were trapped when they tried to return from the open water to clear their breathing holes beneath the ice. Noises that would normally scare seals from using breathing holes had the opposite effect to seals playing in open water. Scratching noises were one sound that was particularly successful in attracting seals toward the waiting nets. For this reason the Inuit made "seal scratchers", from driftwood or walrus ivory. Some of these items included real seal claws which many hunters believed improved their effectiveness. By using slow rhythmic strokes with intermittent pauses a sound not unlike that of a seal scratching on ice was created. This then attracted the curious seals to investigate the unknown "seal". On suddenly realising that the "new seal" was in fact an Inuit hunter the seals would panic and dive under the ice and get trapped in the babiche netting.

Although this was an effective method of hunting it was also a dangerous method. Due to the strong currents, that created the leads in the first instance, the ice around the open leads would often be weak or unstable. On many occasions the ice on which the hunters stood would break away from the land fast ice and they would then be stranded on a drifting ice flow. Tales of hunters being stranded under such conditions for days, or even weeks, abound in Arctic folklore.

The month of March, which is still in the depth of the Arctic winter, is the month when most Arctic seals give birth. This was an opportunity for the Inuit to secure not only adult seals as food but also to capture seal pups for both their meat and also their furry pelts which were highly valued. The female seal excavates a birthing den in snow hummocks on the pack ice. These dens are usually between two and three metres in length with an access hole to the open water at one end. Occasionally a den would be constructed in a natural formed cavity among broken pack ice but in the main it was the snow mound that was the place where a seal pup would be born.

Once a den had been located by the hunter's dog he would jump onto the roof to cave it in. (Polar bears have been observed and filmed using exactly the same technique.) Once inside the den the hunter tried to block the mother seal's escape. More often than not he would fail but as the pups are much less mobile they were usually caught. After dragging the unfortunate pup from its once secure home, using an implement designed for the purpose, the pup was swiftly dispatched by the hunter stepping on its chest. Occasionally a pup would be kept alive and tethered in the hole in an attempt to lure the mother back to the harpoon of a waiting hunter. Although such methods may seem cruel to the point of barbaric to some people, it must be remembered that survival in the Arctic is not, and never has been, easy. Unlike many white cultures, where hunting is regarded as a pastime and sport, the Inuit hunter did not hunt for pleasure but to survive. Both bears and Arctic foxes also take a toll on the seal pups. In the case of the foxes, they will devour the carcass but not the fur coated pelt, which they regularly leave on the ice. If an Inuit comes across such a find it is promptly gathered up as a bonus as its fur is exceptionally warm and highly valued.

When winter finally gives way to the brief Arctic summer, the roofs of the birthing dens give way under the influence of the warm rays of the early summer sun. At this stage the mother seals can be seen feeding their pups while basking alongside the remains of the den. This den is now the escape route for both mother and pup if any danger is sensed. Lone bull seals will also haul out onto the ice to bask in the relative warmth or even to sleep. Swift and powerful as they are in the marine environment, seals are awkward and lumbering when out on the ice. For this reason they stay close to their escape holes. Now, as round the clock daylight approaches, the Inuit hunters adopted a different way of hunting the ever wary seal.

Working in pairs and travelling by dogsled the hunting team would search for seals basking on the ice. The ideal quarry would be a single animal as they are much easier to approach than a group. With seals basking in groups it only takes one to be alerted or frightened for the whole group to disappear down through the ice. So it was often the single but larger males that were the prey at this time.

Once a target had been located one hunter would remain behind to control the dogs while the other would commence the stalk. Before the availability of rifles the hunter had to get within harpoon range, a distance of ten to twelve metres. After testing the direction of the wind by plucking a few hairs from his seal or caribou skin coat and letting them flutter to the ice his stalk would begin.

Starting downwind was essential as even if asleep the scent of the hunter would alert the quarry. Sleeping seals out on the ice are never in the deep sleep like the sleep they have while floating nose up in the water. The sleep on the ice is more like a light dozing with the animal frequently looking up and around to see if there is any imminent danger. The stalker would observe the quarry for some time to enable him to synchronise his approach with the seal raising its head, only moving forward when the creature's head was down. The fact that the alert periods of an individual animal were very regularly spaced between periods of sleep made a predictable rate of approach possible for the hunter. Another indication that the quarry was about to awake was the visible twitching of the seals muscles prior to it wakening. As soon as a movement was observed the hunter would freeze. If the quarry seemed suspicious the hunter would then imitate a seal's movements. Rolling on his back he would wave an arm to look like a seal waving a flipper, or scratch the ice and make a blowing noise like a seal. The sealskin suit gave the correct colour and with its poor land vision the quarry would be convinced that this was another seal and return to its slumber. In some areas, such as the Thule area in North West Greenland, the hunters used a harpooning screen in front of them made of bleached white skin. In a few other areas the white fur of polar bear formed the screen. These screens were mounted on small sleds which could slide silently across the ice toward the prey.

As soon as the hunter judged that he was within range he would launch his harpoon, often aided by the use of an atlatl.

As the summer advanced more open water made hunting either at holes or leads more difficult and indeed more dangerous as well a being less productive. This was the season that the kayak became the chosen method of hunting.

The behaviour of seals when they are in the water, their truly natural element, is very different from when they are ashore on land or hauled out on sea ice. They no longer show the fear that causes them to take to the water at the first sign of anything that unnerves them. Once in the water, fear seems to be replaced by curiosity. This curiosity often proves fatal as the seals would often approach Inuit hunters in their kayaks. The old saying that "curiosity killed the cat", would certainly be applicable to seals when they are playing among the ice floes. Inuit hunters have observed that swimming seals congregate around certain types of features among the ice. The seals will behave more like fish than mammals by congregating around icy headlands where rugged ice floes have packed together to push the ice deeper into the water. This is similar to the behaviour of fish around a sunken reef, or, in the open ocean, congregating around floating debris. (Marine scientists term this the 'Thigmatrophic Effect' and it is the basis of artificial reef technology and the 'FADS', floating aggregation devices used by tuna fishing vessels.) The hunters are well aware that straight, featureless edges of either shore fast ice or a wide lead are more likely to be barren hunting grounds than where hummocks or stranded icebergs are found.

Hunting from a kayak is a highly skilled occupation. The sitting position from which the hunter has to launch his harpoon is far from the optimum for giving either force or distance to his missile. For this reason the harpoon used by the Inuit kayak hunters is much lighter than the harpoon that they would use when "breathing hole" hunting. Again the use of the "Atlatl" was a necessity to increase both speed and penetrating power of the harpoon. Another factor critical to the success of the hunt was that of the manner in which all the necessary equipment was laid out on the kayak. The hunter sat in the well in the middle of the kayak and therefore had to utilise both the deck space in front of him and also that area behind him that was out of his field of vision. The harpoon was secured under a thong stretched across the foredeck where it was readily accessible at very short notice. Attached to the harpoon head was the babiche line, meticulously coiled on a raised platform directly in front of the hunter. The manner in which the line was coiled ensured that it would run freely without tangling when the harpoon was thrown and/or when a stricken seal dived. The end of the line ran behind the hunter to a float perched behind him on the after deck. This float, or "dhan", was usually made from an inflated seal skin. The "dhan" was only lightly secured, if secured at all, on the aft deck. This ensured that when the dhan got pulled off the deck it did so without snatching or fouling in a manner that could upturn the kayak. The method and type of floats used to act as drag to exhaust the seal varied slightly in different regions. Sometimes the sealskin float was replaced by inflated seal bladders tied directly to the harpoon shaft which was connected to the harpoon line. Another variation was that of the shaft being connected to the line in such a way that it lay at right angles to the line when the seal swam off. This increased the drag factor considerably and soon tired the fleeing animal. It was customary for these harpoon shafts to be stained red so that they could be seen more easily by the hunter when pursuing the impaled quarry.

Other ancillary items that are unique to the Inuit culture and worthy of mention are those used in the retrieval and transport of the seal carcass back to the shore. In the winter months the seals were fat with excess blubber. This blubber ensured that the seal was naturally buoyant and easily towed home. The same could not have been said with seals killed in the summer months. Female seals which had reared pups would have little blubber and were much less buoyant and where fresh water ingress had reduced the salinity the problem of the seal carcass sinking was frequently encountered. To overcome this problem the ever innovative Inuit used what is probably the earliest form of pneumatic buoyancy known.

Slits were cut in a number of strategic points on the carcass into which a pointed bone or ivory knife was inserted to free the skin from the meat of the carcass. Once a reasonable area had been separated the hollow wing bone of a bird was used as a tube to inflate the void, the lung power of the hunter was undoubtedly a feature of this technique. Carved wooden or ivory plugs shaped to lock inside the skin were then pushed in to prevent the air escaping. Once all the slits were inflated the now very buoyant seal could easily be towed behind the kayak to the village. Once there the hunter's wife would process the carcass the meat from which would be shared among the community. (This tradition of sharing, even in time of extreme scarcity has over the years been frequently mentioned by those who have lived or worked with the Inuit. In Alex Ritchie's story he mentions this and throughout his life often reflected on the altruistic nature of his Inuit friends.)

The design of the harpoon used by the Inuit is quite unique and is fully explained in a later section.

WALRUS HUNTING

To tackle a beast that is armed with two pointed tusks which can be fifty centimetres long while only armed with a hand held harpoon is brave. When that beast is a bull walrus of around a tonne in weight one needs to be extremely brave. Yet this was a common occurrence among the Inuit people for millennia. But this was no foolhardy or macho enterprise. It was all part of the Inuit survival strategy and was carried out with all the skill and precision that the knowledge of many generations had developed.

Prior to the Inuit having access to metal tools the ivory tusks were used to make tools including knives for cutting snow blocks when building ice "igloos". The tusks were also used for some of the implements used in hunting. The mandible bone was exceptionally heavy and was used in the manufacture of harpoons. Hides were used in the manufacture of harpoon lines and in the covers for the "woman's boat" the Umiak. (Which as well as being used by the women for transport was also used by the men for whale hunting.) Even the membrane that surrounded the liver was utilised, mainly as the "skin" on the traditional ceremonial drums. The organs were eaten as was the blubber but the meat was only eaten when times were extremely difficult. But it was never wasted as it was reserved for dog food. The flippers were regarded as a delicacy, rendered edible by a process of decay and fermentation, which also tended to somewhat increase the flavour. Like most of the creatures hunted by the Inuit, very little of the walrus was wasted.

Walrus are creatures of the ice pack where they haul out both to rest and to rear their young. Otherwise they are creatures of the open water where they dive to feed on clams on the shallow banks around the Arctic seas. This behaviour in turn rendered them a seasonal quarry rather than an "all-year-round" target. Their vast bulk enabled then to burst through the ice from below as the ice formed. Ice up to around thirty centimetres thick would be broken to form breathing holes over shallow clam beds. Once the ice was beyond this thickness they were forced to move out to the open sea or areas of thinner ice. In some parts of the Arctic seas there are areas of permanently open water known as "polynyas". These areas are created by the strong undercurrents being deflected upwards by underwater ridges or banks and this constant surface activity prevents ice from forming. It was here among these "polynyas" that resident populations of walrus were to be found. Unlike their "ice pack" cousins, these walrus were non-migratory.

Those walrus that did migrate did so in a somewhat easy and passive manner. By climbing aboard ice floes during the spring thaw they drifted along the coasts of Alaska and Greenland.

The central Arctic coastline of Northern Canada is an area not frequented by the species. Nor was it the permanent home to Canadian Inuit.

Working in small groups, the Inuit hunters would either use a single umiak or a number of kayaks to journey to the offshore ice pack to locate the walrus herds. Often this would be a journey of several miles. Even when the visibility was reduce by freezing Arctic fogs the hunters would persist until they found the herds by listening for the unmistakeable bellowing of the constant squabbling of the herd. The noise made by an upset walrus is comparable to that of an elephant trumpeting when it wants to make its presence felt. Once located the hunters would paddle to a nearby smaller ice floe and securely tie up their umiak or kayaks. Once this was done a series of holes were cut into the floe to which the harpoon lines were secured. The floe was then quietly paddled toward the herd. Once within range all the hunters would simultaneously launch their harpoons at a single predetermined animal. The impaled beast would roll into the water and immediately try to swim off. The effort of towing an ice floe laden with Inuit hunters soon tired the animal and enabled the hunters to them to get alongside it to finish it off with a spear or lance into its vital organs.

On occasions it was necessary to harpoon the walrus directly from the umiak if no suitable ice floe was available. It was far too dangerous to let an impaled walrus to tow the umiak. If the walrus dived under the icepack while towing an umiak the vessel would be instantly destroyed. So in this instance the use of sealskin dahns

attached to the harpoon lines were used. As soon as the harpoons were thrown the dahns were jettisoned over the side and the drag from these eventually tired the walrus, at this time the following umiak would recover the dahns. This was the most dangerous part of the hunt when the injured beast was brought alongside. The taut hide cover of the umiak was easily punctured by the beast's tusks, so it was better to wait until the walrus was totally exhausted rather than hurry the proceedings.

In the event of the tusks tearing the hull of the Umiak an immediate repair using the repair kit that was always to hand was carried out. This kit of hide, grease and thread of sinew would be used as a temporary fix until the boat could be taken ashore for a more permanent repair. The worst situation that could be encountered was when an irate walrus managed to hook a tusk over the gunwhale. The outcome of this was, in most cases, the boat capsizing and the crew thrown into the frigid waters. Unfortunately this situation was not uncommon. The only other type of hunt that held as much danger as walrus hunting afloat was that of hunting the large baleen whales from an umiack.

Another, rather unusual, form of walrus hunting was unique to certain Inuit tribes of the Eastern Arctic.

Here the Inuit hunter "fished" for the walrus using a lump of either meat or blubber tied on a line. This was done from the edge of the ice, not from either kayak or umiak. The "meat lure" was grabbed by the walrus and held tightly in its front flippers. By gently tightening the line the walrus was slowly coaxed toward the edge of the ice where a second hunter would be ready with a harpoon. The end of the harpoon line was securely anchored to the ice to prevent the beast escaping as trying to restrain such a size of an animal by holding onto the harpoon line would surely have been a recipe for disaster.

When one considers that a bull walrus can weight around one tonne one soon realises that trying to lift one onto the ice is not an easy task. To overcome the problem of this great deadweight the Inuit hunters of bygone days showed a tremendous degree of mechanical skill. First three or four pairs of holes were cut into the ice. These holes were positioned in a line far enough back from the ice edge that would allow the large carcass to lay full length between the nearest holes and the ice edge. The harpoon line was then laced through the holes to form a very effective pulley system with either a three or four times mechanical advantage. In the case of an exceptionally large bull a second line could be added in the same manner. Where possible the hunters would try to haul the carcass from the water where there was a slope on the ice going into the water.

Once ashore the harpoon head was carefully cut from the carcass and thoroughly cleaned for reuse. Any blood that had managed to splash onto the harpoon lines or onto the boat's skin covering was immediately and meticulously washed off to prevent it causing rot.

WOLF HUNTING

As a child, I would sit listening to stories about how the Inuit, or Eskimos as my elderly relative described them, could hunt ferocious polar bears and wolves using cunning rather than foolhardy bravery. Inuit hunting methods, before they had ready access to rifles, were based on using the weak points of their quarry. In the case of the wolf, this was its constant hunger. In parts of Baffin Island and the Ungava Peninsula, the Inuit had a near foolproof method of catching wolves which was totally risk free - the wolves actually got themselves trapped. I will now try to give a step by step account of how this is achieved.

Wolf Hunting, the easy method.

1. Dig a hole no less than 30 inches deep by about 15 inches in diameter.
2. Place a lump of blubber or seal guts in the hole.
3. Withdraw for the night.
4. In the morning remove frozen, dead, upside down wolf from its hole.

What actually happens is the wolf smells the bait but cannot reach it. As it reaches down into the hole with its front legs, its back legs reach a point where they slip on the ice.

The wolf then upends head first into the hole and due to the constrictive size of the hole cannot get back out. Head down with its hind legs up in the air, it soon dies either as a result of blood draining to its head or of hypothermia due to being unable to move. To animal lovers, this will no doubt seem a very cruel method of catching a wolf but to an Inuit, who saw the wolf as a source of fur and both a competitor and threat to his family, it was a form of survival. Although this method is, as far as I am aware, no longer used, have we any right to condemn those who used it to survive?

Two other methods used to kill wolves were equally cruel but, in the Inuit view, "safe" methods.

The "wolf pill", often mentioned in early tales of the Arctic, was an ingenious and deadly method of killing a wolf. Strips of baleen, sharpened at both ends, were coiled up and tied tightly with a piece of sinew then buried in the ice to freeze. Once frozen, the sinew was cut off leaving the frozen coil which was then carefully inserted into a piece of seal blubber. The lumps of blubber would be "wolfed down" whole and once inside the stomach the coil would thaw and spring open. The sharp ends then penetrated the animal's innards, causing massive haemorrhaging and inevitable death. The hunter would watch for ravens indicating the location of the dead wolf, which was never very far away.

The second method was the "knife bone", of which I have two examples in my personal collection of Inuit artefacts. Caribou leg bones were broken lengthwise, allowing the Inuit to eat the nutritious marrow and also giving them an ideal implement to kill even the most cunning of wolves. The bone was sharpened to almost a razor edge on both sides. The knuckle joint end was then planted and frozen into the ice. This was usually achieved using a spear or harpoon to dig the hole then urinating into the hole and allowing the urine to freeze. This prevented the wolf from digging it up. The exposed knife point was then smeared with blood and blubber. When a wolf found the baited knife it would try to lick the blood off and in doing so lacerate its tongue. More often than not, the taste of its own blood kept the poor beast licking furiously until the damage was so severe that it was beyond repair. The hunter followed the trail of bloodstained snow to find the wolf which had rapidly bled to death. Wolf-skin mitts were highly prized as was a wolf furs trim on a parka's hood. (The reason for this trim was not just for decoration. The trim helped to create a sheltered zone in front of the face which trapped heat but allowed the water vapour from breathing to escape.)

WHALE HUNTING.

The subject of whale hunting is a very emotive one and there is little doubt that the industrial hunting of whales in the years between 1750 and the early twentieth century did immense damage to whale populations in the Arctic waters. However we should not confuse the hunting of these magnificent creatures by the indigenous Inuit as a way of surviving with the financially fuelled slaughter of whales by the white man. The following descriptions of whale hunting among the different Inuit peoples, both east and west, is "as it was" for millennia. Not "as it now is", which is dealt with in a later chapter.

The catching of large whales has always been a way of life for the Inupiat Inuit of the North Slope of Alaska and continues to this day. Up until recent years this was carried out using the traditional Inuit skin covered vessel the umiak. With a crew consisting of eight hunters and propelled by paddles it was a highly skilled endeavour which carried with it a high risk of injury or even worse. Nevertheless the whale hunt was a chance for a successful crew to gain great social prestige as well as supply the whole community with not only food but a host of other useful products. The Inupiat Inuit of Alaska were always less nomadic than either the Inuit of the Eastern Canadian Arctic or the Kalaalit of Greenland. The reason for this stability was that the migration paths and timing of the migrations of their quarry were well known to the Inupiat. This enabled settled communities of sod houses to be used over long periods of time, in many cases over hundreds of years.

The whales that were caught, bowhead and grey whale, supplied vast amounts of "muktuk", whale blubber still attached to the whale skin. This was not only high in calories but was also rich in vitamin C, which prevented scurvy. Surplus blubber supplied oil for the Inuit stone lamps. Ribs were used in the construction of roofs for the semi-subterranean sod houses. Jaw bones made perfect runners for sleds and sinews and tendons were ideal for sewing or lashings. What the white man wrongly called "whalebone", the baleen, also had a great value to the Inuit. The white man used this spring like flexible membrane for a variety of items which would now be made of plastic. The whale used it for filtering food from the seawater but the Inuit used it for harpoon lashings, fishing lines, snares and, of course, the infamous 'wolf pills'. Even the innards had uses, so little ever went to waste and due to the huge size of these whales the whole community could share in the kill.

When spring came in both the eastern and western sides of the Canadian Arctic so too did the whales. (It should be noted that the waters of the Central Canadian Arctic are devoid of whales). As the ice started to break up open leads enabled the whales to move in to feed on the rich blooms of zoo planktons which thrive under the ice. It was in the weeks before these leads open that the Inupiat preparations for the forthcoming hunt began. The Umiaks were taken down from their winter storage high above the reach of the ever hungry Malamute sled dogs. From the settlement to their destination out on the ice, where the first leads would appear, could be several miles across piles of rafted ice. Once out there a temporary whaling camp would be established. The track to and from the camp was kept in good order by the womenfolk chopping any obstructive ice out by hand. The men then began their annual vigil. Perching on high outcrops of rafted ice they set a constant watch, first for the opening of permanent leads, then for the approaching whales. As soon as a lead was established the umiacks were set, their bows positioned over the open water ready for a swift and silent launch. The approaching of the whales was noted either by the sighting of the black backs of the whales or by the telltale fountains of spray when a surfacing whale blew. Each hunting crew shared in the round the clock watch. As soon as a hunter came off watch he would drink as much water as he could. These people did not have watches or alarm clocks and relied on Mother Nature to wake them when bodily functions dictated. After relieving himself, the hunter would resume scanning the horizon. In fog when the visibility was poor it was often the sound of the whales blowing that alerted the hunters. For this reason the vigil was a silent affair. It was also thought that any knocking or banging sound might alert the whales so silence was crucial. The Inupiat hunter could even tell which type of whale was approaching by the sound of the blowing. The long deep blow of a grey or bowhead was very different to the sharp exhalations of the much smaller beluga or white whale.

The harpoons used in this hunt were not like those used by the Eastern Inuit of Baffin Island and Greenland for the Inupiat whaling harpoon is a much longer and heavier weapon. With an average shaft length of almost three metres these harpoons were designed for thrusting rather than throwing with an atlatl. This in turn meant that the umiak and its crew were engaging these giants of the sea at very close quarters. Before the coming of the white man, material for harpoon shafts was hard for the Inupiat to obtain. Long, strait timber from shipwrecks was regarded as a bounty. Like the harpoon of the Eastern Inuit, the ivory head was detachable and the barbed design, often tipped with razor sharp bone or slate, was such that it would not pull out of the whale's thick hide. As the bone or slate tips were fragile and easily broken, spare tips were always carried. Often the container for storing the tips was carved in the shape of a whale to bring luck to the hunter.

As soon as the presence of a whale was confirmed the hunting crew sprang into action. The well rehearsed procedure of silently launching the fully prepared umiak was almost immediate and once the crew were aboard the hunt began. Every member of the crew knew his place and what duties he was to perform. The eight man crew consisted of six paddlers, one harpooner and one steersman. The latter guiding the vessel, with a paddle-like rudder, through the confusion of ice floes towards the intended target. The skill of the crew had been learned over many years with each member having started as a paddler before graduating up the pecking order to finally become a harpooner. The whales would be swimming just below the surface coming up to breathe in a slow rhythmic manner which enabled the steersman to follow and close in on the intended target. As soon as the umiak was within striking distance and the whales back was starting to break the surface the harpooner would give the command to go full ahead on the target. Aiming close to the twin blowholes the harpooner would use both the momentum of the vessel and his own strength to plunge the harpoon into the target. As soon as this was done the crew back paddled furiously to avoid being either hit or swamped by the massive tail flukes as the stricken whale dived. Leaving the detached harpoon head or "toggle" in the whale the harpooner would swiftly replace this with another on the retained shaft. At the same time the line which was attached to the embedded toggle would be flowing over the gunnels as the whale sounded. To this line were attached inflated sealskin floats, usually three in number, which were thrown over the side by the leading paddler. Careful coiling of the seal or walrus leather harpoon lines ensured that it flowed freely and without tangles as it went over. The crew would then wait until the floats reappeared before following them with a second harpoon at the ready to strike as soon as the whale resurfaced for breath. Other umiaks would also join in the pursuit. As more harpoon lines and floats were secured the whale would tire and eventually would lie exhausted on the surface due to the drag created by the sealskin floats. Each float had a buoyancy of over a hundred kilograms; three lines with a total of nine floats gave an equivalent drag factor of over a tonne. So the more lines attached the quicker the whale became exhausted. It was then that the surrounding umiaks would move in with lances, which had long fixed pointed heads. These lances would target the vital organs of the whale and soon the blowholes would be expelling blood amidst the exhaled breath of the dying whale. Now the pursuit was over. Quite often the pursuit would have gone on for hours and the hunting party would find itself some distance from home with, in the case of a Bowhead, anything up to sixty tonnes of whale to tow home. Grey whales were not much less in weight. No time was wasted in securing towing lines to the wrist of the tail for the combined fleet of umiaks to start the exhausting journey back to the whaling camp. To prevent the whale's flippers creating drag an ingenious method of tying the flippers into the side of the animal had been developed. Ivory toggles tied together in pairs with a leather thong between them were inserted through the flipper then into slits cut in the side of the whale. These toggles were between twelve and fifteen centimetres in length and made from either walrus or narwhal ivory. Once secured by this means the flippers were much less of a hindrance. Then the long tow back to the whaling base began.

On arriving back at the base the whole community would be waiting to cut the massive beast into manageable sized pieces before transporting it to the village.

Transporting nearly thirty tonnes of Bowhead blubber from the edge of the ice was no mean feat. The butchering could take the entire community more than a day. Added to the blubber they also had to transport all the other usable parts of the animal including the eight hundred valuable baleen plates and the rib bones for roof trusses. To enable the butchering process to be carried out in a safe manner the whale was gradually dragged tail first up a ramp cut in the ice. This was often done using a similar technique to that of recovering large walrus. (See Walrus Hunting.) By slowly reducing the overall weight the whole carcass eventually lay on the ice stripped of all usable parts.

Once back in the village the whale meat was often to be seen hanging up in the frigid Arctic breeze to dry, food for both man and malamute in the leaner times which were sure to come.

Occasionally it was not the large baleen whales of the Mysticeti order that were hunted. Sometimes the Inupiat had the good fortune to be presented with the much smaller toothed whales of the Odontoceti. Belugas, the "Canaries of the Sea", are among the most nervous and easily scared of marine mammals. For this reason they were almost impossible to hunt from a boat in a similar manner to the giant bowhead and grey whales.

The diet of the Beluga includes migratory species of fish such as salmon and arctic char. In the autumn these fish would be found waiting in large numbers at the mouths of rivers flowing into the Beaufort Sea. When this happened the Belugas would herd the fish into the head of the estuaries and this gave the Inupiat hunters an opportunity to catch these wary creatures. Many different methods of capture were employed to give the hunters an easy kill. Using the Belugas natural fear of anything new or strange was one tactic. If a pod were hunting at the head of an estuary at high tide it was often possible to trap them there until the tide dropped. By placing saplings to form a barrier of vibrating stakes across the inlet the frightened animals would not retreat seaward as the tide ebbed. The vibrations set up by the saplings would be sufficient to scare the wary creatures back towards the heads of the creek. If the centre of the channel were too deep to plant saplings, then the hunters would straddle the deeper water with their kayaks and chase the

retreating whales back up the creek. At other times the hunters would place heavily weighted babiche nets across the inlet. These nets, similar to those used in trapping seals under the ice, were made of walrus or seal hide thongs and were sufficiently strong to hold a beluga. Unfortunately if a whole pod of belugas hit the net in their effort to escape then the net was sometimes carried away. Once a pod was trapped in the falling tide and stranded it was easy for the hunters to move in and kill the whole pod.

Occasionally in late autumn the belugas would remain too long at the head of the salmon creeks. When this happened the flowing water would keep the head of the creek ice free but further out the less dense fresh water formed a layer over the top of the salt water. This fresh water would freeze at a higher temperature than the sea water and form a layer of ice across the mouth of the inlet under which the belugas would not swim. It was then an easy task for the hunters to move in using either kayaks or by wading to collect their bounty. The normal method used to kill the beluga was with a long knife stabbing deep into the vital organs but as this lost the valuable and nutritious blood some preferred to stab their prey in the head to pierce the brain. This took skill as the target was roughly the size of a small cantaloupe melon.

Once the beluga was dead a rope would be secured around its tail and it would be hauled from the water and, if not too far from the settlement, it could be dragged or put on a sled to be butchered by the community. When this was done it was common to eat the 'muktuk' still warm. From the oldest to the youngest of the community would all share in the bounty. Not just the flesh and skin but also, as the beluga was a "toothed cetacean", the teeth were of great value before the coming of the white man. This very hard ivory was used as tip holders for weapons and toggles for clothing. Just as with the large bowhead and humpback whales nothing of the beluga was discarded or wasted, all was used.

Another opportunity for the Inuit to hunt the beluga arose when the beluga came into estuaries to exfoliate and rid themselves of ectoparasites. This activity has only been filmed in recent years, but was undoubtedly known to many Inuit

149

groups across the full range of the beluga.

Thousands of miles to the east, around the Pond Inlet area of Canada's Baffin Island and further east across the often frozen waters of Baffin Bay in the Inughuit Inuit settlements around Inglufield Fjord on Greenland a different quarry was sought. The quarry of these groups of what are often referred to as the Polar Inuit was the Narwhal. The Narwhal, or "Tuugaalik" as it is known in the regional dialect of the Inuguit, is the animal from which early Viking traders sourced their mythical 'Unicorn Horns'. Known as the Unicorn of the sea it was the protruding canine of the animal that was valuable to the Vikings, but to the Inuit the whole beast was of value.

The Inuit of Inglufield Fjord first crossed the frozen waters of the Smith Sound millennia ago and right up until recent times continued to traverse it to visit Canadian relatives. The forty miles of frozen sea was not a long journey by nomadic Inuit standards and often only took a day with the help of their teams of powerful Malamute or indigenous Greenlandic dogs, but once the ice started to break up in late summer visiting was put on hold and kayaks and harpoons were made ready for the arrival of the Tuugaalik.

As leads appeared in the ice the hunters would listen for the sound of the narwhal blowing as they made their way through the leads. Often the first sight the hunter would have would be the long tusks of the males prodding the air above a lead. Like all marine mammals the narwhales had to come up to breathe in a regular rhythm and for this reason never strayed far from the open leads. To get trapped under the ice was certain death so the pods of narwhals would only hunt for fish close to the leads. This gave the hunters the opportunity they had been waiting for since the first sign of the ice breaking.

At one time the "Polar Inuit" would not have used kayaks as the sea was never open enough to warrant the use of boats nor were the materials to build such vessels readily available. So these hardy hunters had to hunt from the ice itself, often in competition with the local polar bears. Using only a harpoon attached to a line was no easy way to catch a creature weighing in excess of a tonne and over five metres in length. To overcome this, the hunters worked in teams to try and kill the narwhal as fast as possible by harpooning it multiple times and using a lance as soon as possible to penetrate vital organs. Once dead a rope was put around the wrist of the tail and teamwork soon had it lying on the ice ready for either dragging to the camp or cutting up in situ. As with the beluga, the narwhal was an important source of vitamin C and of vital importance to the Polar Inuit. Further south in Greenland and over west in Baffin Island hunting was done from kayaks. The pursuit of the pod by following both the blowing and sighting of the male tusks enabled the hunters to get within throwing distance using harpoon and atlatl. As soon as the harpoon was secured an inflated sealskin dhan, this was secured behind the hunter on the after deck of the kayak, was released to slow down the escaping narwhal. Other hunters would assist when alerted and add more harpoon lines and dhans to swiftly exhaust the beast before killing it using the long kayak knife. Towing it homeward was again a team effort and as Inuit tradition demanded all, from the youngest to the oldest received their share. The sealskin floats or "dhans" were made from a single sealskin, usually that of a harp seal, and as it was a skill in itself deserves describing. By enlarging the mouth by cutting it back to the throat the complete skin could be drawn back to end up inside out, similar to taking a sock off a foot. Once the skin was inverted as far back as the hind flippers the vertebrae were severed and the internal carcass removed. This meant, that once the skin was turned back on itself, a solid and secure anchorage for the harpoon line was made available. The head end was then sealed round a mouth plug, made of either wood or ivory, through which a hole was used to inflate the skin. Once inflated a wooden plug was driven then soaked to form an airtight seal. The making of a dhan invariably left the craftsman well coated in waterproof blubber. To emulsify this blubber and enable it to be removed the product used was human urine, collected in the community for just such an occasion.

POLAR BEARS

Apart from in Greenland, polar bear hunting is illegal, but it was not always so. At the start of the twentieth century, it was commonplace for the Inuit to hunt polar bears. The bear supplied excellent clothing material as well as food. It was also viewed as a competitor for resources and a threat to Inuit people. So bears were a fair target.

Inuit society meant working as a team, whether looking after children or when hunting. Hunting polar bears and the way in which the bear was divided up amongst the group was no exception.

Before the ownership of guns was common among the Inuit, the only safe way to hunt polar bears was with two or more hunters, their dogs and sledges.

Polar bears are rightfully classified as marine mammals, for it is on the icepack they hunt the seals that are their main prey. The only other predator to regularly hunt on the icepack is the Inuit, who also hunts the seal, with the result that encounters between bears and Inuit were more often by chance than intentional.

If a lone Inuit hunter came across fresh bear tracks, he would often let his lead dog off to find and chase the bear. Inuit dogs have a built-in hatred of polar bears and appear to have little fear of them. The bears show a natural fear of the dogs and always try to avoid them. The natural insulation of the bear's fur is so great as to allow it to survive in its den throughout the winter at temperatures well below 40oC. This, however, means that - although the bear can run at 40 km/h at a sprint - after a few hundred metres the bear overheats as the insulating effect does not allow the heat generated to dissipate. In animals like a horse, sweating enables the animal to control its body temperature. Unfortunately, this does not happen with polar bears. So, when the hunter catches up with the unfortunate bear, it is usually in a state of near collapse, disorientated and showing all the signs of heat exhaustion. This enables the hunter to approach with confidence - after releasing the rest of his dogs to harass the beast - and kill it with his spear.

If a bear was scented by the dogs, or bear prints spotted when two hunters were working together, the hunter whose dogs scented the bear - or the hunter who found the bear footprints - would release all his dogs. Taking his spear, he would then join the other hunter on his sledge and pursue the pack of dogs chasing the bear. Once the pack had driven the bear to a standoff the hunters would approach and the first hunter would have first attempt at spearing the bear, with the second hunter as backup. This was always a much safer method not only for the hunters but also the dogs. If a bear was at a standoff with a lone dog it would often fight and one blow would kill a dog. With a pack of barking malamutes, or Greenland dogs, the bear was seldom able to damage the dogs.

Once the bear was killed and loaded on to the sledge, the dogs were rounded up and taken to recover the first sledge.

Once back at the camp, the bear was skinned and the skin divided in a predetermined manner. The polar bear may be the Inuit hunter's greatest and most dangerous adversary but the value of its hide and fur for making highly prized trousers could not be overstated. The most valuable part of the skin was the upper part and forelegs and this was the property of the hunter who killed the bear. He would carefully measure what length he would require before cutting the skin. The reason this part of the skin was chosen first was that it had the long guard hairs and made the warmest trousers. The second hunter then had his cut and so on until the skin was used up.

The meat was eaten but, unlike most Inuit quarry, it was always cooked. The reason for this is that polar bear meat was always infested with trichinella, and could not be eaten raw. (Trichinella is a parasitic roundworm which causes the disease

Trichinosis)

The only part of the animal, other than its guts, to be rejected is the liver which is toxic even to dogs. Being the richest naturally occurring concentration of Vitamin A, it causes a severe medical condition, known as hypervitaminosis A, when eaten. For this reason, the liver is always carefully disposed of in a manner aimed at ensuring the malamute dogs would not find it. Interestingly the condition of hypervitaminosis A was responsible for the death of Antarctic explorer Xavier Mertz in 1913. He and his fellow explorer Douglas Mawson, who survived, ate the livers of their sled dogs which also contain potentially lethal levels of vitamin A. When the Inuit first realised that bear meat had to be cooked is unknown, but it was most certainly before they encountered Europeans. The method of cooking is strangely similar to the method of cooking used in the Bronze Age house found on the Orkney Islands to the North of Scotland's mainland. By dropping stones heated in a fire into bucket of water containing the chopped up meat it is possible to raise the temperature sufficiently high to kill the Trichinella parasite. In the Orkney case, at the Bronze Age house near the more famous Tomb of the Eagles, there is stone trough adjacent to a hearth. Closer inspection reveals a mound of burnt stone and evidence of where the red hot stones had been pushed across the floor and into the trough. The Orkney site is estimated to be around 3,000 years old. This is not that different in archaeological time from the time the ancestors of today's Inuit would have arrived in the Eastern Arctic Regions of Canada and Greenland. Yet another example of parallel evolution in problem solving.

CARIBOU

Caribou - Tuktu in Inuit - hunting was carried out in the summer months when it was not possible to hunt on the ice. Neither was it possible to use the sledges and dogs. This time of year was often difficult for the nomadic Inuit who would move inland from the coast to live in their Tupiks and hunt Caribou.

Before the use of rifles, the hunters used various forms of deception to trick the often curious but poor-sighted caribou to get them within range of a bow and arrow. One method was to approach from downwind with the bow held above the hunters' heads. To the caribou this would have appeared to be other caribou with antlers.

Another method was for two hunters to get as close to the herd as possible then walk away, one behind the other, using the wind to disguise their scent. To the caribou, this looked like one beast walking away from the herd so others would follow. When the hunters passed a large rock or other similar predetermined hiding place, one would drop into hiding while the other carried on, still being followed by the caribou. As the animals passed the hiding place, the hunter could get a shot at close quarters, which was usually successful. Unlike the famous English "Longbow", as used at Agincourt, the Inuit bow was not made from a springy yew tree branch. The Inuit bow was made by laminating strips of baleen together by binding with sinew from whatever source was available. A photograph of an Inuit named Shoodlue, who visited Dundee onboard a whaling vessel, shows him posing with his bow while dressed in his Inuit clothing. His baleen bow is probably no more than a metre in length and would have been unlikely to kill a caribou at any range over twenty yards.

Knowing the behaviour of the quarry - whether a bear, seal or deer - was the secret to successful hunting and often the difference between starvation and plenty.

The importance of caribou to the Inuit people cannot be over emphasised, the most important element being its hide to manufacture clothing. The insulating qualities of the caribou fur, due to the fact that the individual hairs are hollow, make it the perfect material to withstand subzero temperatures.

The Inuit men's parka and the ladies' amaat are made

of caribou skin with a hood trimmed with either wolf or wolverine fur to trap warm air over the wearer's face.

In the extreme weather often encountered in the Arctic, temperatures can plummet to minus 50oC. Even in these conditions, the traditional Inuit survived by wearing a double-skinned parka. The inside "skin" had the fur facing inward while the outer had the fur exposed. Adopting these Inuit type clothes enabled Amundson to reach the South Pole before Scott! (The heat loss of the cotton clothing worn by Scott's party meant they needed to eat more food and therefore carry greater loads. This is what, in the end, led to their tragic loss of life).

The meat of the caribou is eaten by the Inuit and the bones used to make household items such as needles. The sinews were used to sew covers for both tents and kayaks.

The meat was never, under normal conditions, fed to their malamute dogs as its low fat content was of insufficient calorific value. Dogs fed on the caribou venison would lose condition rapidly and were, therefore, only given it as a last resort. The dogs however thrived on walrus meat which was less favoured as human food.

Another method of catching caribou was by herding them into pitfalls or driving them over cliffs. There is little doubt that the quarry suffered greatly with both these methods. However, as the animals killed were from across all components of the stock, that is both male and female and from young calves to older beasts which were beyond breeding age, a balance was kept within the population. Even today if one searches across the frozen wastelands beyond the treeline one can find remnants of where the "caribou drives" took place. These are often identifiable by stone cairns or occasional inukshuk standing in lines which formed a funnel terminating in either a cliff or prepared pitfalls. This method was not unique to the Inuit as remains of very similar are also to be found in both Scandinavia and in Northern Russia. The traps found in

Scandinavia, in particular Northern Norway, are thought to date as far back as the time of the Komsa People, the forbearers of the modern Sami.

ARCTIC FOXES

The Arctic Fox was of little interest to the Inuit before trade with companies such as Hudson Bay Co. and Revillon Freres was established in the 18th and 19th centuries. They were never really targeted as either a food source of for their skins as the diminutive creatures had little meat and their hides were fragile when compared to either caribou or seals and walrus. The arctic fox is much smaller than the common red fox but it has the ability to change from a dark coat in various shades of brown in summer to a gleaming white coat in winter which, to the white man's fur trade, was luxurious and soft. This made it a desirable winter target once the fur traders arrived. Prior to this arrival, which actually put a high commercial value on a white fox pelt, the only use for any part of the animal was its tail. This use, I have been assured by more than one source, was as a mop to clean up the blood of butchered seals from the family igloo or boat. I have been told that once thoroughly saturated in blood it was then thrown into the cooking pot to add flavour to the stew. How much truth there is to this tale (or tail) I cannot be certain but when I look at some of the other Inuit cuisine I would not be inclined towards total disbelief.

Foxes by nature are scavengers and the arctic fox is no exception. In the winter when little else is to be found the arctic fox will roam the pack ice searching for polar bears. Once a bear is located the fox will follow the bear faithfully cleaning up any remains of its kills. The polar bear, if seals are plentiful, will only eat the high calorific and vitamin rich parts of the seal. After eating the blubber and skin it will leave the rest of the carcass, which is more than sufficient to feed the diminutive fox. Where the remnants of an old polar bear kill are buried, even under several feet of snow, the fox's acute sense of smell enables it to locate these with relative ease. The yellow urine marks of the fox were often used by Inuit hunters to locate their own caches of caribou meat under the snow and it was not unknown for these same signs to have been used by Inuit hunters who had been stranded on ice floes to locate the remains of bear kills and avoid death by starvation.

The scavenging habits of the arctic fox made it a much easier target than the more wary wolf. Many differing types of traps were successfully used to trap the fox, varying from baited box traps to pitfalls. The two following types of trap were, I think, almost unique to the Inuit and were used up until recent years across the Canadian Arctic. The third type of trap, the tension trap was commonly used on the coast and certainly deserves a separate mention, but first we can look at the 'tower trap'. This trap relied on the fox being a habitual creature which would always return to a site where it had found an easy meal. The trap was a very basic tower, round in section and tattering toward the top. Made either of flat stones or, in winter, ice blocks. At first a doorway was left open in the base which allowed the fox to enter and take the bait, which was usually seal guts or other offal, which the Inuit themselves would not be consuming. Once the foxes became accustomed to this being a fast food outlet the door could be filled in and a ramp to the open top of the tower. The traps were of a height just over that which the fox could jump and as the inner walls were sloping toward the centre the fox could neither jump nor climb out. The bait would prove irresistible to the ever hungry fox and inevitably it would enter to its demise. The stone traps were kept in use for generations but those made of ice blocks were only to last for a season as they melted in the spring.

The second type of trap was used by those Inuit who had access to baleen plates from the larger whales. A hole of over a metre deep was dug and using lengths of baleen which extended to the centre of the hole the baited hole was covered over. The outer ends of the baleen were either weighted with rocks or frozen into the ice in such a manner that the length overhanging the hole would flex under the weight of the fox. Relying on the springy characteristic of this material the trap would automatically close once the fox fell through into the pit. As the roof was then sealed above it there was no escape by trying to jump out. Frequently the bottom of the pit would be lined with upward pointing spikes of caribou antler which often either killed or maimed the fox and prevented it from jumping. To further deceive the animal into entering the trap the baleen plates would be covered with a layer of loose snow. This, it is claimed, made the fox think it had discovered a food cache and further encouraged it to venture onto the baleen platform. When the hunter ventured out to check his traps it was very easy to see if a fox had been caught by the snow being disturbed. In the case of a vixen hearing a cub in a trap the vixen would often follow to try and rescue its offspring. The same applied if the vixen was first to be trapped.

The third type of trap was found in areas of the Alaskan Coast and showed the true ingenuity of the Inupiat People. It is reasonable to assume that the reason this type of trap was not found outside this region was that of material availability. Made from a combination of wood sinew and bone or ivory this was a clever mechanical device of the first order. A wooden cylinder enclosed a sheave of sinews which were twisted in a similar manner to that of a Spanish Windlass. This gave the spring power to a lever through which a spike made of bone or ivory had been secured. The lever was held in a loaded position by a small toggle, which could be of wood, ivory or bone dependant on availability. This toggle was attached by a short thong to the bait. As soon as the bait was moved the lever released at speed to impale the fox through the head, usually killing the animal instantly. This also ensured that no damage was done to the valuable pelt.

MUSK OX

The Musk Ox is one of the oldest mega fauna on Earth

having been one of the few to have survived the Pleistocene-Holocene extinction event. The natural distribution of this ancient bovine is confined to the north and north-east coasts of Greenland and the north east Canadian Arctic north of the Foxe Basin, but although found on Ellesmere Island it is absent from Baffin Island. Due to this limited distribution, in areas where even the infinitely resourceful Inuit were few and far between, it was infrequently the target of Inuit hunters. Known to the Inuit as 'Umingmak' it was not just the food value of the beast that was of use. The horns were incorporated into bows while its heavy long wool had many uses from fishing lines to thread while the hide made leather of an acceptable quality.

Hunting musk ox prior to the introduction of guns was a truly dangerous task as the musk ox's horns were dangerously pointed and could be used to deadly effect, particularly when in a herd defending their calves. The normal approach was to use a pack of dogs to break up the herd before chasing a single beast to a standoff. Once this was achieved it was tackled in a similar manner to that of hunting the polar bear. Since the start of the twentieth century these animals have been introduced in many arctic regions in areas such as Scandinavia where they are now well established. In both North America and Greenland reintroductions have vastly increased the areas now inhabited by musk ox, but as the indigenous people of these areas have no history of musk ox hunting they are usually now left in peace.

The only other animal of any consequence that was hunted was the Arctic Hare and this was usually the first quarry of the young Inuit boy. Once the white man came and established his trading posts catching hares was the first stage in commerce for many young Inuit as the winter pelts of these beautiful creatures was a commodity well sought after for making both capes and hats for the wealthy gentry in both Europe and America. Catching was by snares of either sinew or very fine baleen strips. These were set in the low shrubbery where the regular tracks of the hare were visible. The Inuit would use the meat from the hare but the pelts were little used by themselves.

FISHING

Traditional Inuit fishing methods were highly dependent on where they lived and varied depending on the species being targeted. The Arctic seas are very fertile but the number of species that were exploited by the Inuit was not great in number and of these the most important was that quintessentially Arctic fish the Arctic Char. The Arctic Char can be either migratory or sedentary but it was the former that was of greater importance to the Inuit. Strangely enough it is the sedentary form that was of greater importance on the other side of the Atlantic. The Sami of the Scandinavian Arctic, whether Sea Sami or Reindeer Sami fish for the sedentary form of Arctic Char which they call "Rautu " through ice holes on the frozen winter lakes, particularly during the reindeer migrations to the coast. It makes a welcome change to their diet of reindeer meat.

Catching migratory char in the estuaries and creeks was one of the more predictable and reliable sources of food for the inhabitants of both the Canadian and Greenlandic coasts. As a primitive member of the Salmonid family it was not only a source of protein but also of essential fatty acids. The rich oily flesh was preserved by hanging up to dry in the breeze and as it did the oil dripped from its blood red flesh. Whereas the Sami often smoked fish to preserve them this was not an option to a society where wood was extremely scarce and highly valued. Using any available timber for harpoon shafts, fish spears or sled runners meant that wood was never looked upon as a fuel source.

The char would spend the summer feeding in the plankton rich coastal waters putting on weight before heading into their natal streams to spawn then overwinter before returning to the saltwater in spring. It was on the arrival at mouths of these streams that the nomadic Inuit would gather each autumn to trap the ascending fish. Most Arctic rivers are shallow and gravelly where they meet the sea. This in turn gives the ideal opportunity for the Inuit to employ one of the oldest methods of fishing known to mankind--- the weir trap.

By late summer groups of caribou skin covered tupiks would be erected on the estuary banks and repairs to the often ancient fish weirs would begin. In many ways these fish weirs were similar to the "yairs" of the Viking era around Europe or the even older traps of the ancient Celtic people which are still visible in the sea lochs and broad estuaries such as the Clyde in the west of Scotland. The basic principal was the same, allow the fish to enter on the incoming tide then block the way out so that as the tide drops the fish get trapped in shallow water. Once either stranded or trapped the fish can either be picked up or speared. In the Inuit version of the fish weir two low dams of stones were built across the shallows. The upstream dam was strategically placed as near the uppermost limit of the tides influence with the size of the boulders being sufficiently large that the water could flow between them but close enough together that the char were unable to get through. This dam went from bank to bank. The lower dam was in the shape of an upstream facing funnel with a gap at the top to let the fish into the area between the two dams. At this time a constant watch is kept on each incoming tide. As soon as shoals of char are seen to have entered the trap the gap is closed and the process of catching the fish begins.

Armed with specially designed fish spears, known as "kakivak", the hunters enter the freezing water. Having first removed their trousers the men tied their sealskin boots just below the knee. This did not keep the cold water out but what it did achieve was an effect similar to that of a scuba diver's wet suit. The water that got trapped inside the boots was warmed by the heat from the hunters' legs. This was a vast improvement on having bare feet in freezing water and rough gravel that were the only alternative. The design of the kakivak had been developed over many generations and consisted of a central ivory tip with side barbs made of either musk ox horn or baleen. The shape of the outer barbs effectively guided the fish's body onto the central point of the spear. As these outer barbs were facing inward they prevented the fish from sliding back off the central point. This enabled the hunter to lift the fish clear of the water without having to immerse his hands in the freezing waters of the river. As well as his kakivak the hunter would carry a bone needle attached to a leather thong made of sealskin. As each fish was speared they were skewered through the gills with the needle before being released from the spear and slid down the stringer.

When the hunter deposited his catch ashore it was up to the women to split the fish using their ulus then hang them on racks to dry. But before they could do this it was a common practice for the children to pop the fishes' eyes out and eat them. Nothing of the fish, other than the gut and gills, was wasted. Even the now eyeless heads were not discarded. They were buried and allowed to ferment before being dug up some time later and pulverised into a pungent smelling fish paste before being enthusiastically consumed. The majority of the dried fish was cached for use throughout the winter when the only fresh food available was seal-meat. This gave a welcome variance to an otherwise monotonous diet. The caches were constructed on the river bank above highest level the river was known to flow, thus preventing it being washed away. A layer of clean river gravel was spread on the ground around which a ring of large boulders formed a wall. The dried fish were then placed within the enclosure before being sealed in with large flat stones which prevented the cache being plundered by scavenging arctic foxes or other hungry animals.

Once a community had a sufficient catch the dams were once again breached to let subsequent shoals through unhindered. By doing so they ensured that catches of this valuable food source would be available to future generations.

Another fish which was an important part of the Inuit diet in both eastern and western Canadian Inuit populations was the diminutive Tomcod. This small relative of the cod that most people are familiar with looks very like its larger relative and at times are mistaken as the juvenile of the much larger cod. Its lifestyle is also very different from that of the true cod. A really large tomcod will be at most 40 cm long and weight around 700g. However most of the tomcod caught by the Inuit are around 30cm in length and weigh in the region of 550g. It was normal that the womenfolk and children fished for this species during the winter months when inshore waters were covered by thick ice. The ideal location to seek tomcod was in shallow water which was near the estuaries of freshwater streams. Unlike the cod which requires full marine salinity the tomcod regularly inhabits brackish water and is known to be able to tolerate very low salinity level on par with that which may be deemed freshwater.

The Inuit had fished for tomcod for many generations and just as they knew the movements of their land based quarry they also had in depth knowledge of the behaviour of this little fish. Using this knowledge enabled the Inuit women to swiftly locate the feeding shoals of hungry tomcod. Where a large lump of ice protruded above the surface the lump would also be protruding below the frozen surface ice. The Inuit knew that the feeding fish would be found on the downstream side of this and would cut a hole on this side of the hummock. Just to check that the current was flowing in the correct direction a small piece of ice was dropped into the hole and the direction in which it drifted off noted. If the current was not flowing in the desired direction then a second hole in the ice was cut where the flow was more favourable. Armed with a jigging lure made from carved ivory, which had upward pointing spikes to impale the fish, and a fishing line made from fine strips of baleen, the fishing began. Baleen line had unique properties.

Its natural springy characteristics prevented it from tangling and as its waterproof nature meant that ice would not build up on it and could be shaken off if it did. The method of working the lure would appear strange to modern anglers but was highly efficient. Using both a jigging stick and an ice scoop to keep the hole clear of ice the line was spread between the two implements and manoeuvred in such a manner that the lure worked up and down to attract the fish. Once a tomcod was hooked the woman would spread her arms pulling the line over jigging stick and hauling the fish clear of the hole. Once clear of the hole the fish was shaken off the jig to fall on the ice where it froze almost instantly. This method of line retrieval meant that the wet line was never handled. The captured fish were placed around the hole with their heads pointing toward the hole. It was believed that this would encourage other fish to come out of the hole.

Once the white man came lures were made of metal armed with steel hooks and the age old ivory lures, which had often been passed from one generation to another, faded into history.

THE ATLATL

Across the globe many indigenous people, who relied on hunting, developed forms of launching spears more efficiently to gain both distance and accuracy. In the case of the Inuit this was taken to a level of ingenuity seldom seen elsewhere. The spear throwing board know as the "atlatl" by Canadian Inuit and the "norsaq" in Greenland is very similar to the throwing boards of the Australian Aborigines known as a "woomera". Again this demonstrates how different cultures have come up with similar solutions for the same problem. What makes the "atlatl" so special is that it was designed to be used from a kayak. Acting as an extension of the thrower's arm it enables the user to gain both distance and penetration force from a sitting position. The use of this implement also gives the user more consistent results than throwing a harpoon held directly in the hand. The reason behind this is that the user has to hold the harpoon exactly in the same position each throw. As the position in the groove in the atlatl which holds the harpoon is fixed lengthwise by a peg on the harpoon shaft which locates into a hole in the outer end of the atlatl. Greenland 'norsaqs' are identifiably different from their Canadian counterparts by having a second hole at the inner end for securing it to the harpoon when not in use. Other refinements often include a short leather lanyard with a form of toggle to secure it to the kayak. Ranging from around eighteen inches to two feet in length different areas have local adaptations and variations in both shape and decoration. For example those from Eastern Greenland tend to be longer and narrower than those of the west coast. They also are more decorative with bone edges and carved bone or ivory studs. Although there are fewer Inuit hunting from kayaks than a century ago the technique of harpoon throwing with a throwing stick is kept alive in Greenland by the members of the numerous kayak clubs. Most museums which have collections of Inuit artefacts will have examples of this implement on display.

BIRD HUNTING

In the summer months, what ice is left is unstable and what quarry species there were have long since vanished out to sea to feed. This is when the "gatherer" bit of the "hunter gatherer" applies to the Inuit. Many birds, both seabirds and wildfowl, nest in the Arctic regions during the short summer season, hurriedly raising their young before heading south before the sea freezes over again. This gives the Inuit a short period in which to gather eggs as well as catch both adult and young birds.

Fresh eggs were taken from the nests, often from dangerous cliff faces which were scaled in fearless fashion. Young birds were also taken by scaling cliffs before the young had become fully fledged. Adult birds were often caught in nets or by using the specially made bird arrow or bird spear. The bird spear was a very effective weapon during the summer moult of wildfowl such as geese and ducks and was used from a kayak. The wooden shafted spear had a central point with a circle of three or four ivory forward facing prongs mounted further back from the central point. These additional points acted in a similar way to a shotgun by increasing the area of effective cover and hence increasing the chance of killing the targeted bird. When used from a kayak, an atlatl, or throwing stick was employed to give both increased speed and distance.

Another regularly employed method for bring down low flying birds was a bolas made from sinew weighted with teeth from either beluga or walrus. Occasionally sections of antler were used as weights. Even young children would carry a bolas during the waterfowl migrating season and hurtle it at any low flying bird that came within range. The thrower would first swing the bolas around his head to give it momentum. On release the weights opened out to create a shape like a flying spider which, if it hit its target, would wrap around the neck, wings and feet, disabling the bird's flight.

As well as the bird spear and bolas long handled nets were used to catch the little auks that nest in very large colonies on grassy slopes on the coast. The ability of the Inuit to catch these small fast moving birds as they come into land enables a single hunter to catch dozens of the birds per hunt. This also enables the Inuit to store food for leaner times by preparing a dish unique to the Inuit.

This unique Inuit winter food was Kiviak, a dish made from fermented Auks. All you need to make this dish is one seal and as many birds as you can get.

Skin the seal by cutting round the head then turn the whole thing inside out, leaving a thick layer of blubber on the skin and, after removing the seal's inner carcass reverse the skin to put the blubber side innermost. You now have a blubber-lined sealskin bag. Stuff as many auks into this bag as possible (feet, beaks, feathers included). Once full, squeeze out any air, seal up with blubber and stitch closed. Bury under a large pile of rocks (to prevent foxes etc. finding it). Leave for a considerable time, to allow fermentation to effectively take place. After three months or more, dig up and open the bag. Enjoy!!! The only part not eaten is the feathers. The rest, I have been assured, tastes like strong blue cheese. I have long wondered if this is the origin of the phrase 'like spitting feathers'...

In some areas, notably the Belcher Islands and in the Ungava Bay area of Northern Quebec, the skins of birds, mainly eider duck, were used to make clothing. Examples of both the male parka and the female equivalent, the amaat, made from eider skins are held in the Quebec Museum. The Belcher Islands are situated in the south east corner of Hudson Bay and have always been regarded as an area where game of any sort was scarce. This led to the Belcher Inuit being very frugal and their use of any natural resources was quite extraordinary. Bird skins are extremely fragile as anyone who has skinned game birds will readily testify. But if that is one of the few readily available sources of potential clothing material then that is what is used.

THE INUIT HARPOON

Since prehistoric man first became a hunter he has used long, sharp pointed implements as a method of killing his prey. Initially these would have been used to stab the victim. (I intentionally use the word "victim" as the recipient of the sharp end' was quite often another hominid rather than a potential dinner. Millennia later things have not really changed except we now use intercontinental ballistic missiles.)
As time went by the "lance" evolved into the spear, then the arrow then eventually into the gun. When the spear was used to hunt aquatic mammals it became the harpoon and this was

where Inuit ingenuity really came to the fore.

Across the world indigenous people had access to timber. However that was not the case of the Inuit people who lived in the snow and ice covered desert north of the tree-line. Even the Sami of Northern Norway and Russia's Kola Peninsula had access to the vast conifer forests of the Taiga. Where timber was available in such quantities it was not regarded as precious and one could afford to lose or break spear or harpoon shafts without too much serious consequence. But when the only timber available was either found on the shore as driftwood, remembering that the Inuit in the Thule area of Greenland once thought that trees grew on the seabed, or traded for hard earned skins, wood in any form was a highly prized possession. It was due to this shortage of basic materials that the unique detachable head of the Inuit harpoon evolved and is still in use today in some parts of Greenland. Unlike seal hunting where modern high velocity rifles are used, where narwhal and walrus are the quarry the harpoon has remained the method of capture.

The design of harpoon may look at first glance quite basic but on closer inspection it reveals its true identity as a complex piece of ingenious design. Made totally from the materials available to the Inuit since they first ventured onto the ice it is only since the appearance of the white man that the tip of the harpoon has been made of metal. Prior to that event it would have been made of bone, ivory or a hard stone such as flint, if available. Its evolution must have been over many generations and its modifications were localised to suit both the species hunted and the method of hunting, whether from boat or through ice holes.

The loose head is connected to a short fore- shaft, often made of narwhal tusk or walrus tusk. The head itself is a metal tip inserted into another carved bone or ivory piece, sperm whale teeth being a favoured material. The head is connected to the fore -shaft in such a manner that when the impaled animal thrashes about the head comes off beneath the tough hide. The harpoon shaft is usually around two metres in length and the whole three stage weapon is launched with the aid of an atlatl. Attached to the head of the harpoon is a line of between fifteen and twenty metres long. At one time this would have been made from the skin of a bearded seal or walrus but nowadays is more likely to be of synthetic fibre. The hunter would have this line sitting coiled in front of him in a line tray. This in turn was connected to an inflated sealskin float which was placed behind the hunter. When the line to the harpoon head tightens it has the effect of pulling the cleverly designed head at right angles to the line. This then ensures that the head cannot pull free from the quarry.

The detachable shaft also has a float and can be retrieved after the hunter has made his kill. If the quarry is too large for one hunter to haul in further floats are attached to the line, these then act as a drag on the quarry and tire it out until the quarry comes exhausted to the surface where it is killed using a sharp tipped lance.

The skill needed to perform these manoeuvres from a light craft, whether kayak or umiak, bobbing about in the icy Arctic waters was learned from childhood and ensured that future generations of Inuit could be fed.

INUKSHUK

Much of the Arctic lands, particularly in winter, appear featureless. For even the most nomadic of traditional groups, it was difficult to remember what areas would be able to support the food requirements of the group. This problem was often resolved by the construction of the Inukshuk. These structures, often in the shape of a stone man, indicated that the area had the potential to support humans.

With the coming of the white traders, things began to change for the Inuit. Trade with the Hudson Bay Company and, later, the Revillon Freres was to change the way of life for these super self-sufficient nomadic hunters to the ways of the white man.

Now, in the early years of the 21st Century, they have snowmobiles instead of malamutes, rifles replace bow and harpoon, outboard motors on fast speedboats replace the paddle power and stealth of the kayak. Where a child once played with a sled tied to a pup we now have televisions and computer games.

No longer living in either tupik or igloo, they have permanent houses in villages with supermarkets. Most worrying of all is the fact, that like all indigenous peoples of the Arctic, the Inuit have no inbuilt tolerance to alcohol and this has led to a cross-Arctic problem of alcoholism.

INUIT BELIEFS
AND MYTHS

Similar to many other Arctic races, including the Sami of the Warm Arctic, the Inuit are Anamistic Shamanists. But unlike the Sami the Inuit were never persecuted for their beliefs but have been targeted regularly since the 19th century by Christian missionaries mainly from the Anglican and Roman Catholic churches. Other less well known Christian sects have also had an impact on the Inuit. One particular sect, the Moravian Church, had a significant influence during the late 19th and early 20th centuries in the areas of the Hudson Straits, Hudson Bay and the coast of Labrador.

Prior to the coming of Christianity it was the Shaman who gave these people spiritual guidance. This was based on many taboos which had to be observed so as to work in harmony with the animals and environment on which their very existance depended. The Shamans were looked upon as soul voyagers who were able to travel to the spirit world and throughout the winter darkness their tales would hold the community spellbound around the dim glow of the igloo seal blubber lamps.

To cover all the beliefs and myths of the Eastern Inuit would take a large tome on its own so I have just selected a few which have parallels across Arctic societies and in some cases in those of our own.

Ritual and communal bonds.

The inhabitants of the far north live in the most extreme environment inhabited by man and to survive had to work in unison with nature. Limited resources meant that it took a large land area to support a small number of people. This in turn prevented the founding of large, or in some cases permanent settlements. This applied more so in the eastern areas of the Canadian Arctic where regular and reliable food sources and not available. The situation in the Western Canadian Arctic and Alaska is different as coastal settlements of the Inupiat and Aluet could fish and hunt marine mammals for most of the year and store food for during the lean times. There were no cities in the Arctic. Small extended family communities were the norm as was the ability to travel over long distances. The different groups knew one another through marriage, which maintained a viable gene pool and like the ancient Gaelic Culture of the Scottish Highlands memories were long and handed down verbally from generation to generation.

The periods of relative inactivity which were frequent during the long polar winter were the time for community activities and this led to the development of festivities based around the founding myths of each society. Story-telling and music helped to preserve both the myths and beliefs of their ancient cultures.

Reincarnation.

One such belief which appears from as far west as the Nenets of Western Siberia to the Kalaalit of Greenland, many thousands of miles to the east, is that of reincarnation.

The care and affection shown by the Inuit peoples to both their children and the elderly is often commented upon by members of western societies. However, in the not so distant past, starvation was a frequent visitor to the people of the Arctic and it was at these dark times that the belief of reincarnation was shown at its strongest. When the situation was reached that there was insufficient to feed the whole family or village the practice of the elderly to wander off into the wilderness was widespread. Sacrificing their own life to save the younger members of the group may seem very altruistic to western society but the belief that they would soon return into the family as a newborn was great and seemed logical to all concerned. Those left behind accepted the loss and invariably the next child born would be given the name of the lost loved one. It was also believed that the newborn would inherit not only the name but the characteristics of that person.

Similarly if a person was very ill and had become a burden on the group it was common for that person to remain behind as the nomadic group had to move on to seasonal hunting grounds.

Mitaartut

During the period from late November through to the end of January the sun never comes above the horizon to much of the area north of the Arctic Circle. It is during this time that Inuit groups meet up to celebrate. Traditionally this would include, if food was plentiful, feasting. Other activities such as dancing, shamanic displays and games would be interspersed with storytelling from which the younger generations could learn Inuit mythology. From the coming of Christianity these pagan activities have been incorporated into Christmas celebrations. One area where the pagan remnants are more obvious is in parts of Greenland where the celebration of Mitaartut is held. Far to the west in Alaska many indigenous groups hold an equivalent celebration which undoubtedly has similar origins. To many other societies it will bear a resemblence to Halloween as in Mitaartut everthing is reversed, Men dress as women, women as men—often with enlarged sexual adornments to enhance the sexual identification. Mitaartut means, in literal translation, people in disguise. Once suitably disguised,, with faces often blackened or hidden, the paticipants set off round the settlement over a three day period between Christmas and Twelfth Night. Every house is visited and gifts are demanded. Non intelligible garble is spoken and children, usually laughing seek out the safety of their parents. In exchange for the gifts, nowadays most likely cakes, the revellers perform a dance then move on to the next dwelling. The western Arctic equivalent tends to be more elaborate and formalized and has a set series of celebrations which vary from cleaning out the communal house to young boys parading painted and naked in the village, but the hub of the celebration was the Bladder Festival . This could stretch over two weeks and began with all the previous seasons seal and walrus bladders being brought to the Men's House. After feasting the bladders were inflated and hung from the rafters, from then on a series of taboos had to be observed as not to offend the spirits of the seals, which are believed to reside in the bladders. On the final day of the festival the bladders are taken out on the sea ice at dawn to holes cut the ice the previous day and released back to the ocean. To help the spirits in their hunting the bladders are often given miniture paddles and spear heads.

Creation Myths

Most societies and religions have creation myths and the peoples of the Arctic are no exception. The younger generation who have been brought up in an electronic age where television and the internet are the norm are well aware of the Big Bang.
 Their parents, and in most cases grandparents, were most likely brought up on the Christian belief of Let there be Light,and Noah and the Flood. However those Arctic people who were traditionally Anamistic Shamanists have their own

creation myths which are in many cases moralistic and needless to say involve the creatures which were familiar to those who live in the Arctic.

One tale of the creation was that passed down by an elderly Greenland storyteller from the Etah Kalaalit area in the far north of Greenland. Her tales of the creation were many and have been passed down, hopefully without too many additions :

The earth fell from the sky and, once the dust settled, from the soil, rocks and mountains the first people crawled out of the ground. Their existance was hard as their was neither light nor food so they ate dirt. They were so ignorant that they did not know how to die and soon overpopulated the Earth to the point that it started to disintegrate. But before it collapsed a great flood came and washed away all forms of life on the land. However when the flood receded a few people had survived. These people were wiser than the people before them and they traded their immortality for light. So the earth gained light and seasons and people accepted that they had to die.

Now they could hunt and fish and when they died they returned to the sky as stars.'

In the Sami version the dead returned to the sky and their spirits are seen on winter nights as the Aurora. In the Christian version the flood led to the story of Noah.

Another Inuit creation story from the far west in Alaska where both the raven and the whale still carry spiritual significance. This should not cause any surprise as the survival of these people in the past relied heavily on these two creatures. In the case of the whale it was a food source and the raven was used by hunters to find wounded or fallen game.

The story starts with Raven the Hunter spotting a giant whale in the Ocean which covered the world. When Whale leapt into the air then dived Raven had to wait, but he knew that when Whale came up to breath air he would be ready with his harpoon. For a long time he was vigilant and when

Whale surfaced he was ready. He threw his deadly weapon and embedded it into the giants head and a great battle followed.

Raven's line was strong and held fast but Whale was also strong and pulled Raven under the waves. But every time Whale came up to breath Raven took to the sky and also breathed. For a long time the battle went on. Each time Whale came up he was weaker from the wound caused by Raven's harpoon and eventually Whale lay dead on the surface. So high above the surface Whale floated that Raven created a place for man to live. And so the native Inuit of Alaska's north coast explain the creation of their land. In their mythology it also accounts for the whale shaped peninsula on which they live and the whale hunting culture which they depended upon.

The Sun and the Moon.

As previously stated, most indigenous cultures have their own version of how the Earth was created, but the Inuit are the only one I have come across that also have a 'Creation' myth regarding the Sun and Moon. I dare say there will be others but this is the only one I have come across in my travels. This is the Inuit version :-

' Not long after the the Raven and the whale had their battle and the people had crawled from the earth a powerful shaman emerged. He drew power from all things around him until he was so powerful that he raised himself into the sky. But he did not go alone. With him he took his beautiful sister and the magic of fire. To the fire he added great quantities of fuel until the fire was so great that it became the sun we see in the sky. At first both the Shaman and his sister were happy but in time they quarrelled and he started to abuse his sister. She suffered much of this abuse but when he scorched one side of her face with his powerful sun she could take no more and ran away. Destroying her beauty was not to be tolerated and so she became the moon we see in the night sky. The Shaman and his

Sun still chase after her and sometimes get near her but will never catch her. When it is a new moon it is the blackened and burnt side of her face that we see from the Earth. But as she turns her head she slowly reveals her beauty until we see her shine as the full moon in the night sky.'

As well as the Earth and the Sun and Moon myths many North American First Nations people have an interesting myth involving the positioning of the Stars in the night sky. Many different tribes have layed claim to the tale which involves the Coyote, or in the Arctic the Fox. The basis of the tale is that as the wise people were placing the stars in an ordered state in the sky the coyote, a devious and mischevious animal, watched from his hiding place. When he saw the time it took for the wise people to place each star he thought he could do it much quicker. When the wise people had finished for the day he ran over to the basket where the stars were kept. He lifted the basket and threw it over the edge of the earth into the surrounding sky. The stars were spread in confusion all over the sky where they remain to this day.

Hardly a scientific explanation but one that both First Nation and Inuit children have enjoyed for generations.

TUPILAK.

Many tourists to Greenland bring back a form of Inuit carving that has become valued by collectors of what has been loosely termed 'ethnic' or 'indigenous art'. However the origins of the 'Tupilak' were much removed from that of artistic expression and more to do with the power of fear of the supernatural. The original version of the tupilak was not a carved image but a collection of bones from dead creatures. These could be from animals, birds or humans, gathered by the shaman.He would gather these in secret and once tied together he would chant his spells over the assembled bundle. Then, according to Inuit legend, he would allow the tupilak to take its power from his genitals. Once this was achieved the bundle was secretly put into the sea and sent off to destroy its chosen victim. This was not regarded as a foolproof method for if the intended victim had a greater degree of shamanistic power the intended victim could return the tupilak to its origin with increased destructive powers. Hence the apprehensive approach to using such magic. So how did a bundle of bones evolve into the carvings of the grotesque creatures we now term 'tupilak' ? Since none of the original tupilaks remained, due to being disposed of in the sea no-one actually knew what they looked like. When the first Europeans enquired as to what this mythical 'tupilak' looked like the local Inuit carved their own vision of what it might be. Initially these were carved in wood occasionally adorned with skin belts. From these wooden figures the modern carvings evolved. The Inuit carvers were not slow to realise that the more bizarre and grotesque the figure the easier it was to sell. From these strange origins the indurstry we know today was launched. At one time the carvers used ivory from whales' teeth, walrus teeth and walrus tusks. Now they use antler and bone to comply with the international standards of the CITES convention.

EFFECTS OF CHRISTIANITY AND WHITE MAN'S LAW

From the early days of both the whaling and the fur trading companies, such as Hudson Bay Company, Christian missionaries from varying Christian sects set out to capture the souls of what they regarded the godless peoples of the frozen wastelands of Canada's Northern Territories. This race to convert the Inuit was not exactly carried out in a Christian Spirit of brotherly love but more in a form of competition frought with religous biggotry between Anglican, Presbyterian, Roman Catholic Churches and other sects such as the Moravian Church (which is one of the oldest Protestant churches, founded in the Bohemian Reformation of the 15th century.)This rivalry between Christian sects undoubtedly left many Inuit confused regarding Christianity as a belief system and was to lead to a tragic incident among the Inuit who inhabited the remote Beltcher Islands in Hudson Bay.

The following story has intentionally been included in detail so that readers can better understand the phsycology of these people who over millenia had evolved a faith system based on what they observed in every day life, with nature and tales of nature being endowed with spirtual significance. Then along came the whiteman only to tell them they were wrong and that the white man's God was the real God and had to be obeyed.

Located north of James Bay in the south-east corner of Hudson Bay in present day territory of Nunavut, this achepeligo of over a thousand small islands was little known to the white man even into the early 20th century. What happened there in the winter and early spring of 1940 was to shock the whole of Canadian society. It also made many people wonder if the teaching of religion to a people who had been isolated from all other societies for centuries was indeed going to improve their lives.

The Belcher Island Murders.

Christianity came late to the Belcher Islands. Being located around seventy miles off the east coast of Hudson Bay they were known to exist for many years before actually being visited and charted by the white man. Part of the reason was that vessels trading in Hudson Bay in the 19th century would hug the coast from the entrance to the bay at Nottingham Island, past Cape Smith down to Port Harrison before sailing west of the Nastapoka Islands to the Hudson Bay Company settlements of Richmond Gulf and Great Whale River. Those who had ventured west by either design or ill-fortune had found the Belchers barren and desolate and therefore they were regarded as being of little interest to the commerce of the region.

When the Royal Canadian Mounted Police arrived on April 11th 1940 it was the first visit since 1919. That visit had also been to investigate murders but on that occasion no charges had been layed as it was discovered that the two victims had been killed due to their deviant behaviour and had been regarded as a threat to the rest of the islanders. At that time the lot of the islanders was very hard. Inspector Phillips of the RCMP descibed the Belcher Inuit as 'the most destitute natives I have ever seen.' And it was into such a world that the perpetrators of the 1940 murders had been born. This time however it was not greed or threatening behaviour that had triggered the henious crimes but religious fervour.

It all started with an Inuit woman named Mina watching a shooting star. She had heard no doubt of the Star of Bethlehem and promptly connected the two events. She concluded that this meteor shower that she witnessed was signalling the coming of Christ and the end of the world. She set off to tell others. She left her igloo on Camsell Island and made her way to the larger camp on nearby Flahery Island. When she arrived there she found the community in a state of religious frenzy. Two of the community elders, who also had seen the meteors, were leading this mahem. Charlie Ouyerak and Peter Sala were two very repected men who had been infants at the time when Inspector Phillips had visited in 1919 and had been fortunate enough to survive to adulthood at a time of high infant mortality. Their lives had not been easy but their hunting skills had earned them the respect of their community. So when Ouyerak told everyone that they should not care for material things some shot their dogs and broke their guns, these items being crucial to their survival. Even worse was that they not only were telling people that Jesus was coming but that Peter Sala was in fact God and Charlie Ouyerak was Jesus returned to earth. Mina agreed with them whole heartedly as she also had seen the stars. Between them they tried to convince the assembled members of the community and most, probably out of fear, were willing to accept this.

Things started to get serious when a young girl of about thirteen years of age, named Sara, declared that she did not believe that Ouyerak was Jesus nor Sala was God. Even her own brother was infuriated. When she reiterated the statement her brother, Alec Apawkok lashed out at the girl and started beating her with a stick. From there she was dragged outside and constantly beaten before being killed by a blow to the skull with the barrel from a broken rifle. This blow was administered by an Inuit woman named Akiinik.

The only person in the assembly who had resevatuions about this behavior was Ketowieak. He not only had doubts about both Ouyerak and Sala's claims to be Jesus and God but had also read the scriptures more than most. The reason for this was his wife was blind and she liked listening to Ketowieak reading them to her.

These scriptures had been circulated among the Inuit of the Hudson Bay area and more distant parts of what was then the Northern Territories by the Anglican Church. These copies of the New Testament were printed in a syllabic script and had been made available to the Inuit of the Belcher Islands for many years.Two of the Anglican Church's oldest missions were on the mainland directly opposite the Belchers at Great Whale River and Little Whale River. Although the church had no resident preacher on the islands some had visited there in the past to distribute the syllabic script translations of Rev. E.J. Peck.

When Ketowieak challenged Ouyerak's claims to be Jesus a fight between him and Ouyerak ensued. When the two separated, Ketowieak left the meeting house, passing Sara's body on the way. He returned some time later but rather than go in he stayed outside and called for his relatives to come out and join him and to believe in the 'true God'. In reply Peter Sala threw a piece of wood at him through an ice window hitting him in the mouth. Not even his wife came out to support him and the others were too scared of Ouyerak and Sala to do so. Ketowieak retreated to another igloo for the night. The next morning Sala entered the Igloo carrying two harpoons and attacked Ketowieak but it was another Inuit, Adlaykok who dealt the fatal blow by shooting him with a rifle. Everyone watched but no-one went to his aid. Adlaykok declared that he had killed Satan. The igloo was pulled down over Katowieak and his frozen body lay there until the police arrived many weeks later.

Those not directly involved gathered up their possessions and moved away from the scene, but remained silent about the events that had taken place.

Meanwhile Mina was happy to go along with it all as she

had moved in with Charlie Ouyerak.

It was some time later, in early February that the religious mahem raised its ugly head again. This time the victim was Alec Ikpak, brother of the murdered Sara. He approached Ouyerak and tried to reason with him, insisting that the madness had to stop. However Ouyerak had already convinced oothers that Ikpak was Satan and that Satan, like the serpent, must be expelled from the garden. This led to the third murder when on February 9th Ouyerak went into Ikpak's igloo and confronted him to accept that he was Jesus. When Ikpak refused he was called outside where he was told to walk out on the sea ice where his father-in-law shot him twice in the back then once in the head as his wife looked on. His body was then retrieved and buried under stones near the beach. At this time, the outside world were totally unaware of the goings on on the Belchers. Even the two white men employed by the government subsidised Hudson Bay Company trading post were ignorant of the murders.

The two whitemen on the Belchers were the Hudson Bay manager Ernie Riddell and his assistant, Lou Bradbury. It was fairly normal for the employees of HBC to work for great periods without having much contact with the outside world other than by radio. In the case of the Belchers this also meant that mail was only collected infrequently due to the remoteness and the fact that in winter the only way across the ice was by dogsled. This had to be done before the thaw set in around the beginning of April. (now it is earlier due to climate change). The normal way was to employ a native hunter with a dogsled and team as they knew the ice and their dogs would not cross unsound ice. The best hunter and dog team were Peter Sala and his dogs and they were soon located and hired by Ernie Riddell to take him the seventy miles across the sea ice to Great Whale River. Totally unaware of the murders Riddell set off for great Whale River with an only too keen Peter Sala on March 12th 1940. They knew that it would take around three days to reach their destination and that they would have to build igloos on at least two nights. It was just as they settled in for the first night that Sala told Riddell that he had been a 'very bad man'. Initially Riddell tried to assure him that he was a good man, a good hunter and provided well for his family. However, Sala insisted that he was a 'very bad man' but did not elaborate on the subject. This puzzled the normally quite self assured Riddell.

On reaching the HBC post at Great Whale River, Peter Sala went off to see his old friend, a half breed Indian who had been employed by HBC for many years. It was to Harald Udgarden that Sala confessed about the murders. It was then that Udgarden ran to the HBC office and blurted out the question, 'Have you heard about the murders on the Belcher Islands ?' This was how the outside world were informed of Ouyerlak and Sala's deeds. Imediately Riddell radioed his bosses in Winnipeg of the events requesting immediate police response. Nearly three decades later he said he could still hear Udgarden's trembling voice asking that question.

By 15th March the authorities in Ottowa were aware and started to take action. All they had to go on was what Peter Sala had told them. This meant that they needed to return as soon as possible to the islands and, since it was obvious religion was at the core of the situation, a clergyman in the party would be an essential asset.

That clergyman was the eccentric Anglican missionary the Reverend G. Neilson. When Neilson was told what was happening he immediately made himself available. In under two weeks they were on their way back to the Belchers but what they were yet to find was only to add to the already dreadful situation.

On their final stretch they came across Quarak who was out hunting. When Peter Sala spoke to the hunter he burst into tears, a thing that Riddell had never seen before was an Inuit hunter cry. Riddell asked Sala what was wrong and got the simple reply of 'Very bad ! Very bad !

It was soon realised that since they had left further

tragic events, this time with Mina at the centre, had led to the deaths of six more people. Even sadder was that this time it was two women and four children who were the victims. These included Peter Sala's two young sons .On March 29th a group of eight adults and their children were camped on the small island of Camsell about five miles from the main camp on Tukarak Island. This was a month and a half after Ikpak's death andmost of the Inuit thought that the religious frenzy had subsided. Mina had left Charlie Ouyerak and returned to her husband Moses. Peter Sala was in Great Whale River and Charlie Ouyerak was away at another camp. Mina had started to act strange again and insisted that they all go out onto the ice as Jesus was coming. Only Sara, Quarak's wife with her own children hid from Mina who was busy forcing the others onto the ice. Once well out from shore she then told them to take off their clothes so that they would be naked when Jesus came to them. She forced the women to remove their amaats, the female equivalent of the parka. Then she removed the childrens trousers. The only ones to escape were Moses, Mina's husband and Peter Sala's wife, also named Mina.

These two and Mina were the only ones to come off the ice alive. Two women and four children lay dead, one of them Mina's mother the other woman a widowed sister, Sara Kumudluk.

In many ways the Belcher murders parallel the Sami uprising in 1852 at Kauto Keino in Noway's Finnmark region. The leaders of that uprising had been influenced by the teachings of Swedish Lutheren Pastor, Lars Levi Lastaedeous. The Sami involved saw themselves as God's Children and sin free who were driving out the sinful and evil members in their midst. Unfortunately the Norwegian authorities handled the outcome in a very different manner in 1852 to the way the Canadians of 1940.

The Belcher Island Trials

It was the 11th April before the RCMP arrived on the Belcher Islands. On their previous visit, twenty one years before, they were investigating the murder of two Inuit hunters. On that occasion they remained for twelve days and left without charging anyone with the killings. The reason given for not making any arrests nor pressing charges was that the two men concerned had been killed by the community because they were a threat to the people on the islands. By taking this view they had recognised the fact that people living in a sparsely populated and remote society had to make decisions differently from those in an urban society. This set a precedent for the ensuing trials on these still barren and 'uncivilised' islands where there were neither a resident law enforcement nor formal government presence.

The natural self reliance of the Belcher Inuit had been clearly demonstrated back in 1919 when, before the RCMP left, the residents asked if the Government could supply them with a suitable boat so they could move families to different hunting grounds and be able to visit Great Whale River in the summer. They also asked for rifles and fishing nets. Noticeably they did not ask for any food supplies but only for the means to enable them to source their own food in an easier manner. Such was the way of the Inuit. Unfortunately, despite this request being put to the Canadian Government by Inspector Phillips who led the inquiry, nothing was done. Life on the islands remained at subsistance level with the ever present threat of starvation. It was not until the 1930's when the Hudson Bay Company constructed a permanent base on the island that things improved. Even this improvement was small as, other than the HBC employees, few white men ever visited this isolated outpost of the dominion.

When on the 11th of April 1940 the plane carrying both the RCMP and Indian Agent and Justice of the Peace, Dr. T.J. Orford, it caused great interest. It was two days before the party of officials reached Tukarak Camp despite it being only six miles from the HBC post, the reason being that there was a lack of available dog teams. Once at Tukarak they soon uncovered the body of Ikpak as his wife led them to where it was buried. Dr. Orford confirmed that death was caused by two bullet wounds in the back and one in the head.

By April 15th Inspector Martin, Investigating Officer RCMP, reported by radio that he and Dr. Orford had examined and identified seven bodies. He confirmed that one man had been shot and two women and four young boys had been driven naked on to the sea ice and frozen to death. He stated that he had the perpetrators in custody and although he knew the location of another two bodies, these had neither been recovered nor examined.

When the plane left the Belchers on the 16th it had all the party that had come with it plus three prisoners, Mina, Quarak and Adlaykok. Mina was charged with the deaths of four children and two adults, Quarak with the murder of Ikpak and Adlaykok with the murder of Ketowieak, whose body was still to be recovered. Sala was away at Great Whale River at the time with Lou Bradbury.

From the plane leaving until it returned was a worrying time for Ernie Riddell as it was judged by the locals that he had been responsible for three of their people being sent away. If he left the post he carried a rifle, such was his fear of reprisals. Fortunately the locals had enough respect for him and had decided not to cause him or the property of HBC any harm.

The decision had been made to try the accused on the islands rather than take all those concerned to Moose Factory. Not only did this mean less transporting of people but it also showed to the local Inuit that the trial would be fair. It also was closer to the scene of the crimes.

The RCMP arrived ahead of the judiciary and had arrested Ouyerak, Sala, Akiinik and Apawkok. Quarak and Adlaykok had been brought back from Moose Factory and Mina from a psychiatric unit in Toronto where she had been held for assessment.

The arrival back on the islands of the three prisoners led to what was described as a 'party atmosphere'. This in itself gives one an indication of the Inuit mindset regarding community and family matters.

In the intervening period the Inuit hunter who' back in 1919, had acted as guide to Inspector Philips, Anawak, had retrieved the missing bodies of both Sara and Ketowieak and brought them back to the Hudson Bay Company post for proper burial.

Judge Plaxton from Toronto and the rest of the judiciary arrived on Monday 18th August after being delayed by weather. The SS Fort Charles had to wait until the weather eased before making the crossing frommGreat Whale River where it had taken refuge en route from Moose Factory. So the scene was set for the trial.

The trials were conducted in a marquee erected near the trading post. The judge presided from a raised platform which had enough space for his desk and chair, but little else. The jury and prisoners sat on wooden benches while others, including the witnesses sat on the mossy ground. The trials started on the 19th and ended on the 21st. A much shorter time than would be appropriate in an urban located court of law. Despite this all was in accordance with the Dominion of Canada's legal framework.

Most of the debate centered around the Inuit's cultural ways where 'things were done as they always had been done'. The responsibilities of both native and white man and the influence of the church were also debated. The outcome prompted Major D McKeand, Commander of the East Arctic Patrol to write to the Deputy Commissioner of the North West Territories stating ;-

' Eskimos have no tribal system and the family is the independant unit. In time, to ridicule or inflict whipping on the Canadian Eskimos would bring forth a vigorous protest from all white persons who know them personally.'

A senior solicitor had written to McKeand as early as

31st May expressing the need to install the right judge. In his letter he wrote :-

' --- someone conversant with native phsycology, customs and habits should be in charge. ------ As it is unthinkable that a native would receive capital sentence the further question of detention and punishment will also arise. Detention at any of the peneteniaries would, I think, be equivalent to execution by slow torture, but detention at any of the northern police posts would be equivalent to a holiday with pay and the matter must be carefully considered.'

Carefully considered it was and in Judge Plaxton a man of unquestionable intelligence and integrity had been appointed. The findings of the jury, which consisted of not only Ernie Riddell but also members of the press, a prospector, mining engineer, the ships engineer and RCMP members, were unsurprisingly guilty on six of the accused with onlyApawkok being aquited.

The manner in which the sentencing of those found guilty was carried out demonstrated clearly that Judge Plaxton fully understood the situation and acted accordingly. The sentences were as follows :-

Quarak :- Released on a two year suspended sentence to keep the peace and be of good behaviour. He was also to protect and provide food for the families of Sala, Outerak and Adlaykok during their terms of imprisonment.

Adlaykok :- One year imprisonment

Sala and Ouyerak :- Two years imprisonment,

Mina and Akiinik were both deemed to be insane.

Before the prisoners were taken from the Belchers on the 22nd of August orders were issued that the HBC would issue weekly rations to the families of the three male prisoners. A further order dictated the issue of either ten rounds of ammunition or equivalent be given to any hunter who undertook to provide meat and fish for the prisoners families. These stipulation then ensured that the families would not suffer and also showed to the Inuit that the white man's justice could be fair. However, although sentencing had been carried out and as far as the legal situation was concerned the case closed, the debate on the issue was far from over. The following, lengthy memorandum was sent from R. Olmstead, Crown Prosecutor at the trials to the Deputy Minister, Department of Justice, more than a year later on 11th October 1941. Its sentiments were in line with the thinking of many in legal circles in Canada at the time.

'It is my opinion that it would be very difficult to secure a jury of white men in the James and Hudson Bay districts who would convict an Eskimo of murder arising out of the killings of last winter or any other time. White men resident in these areas appear to have what amounts to almost an affection for the Eskimos. They understand that he is probably the friendliest, happiest aborigine anywhere in the world and that he lives in a country and in conditions far more rigorous than existance elsewhere outside the Arctic region ------- Any killing that may occur is due very rarely to malice but has behind it some motive, belief, transgression, or tradition that justifies it in his eyes.---------

Similarly with regard to punishment. It is not understood as punishment unless it is associated with physical pain. It is the only form of punishment he knows. He whips his dogs frequently and hard when he thinks they deserve it. To take him away and shelter, clothe and feed him for months on end, meanwhile giving similar treatment to his family is not his idea of punishment. Being complacent and easy going by nature, a term of imprisonment is a holiday about which he will be able to talk the rest of his life------- In fact one of the accused was begging to be taken away before the trial. He frequently asked, 'Moosonee, me, plane ?' He actually gloated and beamed with pleasure when he learned he was to go.'

I have cut the length of this memorandom considerably but I think one can easily gain the general feeling about the application of white man's laws on a people who were at the time viewed as 'childlike and sometimes childish.'

Olmstead further went on to make recommendations :-

' I recommend and strongly urge that never again should the provisions of the Criminal Code be applied to the Eskimos. The cap of Canadian criminal jurisprudence cannot be made to fit the head of this primitive people. The Criminal Code is not applied to white children of tender years ----- it ill behooves the most advanced race to apply its rigid rules of conduct to another race which by reason principally of geography has made little or no advance in the last two or three thousand years.'

After various dissertation on the Inuit situation and development he looked at the financial cost of supporting the natives of the Belchers. Noting that this was less than a decade after the UK Government depopulated the St. Kilda Archipelago, a precedent had already been set. The difference being that the St. Kilda people were requesting resettlement whereas the Inuit of the Belcher Islands were not.

' Personally I cannot see why two white men should be asked to live in that region at great expense to their government in order to supply certain commodities to a few dozen Eskimos who might or might not need them.

These Eskimos should not be on these islands and should not be allowed to remain there, If Government insists in supervising their welfare then it should move them to localities where they would have a better chance of avoiding starvation, where RCMP posts are already established and serviced, where it would cost less money to supervise them and where there are more of their own kind-----'

In reflection the careful handling of the Belcher case was without doubt the correct line of action. Charlie Ouyerak never returned to the islands as he took ill and died of tuberculosis a few months into his sentence. Mina was released from custody and eventually set her self up as 'housekeeper ' to an RCMP officer and his wife, This officer had looked after her when she was initially in custody. But the Belcher Islands were never depopulated as Olmstead advised.

This all took place nearly eight years ago, The Inuit are still on the Belcher Islands but life now is very different.

The Belchers are located in the most southern reach of Nunavik . The nomadic existance has gone, the local people are 'Screened out,' as one inhabitant claims, meaning that smart phones and computers with internet access are prevalent. The current population of around eight hundred are based in the settlement of Sanikiluaq on Flacherty Island ninety three miles of the coast. This is the only permanent settlement on the archipelago of over eleven hundred square miles. It has two schools and an airport.

Industries are based on Inuit traditional ways. An eider down factory, which closed down in 2005 after twenty years of production reopened in 2015. Wildlife tourism, in particular kayaking in two man kayaks, is popular as many of the small islands are breeding grounds for seabirds, ducks and geese. Seals, walrus and beluga whales frequent the coastal waters and the soapstone carvings of the native Inuit are much sought after. Sanikiluaq women are famous for their unique handicrafts including dolls made from fish skins and clothing such as parkas made from eider ducks.

Whether white mans religion and law were ever good for the Inuit I will leave up to the reader to decide. The effects of modern society on the Inuit are dealt with in a later chapter.

One group of people who had a great influence on the Inuit of both Western Greenland and of Eastern Canada were the Scottish whalers who operated in the region for a period of over one hundred and sixty years. Ending in 1914 at the outbreak of the First World War, the partnership involving these two groups of hunters is a history in itself and no work on the Arctic would be worth reading without a section on this relationship.

The following section is nowhere near a complete anthology, merely a small collection of facts and stories to give an insight into this unique relationship between two very different races. Hopefully, what is portrayed will do justice to all concerned.

THE WHALERS
AND THE INUIT

The port of Dundee on Scotland's east coast is known as the city of three "Js"

Jute, Jam and Journalism. Whereas jam and journalism were controlled or dominated by two families, jute was different as it was owned by many wealthy business families known as the 'Jute Barons'. The jute industry at its peak employed tens of thousands of both native Dundonians and immigrant workers who took refuge there during the Irish potato famines of the 19th century.

Overseas, in what was then British India, it employed thousands more in growing the raw materials. But one ingredient it could not grow was the oil that was used to soften the jute fibres. That oil was whale oil.

In the early 1750s, Captain William Cheyne sailed the first recorded Dundee whaling ship into the Arctic, the appropriately named 'Dundee'. From the success of this voyage, an industry was spawned that was to endure for over 160 years. A successful whaling voyage brought wealth to ship-owners and crew alike. The Arctic is by nature a harsh and dangerous place. There were setbacks, triumphs, tales of courage and endurance. There were also friendships forged between the hardy and brave Scottish whalers and the friendly native Inuit of Greenland, Baffin Island and the Ungava Peninsula.

With one or two notable exceptions, whaling was not

there to provide excitement for brave and daring men nor was it an excuse to slaughter magnificent animals. It was a vital component of the industry that supported thousands of families on the other side of an ocean. The men involved were ordinary family men earning an honest living in one of the world's harshest environments. It is strange to think that these same whaler men were to change the lives and ancient ways of the native Inuit of these frozen lands forever.

One Dundee whaling captain who built a long-lasting relationship was William Fraser Milne. Although he was only five feet tall he was, in many ways, a giant personality in Arctic folklore and trade. At one time he was described as having more knowledge of Inuit life than any other European. His career in the Arctic started at the age of seventeen when he first entered the whaling industry. He subsequently made 42 voyages to the whaling grounds, during which he built up a lasting relationship with the Inuit as well as a reputation as an authority on Arctic life.

He was held in great esteem, not only by his crew and the Inuit with whom he had dealings, but also by an impressive list of Arctic explorers. Both Nansen and Peary claimed him as a friend. Amundson sought his advice before setting out across the Arctic and Antarctic. The advice he gave to Amundson was what he in turn had learned from his Inuit friends.

His knowledge of the Arctic earned him a Knighthood of the Order of St. Olav from King Haakon of Norway. He was the only Dundee whaling master ever to have been so honoured.

William Fraser Milne commanded the whaler 'Eclipse' for a term of fifteen years. Photographs of ship masters with their crews are rare, but among the photographs held in the internationally important collection of whaling and Inuit artefacts in Dundee's McManus Gallery is such a photograph. So one can guess that Milne had a special bond with his men. A bond that also extended to his relationships with the Inuit.

Another picture in the collection shows the whaler 'Eclipse' being met by a group of Inuit on the pack ice.

The Inuit are boarding by a ladder from the starboard bow. The crowd standing on the bow of 'Eclipse' are waiting to welcome them on board and show the friendship that had developed between the men of the whaling fleet and the Inuit. What we see in this picture is just one moment in time, frozen for posterity, which demonstrates the close links fostered by two very different cultures at a time in history where one culture was still at the hunter gatherer stage while the other led the world in science and engineering. Not only did the Inuit learn from the whalers, the whalers gained knowledge of the Arctic and its wildlife from the Inuit. One example of this is the fact that the crew of the 'Eclipse' learned to use paddles rather than oars when approaching a whale. Paddles are quieter than oars as the Inuit in their kayaks willingly demonstrated.

As time went on, the number of whales in the Arctic waters declined. The waters west of Greenland, the Davis Strait and Hudson Bay had been drastically over exploited. The once sought-after 'right whales' (named 'right whales' as they floated when dead, so were the 'right whales' to hunt) all but vanished. The much smaller narwhals and belugas, which would have been ignored a few years before, were now hunted. To make voyages viable, other products had to be found and that is when the Inuit became a key factor in the annual voyage to the cold waters of Western Greenland and Baffin Island.

Seal and walrus colonies were numerous all the way from the Gulf of St. Lawrence to Ellesmere Island at the north end of Baffin Bay. These two species could supply not only blubber but also quality skins which the then thriving leather tanneries of Dundee were eager to buy. The ivory tusks and teeth of the walrus were also a valuable commodity.

Hunting seals and walrus for food, clothing and leather for harnesses and harpoon lines had gone on since time began among the Inuit. Now they could hunt it for profit. Soon the way of natural conservation that the Inuit had always practiced was abandoned as desire for the goods of the white man took hold. It didn't take long before the whalers supplied guns and ammunition to the Inuit and wholesale slaughter ensued.

Records show that this seal-hunting started as early as the eighteenth century, when in 1787 the whaler 'Dundee' brought home 1500 seal skins. The same year, the whaler 'Tay' brought home 1400 skins. Add to this the oil from the seal blubber and the voyages of both vessels went into profit.

By the second half of the 19th century, the importance of the seal trade became even greater as some species of whales had totally disappeared and other less valuable cetaceans were vanishing, as evidenced by the figures from 1878, when the 'Arctic 11' returned to Dundee with 33,000 seals. Many of these seals were taken by sealers from Newfoundland as well as by the native Inuit. What the following picture shows is a Seal Pan, where seal skins - still with blubber attached - were stored until ready to be taken aboard. These 'Pans' were little more than a mound of sealskins marked by a flag signifying which ship owned the skins.

Over the years, relationships between whaling men and Inuit women often progressed beyond barter and dancing when they went aboard ship.

Boats started overwintering in ports in the Hudson Straits and elsewhere. Kinnes House vessels used Lake Harbour on Baffin Island's Hudson Strait shoreline, where they had a shore based trading post. In 1885 the Dundee whaler 'Esqimaux' overwintered in Hudson Bay and some of the crew brought Inuit women aboard for the winter. The inevitable outcome of such close liaisons was a number of children with Dundee fathers and Inuit mothers. It says a great deal about the philosophical attitude of the Inuit people that they accepted these children into their society without fuss or discrimination. The Inuit of Eastern Canada and Greenland were naturally humanitarians and politically correct when, at the same period in history, racial discrimination would have been prevalent elsewhere. Another picture from the McManus demonstrates this as one Inuit lady in the group of whalers and Inuit women is clearly 'with child'. The chances are that a few people in the Dundee area will have Inuit relatives; on the other hand the Inuit of the Davis Strait and Hudson Bay probably have a high incidence of Dundee genes.

Dundee whalers and the Inuit were usually on the best of terms and wherever the ships put in they were welcomed by the local population. The Inuit taught the Dundee men the ways of the Arctic and guided them over the ice on the hunting grounds. In return the Dundee men brought the Inuit onto the whaling ships. The Inuit had many happy memories of the Scottish whalers. In the book 'When the whalers were up North', Dorothy Eber quotes an elderly Inuit named Nutaraq, saying: 'When ships came my grandmother said 'If they ask you to dance for them, dance so they'll like you.' On one ship there was a man who would tease me and make fun and chase me round the deck. This man who was so kind to me must have had children of his own.' Another Inuit woman named Anirnik said that Inuit children would have pretend fathers on the ships who would give them presents. One favourite present for Inuit girls to receive was that of an old penny. Apparently, the ones most sought after were the ones with Queen Victoria's head on them. These were said to make a better ringing sound when attached to a girl's belt as jingles.

Yet another McManus picture shows a group of Dundee whaling men with Inuit on board a ship. The affection being shown to an Inuit child by the whaler standing behind him is obvious. Was the child his from a voyage years before? Not an unlikely scenario. But, sadly, I do not know, so that question will forever go unanswered.

Victorian Anthropology

The Victorian era was one of exploration and discovery. Explorers pushed the boundaries and, with the developments in photography, photographers were never far from the scene to record happenings for posterity. Public interest in everything from exotic animals to what were viewed as 'primitive people' was aroused like never before. Photographs showed actual reality as opposed to the drawings of early explorers which were often subject to artistic license. Because of this interest and the daring nature of young Victorian photographers, we have a wealth of pictorial evidence about the daily life and ways of the different races that inhabited Victoria's vast empire. The Inuit of eastern Canada fell into this category. Not only did the adventurous Victorians think that it was their duty to record all for posterity, they also thought it was their duty to introduce these same 'primitive people' to modern technology and materials. It was as a result of this that what is now regarded as Inuit 'traditional dress' evolved.

A few years ago I had the pleasure of attending a 'kafemik' at the home of an elderly Kalaalit lady from Qaqartoq in south west Greenland. Over the years she had won many competitions for making highly adorned Inuit dolls. Her dolls were clad in the most amazing bead collars boots. Classic examples of the 'traditional dress' which came into being in

the 19th century. The Inuit had always made bead collars but the original beads were made from vertebrae from a small fish, the capelin. These vertebrae were dyed using dyes made from lichens and mosses. When the whalers saw these collars, they saw the opportunity to trade coloured glass beads and this went down really well with the Inuit females. It soon started a trend for large colourful collars and decorative clothing which evolved into what we see today. It has also created a form of cottage industry among some of the older Inuit ladies who now produce bead jewellery to sell to tourist arriving from cruise ships. Buying these items on the quayside costs a fraction of the cost of what is charged in the souvenir shops in the main towns, such as Nuuk. It also ensures that the creator of the item earns a realistic sum for their endeavours. I purchased two beautiful bead necklaces for my granddaughters from a lady on the pier at a small west coast port only to see similar items on sale at an up-market shop in Nuuk a few days later for nearly five times the price.

The public perception that the Inuit lived their lives in igloos is nigh on universal. However, that is not the case! Even back in the early days of the 20th century, the Inuit only used the Igloo as a winter refuge. The semi-nomadic life of the Inuit meant that they would move their base camp three or four times each year to follow the species on which their existence depended. As animal migrations follow a predictable annual cycle, so too did the migration of the individual Inuit groups.

In winter they lived in igloos on the coast and hunted the seals on the frozen sea ice. When spring came and the ice started to melt they moved out of the ice igloo and into the tupik, still hunting seals and also fishing. In the short summer months they moved inland to hunt caribou.

Before the white man came, this was a pure hunter-gatherer society where mobility was essential. After the arrival of the Dundee whalers, who built trading posts and stores for the Inuit produce, things began to change. Semi-permanent Inuit settlements grew up around these bases where trading of skins, walrus tusks etc. became the norm. What the Inuit were given in exchange for these items may come as a surprise to many.

In many ways, this was beneficial to the Inuit. If a severe winter of storms prevented them hunting for their food, the whaling company manager at the base would be able to supply things like beans and bacon on credit. The whalers knew that an Inuit hunter's credit was good and that whatever was owed would be repaid as soon as the weather allowed. As well as the obvious hunting requirements such as guns, ammunition and ropes for harpoons there were many other metal items that were previously unknown to the Inuit until the coming of the white man. Metal cooking pots to replace the heavy stone pots were popular among the women as were other domestic utensils such as knives and spoons. If the hunter had a good season it was regarded as a status symbol to own a phonograph which was invariably used to play music and songs of Scottish origin. In particular it was the music of Sir Harry Lauder that was favoured among the Inuit of both Eastern Canada and Greenland. Young Inuit who, by the age of around ten, were already becoming skilled hunters would trade both Arctic hare and fox pelts for harmonicas. In the early years of the twentieth century sewing machines, often made in Clydebank, of Singer manufacture were a status symbol among the womenfolk. Many of these machines are still around to this day, some in the Inuit Museum in Nanartalik in South West Greenland.

The Inuit are by nature a cheerful race, so the rather flamboyant music of Sir Harry Lauder appealed to their sense of fun, even if they didn't fully understand the words. Laughter is infectious among the Inuit so when one laughs they will all laugh. This spilled over into dancing, much of which was influenced by the visiting Scottish whalers. When Inuit went aboard they learned Scottish dancing to both fiddle and accordion music played by the crew. It was also from this source they discovered phonographs. Just as European youngsters would go to dances or listen to music at home the Inuit were no different. If one looks at the notice outside the village hall in Nanartalik, where locals demonstrate Inuit dancing to tourists from cruise ships, they will read that this dancing is highly influenced by the Scottish whalers of the late nineteenth and early twentieth centuries. If I were asked to describe this dancing I think I would probably say it was 'akin to a Gay Gordons with sealskin boots on.'

Prior to the establishment of the whaling based trading posts and those bases belonging to both the Hudson Bay Company and Revillon Frères, the interior of a traditional Inuit summer tupik held the entire range of an Inuit family's household goods. These consisted mainly of caribou skins and the few personal items of adornment such as girl's belts and amaats (the female equivalent of a parka) adorned with trinkets such as pennies or the heads of spoons. Hunting equipment was stored outside along with dog harnesses and other similar items but held high above the ground. If harnesses or harpoon lines made of hide were left at ground level they would soon be devoured by the ever present and ever hungry Malamute dogs. Boots were often seen held aloft on spears or harpoons stuck into the ground. When the time came for the seasonal move on to fresh hunting grounds everything an Inuit family possessed was loaded onto sleds and hitched up to teams of the ever willing Malamute dogs. Often the movement of the camp was over several days and many kilometres. Such annual migrations had evolved over centuries, maybe even millennia.

Once permanent settlements became established around these shore bases and trading posts the Inuit followed the way of the white man and became more consumer orientated. Within a few years many Inuit families would have found it impossible to load all their worldly possessions onto a sled pulled by a team of oxen let alone a team of Malamute dogs. With this came the end of the nomadic existence of the Eastern Canadian and Greenlandic Inuit.

Osbert Clare Forsyth-Grant,
an Arctic enigma.

Cape Haven was the Baffin Island shore base of one of the most enigmatic of all the Dundee whaling ship owners, Osbert Clare Forsyth-Grant.

By the time of his mysterious death - in a suspected mutiny, when his vessel 'Seduisante' was wrecked on rocks off Nottingham Island in Hudson Bay - he was already a legend in the Arctic. He was the eldest son of minor Scottish aristocracy, related to the founders of the Hudson Bay Company. He went to the Arctic to hunt as a sport more than as a business and yet his first vessel 'Snowdrop' was not only the smallest of Dundee's whaling vessels but also among one of the most successful.

On his second voyage to the Arctic, his hired captain was afraid to enter the Davis Strait icepack and engineered a mutiny which saw most of his crew abandon the Snowdrop in Greenland.

Most people would have given up at this point, but not Forsyth-Grant. He was left with only three crewmen - one of whom, Alex Ritchie, will be mentioned later. As it would not have been possible to carry on with such a small crew, he did what no other whaling owner had ever done - he crewed Snowdrop with Inuit. This started a relationship which remained solid until his untimely death in 1911. After a costly court case, in which he had been accused of piracy, he had become the owner of the shore base at Cape Haven, which the Inuit called Signia, meaning the 'pregnant place' as many of the Inuit women went there to give birth. When 'Snowdrop'- and then its successor 'Seduisante' - returned to Dundee with the year's produce, Grant would stay on at Cape Haven and live with 'his' Inuit who had become known as 'Grant's People'. One of these Inuit was his concubine Nannurak. An old photograph album at Forsyth-Grant's ancestral home at Ecclesgrieg has a number of photographs showing this lady at the centre of the picture. From the outset the relationship between the tall, aristocratic Scotsman and the Inuit, some of whom he had originally brought from Greenland was a harmonious one founded on mutual respect. It was this relationship that made his little vessel 'Snowdrop' beat the larger vessels of the Dundee fleet as 'Grant's People' would hunt throughout the winter while his Scottish crew were at home.

After the death of Forsyth-Grant in 1911, his Cape Haven trading post fell into the hands of the Sabellum Trading Company, a London-based company involved in the fur trade. From 1910 to 1927, Sabellum operated shore trading bases in the Davis Strait area. They purchased furs and sealskins from the Inuit who, by this time, had settled around such bases and were to a great extent dependent on this barter trade to survive. However, Sabellum frequently did not turn up with the annual supplies for these resident Inuit and this often led to extreme hardship. Unlike Forsyth-Grant, who - prior to the loss of his vessel on Nottingham Island in September 1911- sent his Inuit hunters and their families ashore when the vessel went aground on a reef, leaving himself exposed to a mutinous crew, Sabellum cared little for the welfare of the Inuit.

Sabellum were not the only company to have treated the Signia Inuit in such a manner. Indeed it was due to the Boston firm of Wrightington & Company that Osbert Clare Forsyth-Grant ended up in the Court of Session in Dundee in a prolonged court case. This case started on the 14th March 1907 and continued intermittently until the second half of May that year. How this came about was that when the Snowdrop arrived off Cape Haven the previous year Forsyth –Grant found the local Inuit in a perilous state. After being approached by the Cape Haven Inuit he found out that, as Wrightington's supply vessel had not arrived the previous autumn, the Inuit had neither food supplies nor ammunition to hunt for food. Forsyth Grant immediately traded guns, ammunition and other trade goods for all the produce these people brought to him. What he didn't know at the time was that a number of the walrus hides had already been paid for by Wrightington & Co. and carried their tags. It was only when Snowdrop arrived in St. John's, Newfoundland, that this was discovered. Wrightington accused Forsyth-Grant of piracy as he, rightfully I believe, refused to hand over all the produce he had paid for. Added to this produce was all the other produce that both his crew and the Cape Haven Inuit had gathered when he took them aboard and transported them to more lucrative hunting grounds on what was then termed Meta Incognita. Once there the Inuit were able to hunt large numbers of caribou to feed and clothe them through the winter of 1906. There is little doubt that if the Snowdrop hadn't arrived many of the Cape Haven Inuit would have perished that winter, for by 1906 many of the traditional hunting skills of the Inuit, such as with harpoons and bow and arrow, had been replaced by the rifles of the white man. To relearn these skills to a degree good enough to support the community would have taken a great deal of time—time that these people just did not have. The court case was held in Dundee with none other than Robert Kinnes of the Dundee whaling firm of the same name being a witness for Wrightington and Co. This was not really surprising as Kinnes viewed Forsyth-Grant as a very unwanted competitor in the whaling industry around the Davis Strait. The outcome of the case was that it cost Forsyth –Grant three thousand pounds to Wrightington & Co, plus a further seven hundred and forty five pounds in legal and court costs. This no doubt gave a great deal of satisfaction to Robert Kinnes. The settlement did however give Osbert Clare Forsyth –Grant the Cape Haven station as neither Wrightingtons nor Kinnes wished to have any more dealings with what they regarded as a commercial liability. This left the Cape Haven Inuit in the hands of Forsyth –Grant who, unlike either Wrightington or Kinnes, they both respected and trusted. Even to this day the Inuit of that region remember Osbert Clare Forsyth – Grant in a good light.

A photograph was taken at Cape Haven in 1927 just before the collapse of Sabellum's Arctic trade. The number of Inuit in the photo includes children, indicating that there was an Inuit settlement of near permanent status in the vicinity of the trading post. The photograph was taken by Dr L D Livingstone of the then Canadian Department of the Interior, now incorporated into the Department for Northern Development.

ALEX RITCHIE

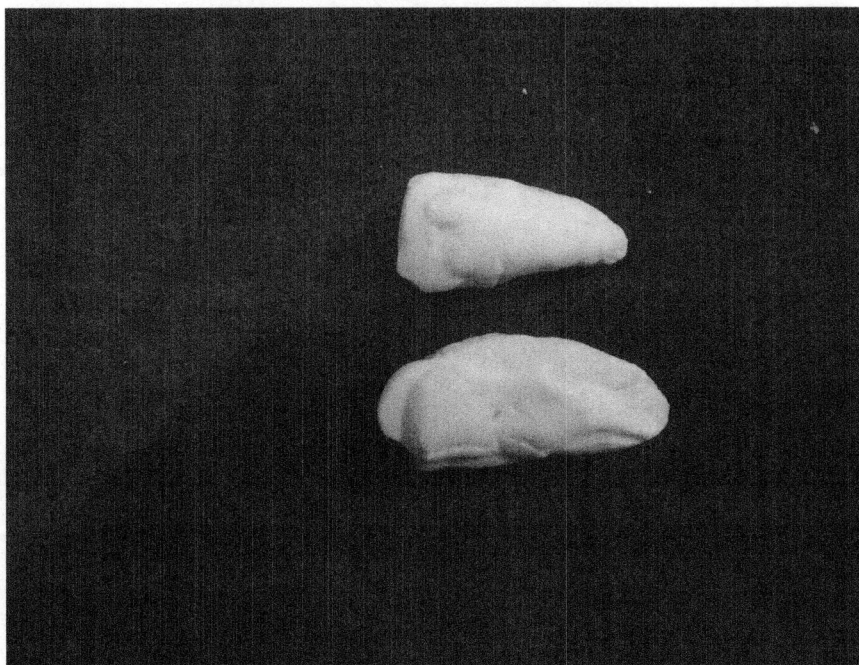

The carved walrus teeth shown above are possibly the final piece of a jigsaw that started back in the winter of 1908 when the Dundee Whaler 'Snowdrop' got wrecked on Baffin Island during a hurricane. The only thing being rescued, other than the people on board, was a bag of walrus teeth. These two teeth were removed from the bag by an unknown person and turned up more than a century later, and are as far as we know the only carved teeth of this nature in existence. The teeth have now been returned to the family of Alex Ritchie. Below tells the tale.

The story of Alex Ritchie reads like an adventure story of

Herman Melville calibre. But unlike Moby Dick and Captain Ahab, nothing about Alex Ritchie's story was fiction.

Born and brought up in the Kincardineshire fishing village of Gourdon, just six miles north of Ecclesgreg Castle at St Cyrus - the home of Osbert Clare Forsyth-Grant - Alex Ritchie sailed on the 'Snowdrop' from her first voyage under the ownership of Forsyth–Grant. When the crew under Captain Walter J Jackson mutinied while in Greenland (encouraged by Jackson, who did not want to sail into the ice of the Davis Strait), one of the three crewmen who stood by Forsyth-Grant was Ritchie. From this, he became one of Forsyth-Grant's most trusted shipmates. He also earned respect among the Inuit who hunted for the 'Snowdrop'. But, in the autumn of 1908, disaster struck while the 'Snowdrop' - fully laden from a successful year - lay anchored in Countess of Warwick Sound near the place the Inuit called Topjuak, prepared to set sail for home.

What happened that September day was to propel the quiet, bible-reading fisherman from Gourdon to legendary status for both his bravery in saving all aboard the Snowdrop and then his epic 500 mile journey across the frozen wastes of Baffin Island. It also earned him the Inuit title of 'Qivitoq'. Depending on where you are in the Arctic the legend of Qivitoq can vary dramatically, from a malevolent evil being to a benign giant. According to the legend of the time among the Baffin Island and West Greenland Inuit 'Qivitoq' was an immortal giant who lived alone in the mountains and came to the aid of the Inuit in times of dire need. Ritchie's journey across Baffin Island from Signia to Lake Harbour still rates as one of the greatest Arctic survival stories of all time. When he set out on this journey all he had was a packet of biscuits, a rifle and fifty rounds of ammunition.

Alex Ritchie was a big strong man - taller than the average at that time and certainly, to the much shorter Inuit, he and Forsyth-Grant must have appeared as giants.

When 'Snowdrop' got stranded there was a full-blown

easterly gale with surf breaking on her decks. Inuit never learn to swim as they believe that only prolonged the pain if one ended in the water, so it was Alex Ritchie who volunteered to swim ashore with a rope to secure a way to rescue all aboard. After braving the breaking surf, he secured the rope to a large boulder on the beach and pulled himself back along the rope to the ship. From there, he assisted everyone on board to reach the shore safely and not one casualty was sustained. The number of Inuit aboard is uncertain - depending on which account you read, it was either 42 or 65. It may be that both figures are correct as there were Inuit men, women and children on board. The figure of forty two is likely to have been the number of Inuit adults; sixty five is probably the figure including children, some still being carried in their mother's hoods. Whichever figure you opt for, it is more than significant as it was effectively a whole Inuit group. As well as the Inuit, the other nine white men were also saved.

What happened next is a bit confusing. Whether you believe what Alex Ritchie said later in life or believe what the newspapers of the day told us is almost immaterial. From both accounts, only one conclusion can be drawn and that is that Ritchie's epic stories of survival in the Arctic wastes of Baffin Island in the winter of 1908/9 were heroic. Due to his trust in his Inuit friends, he accomplished what Franklin's expedition failed to do - he survived. (See Appendix 2)

On 16th December 1908, Ritchie decided that, after a year of awaiting rescue, he would head off for Lake Harbour on the Hudson Strait to seek out the Dundee whalers that used this as a base each summer. The Dundee firm of Kinnes also operated a mica mine nearby. Rather than go into the full details of his journey, I have included a short piece from an American newspaper of the time.

Dundee Whaler's Pluck

CROSSED HUDSON STRAIT IN OPEN BOAT AND SAVED COMRADES.

The pluck and hardihood of a young Scotch harpooner,

Alexander Ritchie, who crossed the stormy waters of Hudson Strait in an open boat to the Moravian settlements in Northern Labrador, were the means of bringing word of the safety of the eight members of the Scotch whaling ship 'Snowdrop'.

It then goes on:

With the coming of the brief summer in those northern latitudes, Ritchie decided to make an attempt to reach civilization to bring succour for his comrades. With an Eskimo guide, he travelled on foot and by dog sledge 500 miles until he reached a spot on Hudson Strait favourable for crossing. There he found a boat and fought his way through drift ice and storm single-handed to the Labrador coast, where he found a Moravian settlement.

Unfortunately, the highly detailed archives of the Moravian Church have no entries referring to this episode. Nor did Alex Ritchie mention such a crossing in his recollection of the events when his son recorded them for the BBC in the 1950s. His nephew, Neill Ritchie, wrote his uncle's story down verbatim for Canadian writer, Robert James Fraser, for inclusion in his book 'Arctic Adventurer, Grant and the Sedusante'. Another point which is also in dispute is that Ritchie's epic journey was not during 'the brief Arctic Summer' but in the depths of Arctic winter. He spent New Year stranded in blizzard conditions in a rather small igloo.

At no time did Alex mention crossing the Hudson Strait, although at one point he and Osbert Clare had tried from a point near the wreck of the Snowdrop but returned due to storms.

As a youngster, I had heard all the stories about Alex and the Inuit, but cannot honestly recall any of him crossing Hudson Strait. I heard these tales not from Alex himself but from his brother Edward and from my late father, who was a friend of Alex's son. One thing is certain - he was the first white man to cross Baffin Island's fearsome Grinnell Glacier, ill-equipped except for the trust of his Inuit companions and a determination to survive. He was eventually brought back to Newfoundland on the 'Lorna Doone,' a ship owned by the legendary Dr Grenfell of Labrador.

While giving a presentation, at the Maggie Law Maritime Museum in Ritchie's home village of Gourdon, a strange thing happened. The presentation was on the influence that the Dundee Whalers had on the Inuit. After the presentation I was approached by a young lady who introduced herself as Alex Ritchie's great grand-daughter. She was convinced that he had indeed crossed the Hudson Strait and back in the spring of 1909. Did he or didn't he? If he did, which is not impossible, was he unable to find a Moravian settlement and so returned to the Saddlebacks? I personally do not think he did or his account to his nephew would surely have included this adventure. Nevertheless his account of his journey with his Inuit friends is still worthy of a place in Arctic history without further embellishment.

The Ballad of the 'Snowdrop'

We're sailors, we're whalers, we sail the cold sea.
Aboard the sweet 'Snowdrop', which hails frae Dundee.
The 'Snowdrop was pretty, queen of the sea.
The smallest ever whaler to sail frae Dundee.

We're sailors, we're whalers, we sail the cold sea.
Aboard the sweet 'Snowdrop', which hails frae Dundee.
We're sailors, we're whalers, hunt walrus and seal
And the cold Baffin waters to us does appeal.

We're sailors, we're whalers, we sail the cold sea.
Aboard the sweet 'Snowdrop' which hails frae Dundee.
Our hunters are Eskimos who don't feel the cold.
With walrus and seals they fill 'Snowdrop's' hold.

We're sailors, we're whalers. We sail the cold sea.
Aboard the sweet 'Snowdrop' which hails frae Dundee.
For four long years the Arctic we'd sail
With bold Captain Grant we went huntin' the whale.

We're sailors' we're whalers, we sail the cold sea.
Aboard the sweet 'Snowdrop' which hails frae Dundee.
Then one autumn day down in Frobisher's Bay
A storm it broke out, 'Snowdrop's' anchor gave weigh'

We're sailors, were whalers, we sail the cold sea.
Aboard the sweet 'Snowdrop' which hails frae Dundee.
On board the 'Snowdrop' all felt the fear
As she hit the rock and the shore it was near.

We're sailors, we're whalers, we sail the cold sea.
Aboard the sweet 'Snowdrop' which hails frae Dundee
Then up stood young Ritchie, so tall and so brave.
He took the rope and dived into the wave.

We're sailors, we're whalers, we sail the cold sea.
Aboard the sweet 'Snowdrop' which hails frae Dundee.
The waves they did surge and the storm it did roar
As young Alex Ritchie he made it to shore.

We're sailors, we're whalers, we sail the cold sea.
Aboard the sweet 'Snowdrop' which hails frae Dundee.
The rope it was strong to a rock he did tie
And thanks to young Ritchie no-one did die

We're sailors, we're whalers, we sail the cold sea.
Aboard the sweet 'Snowdrop' which hails frae Dundee
Forty five Eskimos and the Scot's crew
We're saved by young Ritchie, we know that is true.

We're sailors, we're whalers, we sail the cold sea.
Aboard the sweet 'Snowdrop' which hails frae Dundee.
For over a year no rescue came by
To cold Baffin Island though some they did try.

We're sailors, we're whalers, we sail the cold sea.
Aboard the sweet 'Snowdrop' which hails frae Dundee.
Young Ritchie then took off and left us behind

He went off for Lake Harbour a ship for to find.
We're sailors, we're whalers, we sail the cold sea.
Aboard the sweet 'Snowdrop' which hails frae Dundee.
Five hundred miles o're Baffin's white hell
Went young Alex Ritchie and he lived to tell.

We're sailors, we're whalers, we sail the cold sea.
Aboard the sweet 'Snowdrop' which hails frae Dundee.
Then we got rescued and soon we came home
And the cold Baffin Island no more will we roam.

We're sailors, we're whalers, we sail the cold sea.
Aboard the sweet 'Snowdrop' which hails frae Dundee.
In Eskimo legend the 'Snowdrop' still sails
With Captain Grant's ghost she's still chasing the whales

We're sailors, we're whalers, we sail the cold sea
On the brave little 'Snowdrop' the pride o' Dundee.

INUIT BOATS

To write about the Inuit without mentioning their unique vessels would be unthinkable.

The Kayak

Most people are familiar with the Inuit Kayak. This slender and fast hunting canoe, which evolved in the Arctic waters, was originally built out of whatever was available then covered in sealskin. Unlike the modern glass-reinforced plastic, or GRP as it is termed, the Inuit used driftwood, bone and baleen (whalebone), bound together with deer sinews or sealskin cords to form the framework.

The covering of waterproof sealskins was stretched tightly over this frame and, with a stitching of sinew, was made totally watertight. The Inuit jacket or tuilik- a parka sometimes made from seal intestines, which was used in conjunction with the kayak - was held securely in place over the kayak's cockpit so that, even if the kayak capsized, no water would enter the vessel. Each kayak was unique and each Inuit hunter knew exactly how his vessel would react to wind and wave. For this reason, no-one would ever even think of using another hunter's kayak.

The famous 'Eskimo Roll' where the vessel is intentionally capsized - sometimes unintentionally - was not developed for show. It was a method of survival in rough seas. If a large breaking wave was to hit an upright kayak, the force of the wave hitting the paddler might be sufficient to snap his spine. However, if the vessel was bottom up with the paddler on the underside, there was no shock loading and hence less chance of injury. The ability of the Inuit kayaker to carry out the 'Eskimo Roll' was greatly assisted by the purpose made kayak spray suit known as the 'Tuilik'. When worn outside the confines of his kayak the tuilik looks like an over long anorak which reaches down to the wearers knees. It is only once he is sitting in his kayak that the full ingenuity of this garment can be fully understood and appreciated. Made of the softest sealskin, which has had all the hair removed, it effectively makes man and boat one single unit. Its watertight seal around the cockpit coaming keeps the water out, whether upturned or upright in heavy weather. This is achieved by a draw -string made of leather around the bottom of the garment fastened with a toggle made either of bone or ivory. Similar draw- strings around the cuffs and face prevent the ingress of water in those areas. The stitching of the tuilik has to be of the finest quality and is always in the form of double seams sewn with fine stitches. To increase both its watertight and waterproof capabilities it soaked with seal oil. This also increases the supple qualities of the seal skin. What appears to be overkill in the length of the garment is totally intentional to allow the wearer to push himself up higher in the kayak. By doing so he can, in the event of a capsize, get his head above water without breaking the seal around the cockpit. From this position it is easier to use the paddle to lever the kayak back into the upright position and complete the 'Eskimo Roll' manoeuvre. Modern kayakers still use spray suits but made from modern materials such as neoprene similar to that used in diving suits. In warmer climes, such as around the coast Scotland and Southern Norway, the spray cover tends to be fastened around the wearer's waist. This prevents water entering the kayak but the kayaker gets his upper body wet, unless of course he is wearing a modern 'dry-suit', which most of them now do. In some areas matching mitts of soft sealskin are worn by the kayaker, these help retain heat in the extremities and prevent the potential loss of fingers from frostbite.

The Inuit that Forsyth–Grant had as crew, taught him and other members of the 'Snowdrop's' crew how to use kayaks to improve their hunting skills. A very rare group of photographs, kept at the home of Maurice Forsyth-Grant, Osbert Clare's grand-nephew, show crew members from the Snowdrop learning to kayak. This included learning how to 'Eskimo Roll.' It is highly likely they were among the first non-Inuit ever to master this technique.

The use of the kayak is pretty well universal throughout the Inuit world although those who lived inland used shorter kayaks than those who hunted the coastal ice. The exceptions to this were the 'Polar Inuit' of North West Greenland who did not have the necessary resources of driftwood to build kayaks. Even if they did have the resources, there was seldom, if ever, enough open water for them to be of use.

The Umiak

The umiak is the Inuit version of the family car or, more realistically, the family minibus and removal van rolled into one. Sometimes it also doubled as a hunting vessel for both whales and walrus. The framework of the umiak, like that of the kayak, was made from whatever materials were available, baleen and driftwood being the main components, to which a covering of tough walrus or sealskin was fastened. It is thought that the umiak was originally designed as a whale hunting vessel but when whale hunting declined along with the Thule Culture, it became the 'Woman's Boat'. Although the umiak is found in both Alaskan and Eastern Inuit areas it is notably absent in the central Arctic where whales were also absent. Umiaks vary widely in size from around six metres to double that length. After a hunting expedition, the Inuit women would carefully wash the vessel to remove all traces of blood to prevent it rotting the hide covering. When not in use, the vessel was held aloft on poles to prevent the ever-hungry Malamute sledge dogs from eating it.

The women would use oars when transporting their goods and belongings from one camp site to another while the men always used paddles when using the umiak for hunting. Both would use a small sail if the wind was favourable.

The concept and design of the umiak is very similar to the curraghs of Ireland which go back centuries and in which Irish monks such as St. Brendan and St. Columba crossed to Scotland and the Faeroe Islands in early medieval times (again proving the concept of parallel evolution where two indigenous cultures, thousands of miles apart, come up with the same solution for a basic problem.

A further use of the umiak was that of a portable shelter during summer migrations or hunting expeditions. The umiak was turned upside down and held clear of the ground on the side away from the wind by using either a piece of timber or available rocks. This gave a comfortable dry area in which the hunters could sleep or shelter. When Eric the

Red's son, Thorvald, retraced his brother Leif's route to the fabled 'Vinland' in 1004 he overwintered in Leif's temporary camp before going south again in the spring of 1005. After rounding a cape south of what is now known as Cape Bauld he spotted three skin boats on the shore. These boats were undoubtedly umiaks on a hunting trip. Beneath each of these slept three 'Skraelings' as the Vikings called the Inuit. With typical barbarity he and his crew killed eight of the Inuit, the ninth escaped. This act cost Thorvald his life as the Inuit who escaped soon returned with reinforcements to the murder scene. Thorvald ordered his men to retreat to the safety of their beached longship to hide behind the gunnel hung shields. The 'Skraelings' let fly a hail of well aimed arrows, one of which penetrated between the wall of shields and lodged in Thorvald's armpit. Although the Vikings escaped Thorvald's wound festered and he died. Supposedly being a Christian he was buried on the Newfoundland shore, his grave being marked with a cross. The only conclusion is that he hadn't got to the bit in the book that told him to 'love thine enemy' or ' thou shalt not kill'. It was probably just as well he was a slow reader otherwise he would not have gained fame as the first European to be buried in the 'New World'. This was also the first recorded contact of Europeans and the Inuit outside Greenland.

PHOTOGRAPHY

As previously mentioned, photographers were quick to take advantage of the opportunities offered by a whaling voyage. One such photographer and self-styled 'explorer' was Sandon Perkins, who took the pictures on board a Dundee whaler in the early 20th century.

In one photograph, held in Dundee's McManus Galleries, two Inuit from the Etah group from North West Greenland are to be seen eating on a whalers deck. At one time this group lived on the Inuit migration route from Greenland to the Canadian Arctic. These seasonal migrations ceased in 1865 as the impact of the European and American whaling industries changed the Inuit from a hunter-gatherer society to commercial trading society. These Inuit were the descendants of the Polar Inuit encountered by John Ross in the early years of the 19th century. In this picture, they are wearing the traditional sealskin parka and polar bear trousers, but what is probably more interesting is what they are eating. The delicacy being consumed is raw seal flippers. These will have been left to 'mature' for some time before being eaten (similar in many ways to the 'Auk in a Sealskin'). The photograph has obviously been carefully posed as the Inuit are facing the camera, as is the whaler in the background. It is noticeable that, whereas the Dundonian is lightly dressed (indicating that it is around midsummer), the Inuit are dressed in their autumn hunting gear. The object of this was to enable Perkins to show the better educated in society, who were greatly interested in ethnology at that time, exactly what northern Inuit looked like.

Nowadays, they would be wearing Gore-Tex and eating burgers!

Over the years, many Inuit came to Scotland aboard whaling ships. Indeed, this form of Inuit travel continued well into the second half of the 20th century, by which time they travelled on cargo vessels from the Clyde, taking stores to Greenland. One Inuit resident of Nanartalik in South West Greenland told me of his childhood adventure aboard a Scottish ship with his father. They went to Glasgow and stayed there until the next ship bound for Greenland left the Clyde. That was in the 1950s.He was put up in the Seamen's Mission, free of charge as they had no money other than that given to them by the ship's crew. He told me that he was really made feel welcome by the Scottish people.

Back in the days of whaling, it was not Glasgow, but Dundee, that the Inuit adventurers chose as a preferred destination. One of the best known and recorded was Schoodlue.

REPRODUCED 1941 BY J.A. TRANTUM.

This 'Gentleman of the North' was an Inuit shaman who arrived in Dundee with none other than Captain William Milne in 1894 on board his ship 'Eclipse'. Schoodloe had approached the 'Eclipse' off Cape York as she was preparing to head home. He was in his kayak when he requested to be taken to Scotland. He had known many Dundee whaling men over the years and was a friend of Captain Milne. He spoke good English - not surprisingly, with a Dundonian accent! – And, as he was willing to work his passage, he and his kayak were promptly taken on board. From the moment of his arrival at the Earl Grey Dock, he was an instant hit with the residents of Dundee. While in Dundee he stayed at the Sailors' Home and took part in temperance meetings. When he visited Broughty Ferry and Tayport, wearing his native dress, crowds of local people turned out to greet him and give him gifts. On two occasions he gave kayaking demonstrations to crowds of onlookers lining the Tay Esplanade. He was always happy to pose for photographs in his Inuit costume and the McManus Gallery displays a photo of him with his laminated bow made of baleen.

When he travelled back home with Captain Milne the following season, he had been given so many gifts from the people of Dundee and the surrounding towns it took two trips in a whaling boat to carry them all to shore. The Dundee men were always made welcome by the Inuit of Greenland and Canada and this was fully reciprocated by the citizens of Dundee. However, one has to consider the fact that, in some of the early cases of Inuit being brought to Dundee aboard whaling ships, they were being displayed to the public as a curiosity show.

As a youngster, I heard a tale about a young Inuit male, Iniaq, who lived a winter in the tower of Ecclesgreg Castle - at that time home of Osbert Clare Forsyth-Grant. The Forsyth-Grant family were heavily involved in the salmon netting concern of Joseph Johnston and Sons, the netting proprietors on the North Esk. Legend has it that the young Inuk protected the salmon bag nets from marauding seals by hunting them in his kayak. He reputedly lived in one of the turret rooms in the towers which are still visible today to travellers on the A92 coast road between Montrose and Inverbervie. The castle lies inland on a hill overlooking the village of St. Cyrus.

SCRIMSHAW

Scrimshaw is an art form which most people associate with the crews of sailing ships and, in particular, whaling ships. Indeed the word 'Scrimshaw' is a nautical term meaning "to waste time". The word probably has its origins in the days of sail when ships could be becalmed for days but latterly the term was used to describe the items carved during that period of inactivity. Different groups of whalers used different materials, dependent on what species of whale their quarry happened to be. In the British and American fleets which worked in the Southern Ocean or the Pacific most scrimshaw was made from the teeth of sperm whales. In the Arctic, the preferred medium was that of baleen from the 'right whales', although other mediums such as narwhal and walrus tusks were often used.

However, long before the arrival of the white man or the whalers, the Inuit of the Arctic had carved and drawn on ivory from their narwhal and walrus captures. It is thought that some of the earliest examples of scrimshaw may have held religious significance but that is difficult to verify.(It is not unusual for archaeologists and anthropologists to attribute 'may have been of religious significance' to any object which did not have an obvious purpose.) When the whalers arrived, they often bartered with the Inuit and there is little doubt that the piece shown in the McManus collection was obtained in this manner. This item is carved on part of a walrus tusk but, presumably, the complete tusk would have originally been traded. Unfortunately, it has been broken. Much of the scrimshaw on sale nowadays is modern reproduction work and has no connection with the whaling industry. Genuine pieces are rare and can command high prices.

Two very unique carvings are those of a sperm whale and a walrus. They are carved on walrus teeth which were salvaged from the wreck of the 'Snowdrop' in 1908. As far as I am aware, they are the only ones of their kind in existence, although Maurice Forsyth-Grant still owns the remaining teeth from the sack of teeth recovered from the wreck when it went ashore. Walrus teeth are an exceedingly hard form of ivory and were ideal for the carving of the iconic Japanese Netsuke.

CONCLUSION

Was the mixing of these two cultures beneficial to both parties?

Certainly, it was very beneficial to the port of Dundee as it created wealth for many of its merchant classes for a period of more than 160 years.

For the working classes in many occupations other than the whaling and jute industries, it created the wealth and employment that enabled them to function (e.g. the leather and tanning industry employed hundreds and leather was in demand as belts and boots by those in jute and whaling). It was of particular importance to those Irish emigrants who fled the potato famines of the 19th century, for without the jute employment many of them would have perished from starvation.

The situation with the Inuit is not quite so clear-cut. At the time, it probably was good for the people involved. The whalers' trading bases often prevented hunger and starvation in the local Inuit populations when hunting was poor or weather prevented them from venturing out on the ice. The fact that the whalers and traders - like the Hudson Bay Company or Revillon Freres - supplied them with rifles made hunting safer as well as easier. Unfortunately it meant that many ancient arts, such as cutting a leather rope from a walrus hide using the unique half moon shaped knife know as an ulla, were lost. However, where companies failed to turn up with supplies, as happened on numerous occasions, this led to terrible hardship among the indigenous people. By the time the whaling ceased in 1914, the Inuit were totally dependent on the white man's goods such as rifles and other metal products.

WHAT EFFECT IS MODERN CIVILISATION AND CLIMATE CHANGE HAVING ON THE INUIT?

Greenland.

Back in 2011, Danish documentary film maker Jan van den Berg premiered his film "Silent Snow". A hard hitting documentary which may only be described as thought provoking. Some people try to claim it as alarmist and propaganda. But to many others, including myself, it is a revealing work which should be shown in schools and colleges worldwide. The points it raises should be cause for concern to every human being on the planet, unfortunately its issues are not regarded high on political agendas. The following paragraphs give a brief insight into the issues raised in the film.

A teenage girl looks east across the frozen sea to watch the sun rise above the horizon.

It is the first day that the sun has come above the horizon since the previous autumn.

The place is the Inuit town of Uummannaq, on the island of the same name. Positioned 300 miles north of the Arctic Circle, off Greenland's west coast, Uummannaq - which in the Greenlandic Inuit language means 'heart shaped mountain'- is the central hub for the population of around 2200 people who live in the settlements around the fjord.

The girl is not alone. Her name is Pipaluk, and around her are many of the other occupants of the town, turned out - as they have done for many years - to welcome the sun which brings light after the dark long night of the Arctic winter.

But this year is different from the past. The sun has come two days earlier than its traditional appearance day. The reason is that the icecap on the mainland of Greenland has decreased to such an extent that the sun is able to be seen earlier than in previous years. Greenland is melting!

Pipaluk, like many of her friends, lives in a tidy wooden house with modern facilities - electricity, water, video games and television - similar to the homes of teenagers in towns and cities across the globe. The main difference is that Pipaluk is living in a world of uncertainty, for hers is a world being destroyed by climate change and pollution from the so called 'advanced industrialised societies'. While watching a video on her television, she asks her friend Sarah if she will continue to eat their natural diet of seal meat and blubber, to which her friend, also still a teenager, replies 'yes'. The reason for this, ostensibly strange question is that due to the amount of toxins present in seal meat - toxins such as PCBs, polychlorinated biphenyls - the breast milk of Inuit girls is now so toxic it would harm their offspring.

The Inuit's diet of fish, seal, walrus and cetaceans such as narwhal and beluga, occasionally supplemented with polar bear and birds, all have one thing in common - their food chain base is plankton! This is where the problem starts, as all the plankton derives its nutrients from the sea which in turn has carried pollutants from our so called 'consumer society' to every corner of the globe into which the ocean currents travel. By the time the Gulf Stream and North Atlantic Drift have carried the outfalls from industrial zones in the Gulf of Mexico and the Eastern seaboard of the USA they are laden with everything from residual agrochemicals to heavy metals. The destination for most of these is first the Arctic Ocean then, via the Fram Strait to the eastern side of Greenland or between Canada's Ellesmere Island and Greenland, to Baffin Bay. Once in the bay, the seaborne contaminants are joined by the ever increasing fresh water runoff from the Greenland Icecap to the east and runoff from the glaciers of both Ellesmere and Baffin Islands to the west.

This fresh water, whether as direct runoff or as melting icebergs also has contaminants. These contaminants were originally airborne and, now that the surface layers are melting, they also flow into the sea.

It is easy for us to say: 'Well, why don't you eat imported foods or become vegetarians?'

Have you tried growing cabbages in Greenland? Being a vegan in the Arctic is not a realistic option.

For many years, I was a farmer growing organic vegetables. I also kept sheep and pigs in an attempt to balance the ecology and retain fertility in the soil for future generations.

Unfortunately, this is not an option for the Inuit either.

Unlike the Sami on the other side of the Atlantic, the Inuit do not have the benefit of warmth from the North Atlantic Drift. Their land is one of permafrost and icebound seas for most of the year … but even that is changing.

Growing vegetables is out of the question. Importing vegetables and meat which does not contain unwanted additives is expensive, not only in financial terms but also in terms of CO_2 emissions from the freight miles, whether by sea or air. Also, since would-be conservationists, including organisations like Sea Shepherd have exerted their influence on both public and politicians alike, the Inuit of Uummannaq - and all the other Inuit settlements - can no longer sell their seal skins to former markets such as Europe.

As young Pipaluk Knudsen- Ostermann states in Jan van den Berg's film 'Silent Snow': 'They expect us to eat hamburgers!'

If a teenage Inuit girl can understand that eating 'high carbon footprint' hamburgers, instead of natural, sustainable food like seals, is not going to 'save the planet' or the seas, why can't people like Sea Shepherd?

Unfortunately, seals, fish and polar bears are so high up in the food chain that the concentrations of toxins are well above the recommended levels set by the World Health Organisation. As it is the Inuit who sits on top of this Bio-accumulation Pyramid they are the species most at risk. What the health risks will be in the future is currently unknown, but one thing is certain - the current situation cannot be allowed to continue.

Since breast-feeding is not advised, it will bring another factor into the equation of Inuit life. Inuit traditionally breast-fed for up to three years, which depresses fertility. Now young girls are able to conceive far more frequently, bringing all the usual problems of population versus resources into play. In one settlement I visited in South West Greenland I saw several young Inuit mothers with two and three children under the age of five. This would certainly not have been the case even fifty years ago. Thankfully, despite this noted case, the population of Greenland is not showing a rapid growth. In fact, the opposite is happening. Greenland's population is ageing and young people from the outlying areas are moving to the larger towns or moving out of Greenland altogether. This has led the Greenlandic Government to consider evacuating some of the northern settlements which are currently only viable due to government subsidies. These subsidies are only affordable due to the Danish Government giving Greenland a very large annual grant - no longer are the Inuit masters of self sufficiency!

If the Inuit are not allowed to export their sealskins,

how are they expected to pay for the imported hamburgers?

One source of income in recent years was that of tourists from ships coming ashore.

However, since the ice is too thin to land on and also too thick for tender boats to break through, the ships are no longer going into Uummannaq Fjord. The same problem is affecting Sarah when she heads home for the school holidays. She once travelled the whole way by dog sledge, but now the ice is too thin. Now she travels part of the way in a small 'ice hardened' coaster. The final leg home is then by dogsled. The Greenlandic Government is considering closing some of the smaller settlements and relocating the inhabitants to larger towns as the economic state of the settlements is getting worse. Just as the Highlands and Islands of Scotland were cleared of people in the eighteenth and nineteenth centuries the Inuit living in remote areas of Greenland fear that they may have to leave their ancestral lands. Unlike the Scottish clearances, where the people were replaced by more profitable sheep, there will be no species to replace the once self sufficient Inuit.

Even hunting seals is becoming more difficult. Due to the thinning ice, the traditional Inuit method of hunting on the ice is now limited only to when there is thick enough ice in deep winter. This shortening of the season means that more of the seal hunt is carried out from boats using high-powered rifles, as opposed to harpoons. But even using this method has encountered climate change-related problems. The seals that the Inuit hunt are naturally buoyant - in sea water, that is!

What is now happening is that the less dense fresh water run-off from the melting glaciers is forming a layer on top of the dense saline water below. The seals which have been shot sink onto this sub-surface layer. Where the fresh water surface layer is around a foot deep it is reasonably easy for the marksman to find and retrieve his kill. But sometimes, particularly at the height of summer, so much glacial ice melt is coming into Uummannaq Fjord that the dead seal sinks out of easy reach or cannot be found in the cloudy glacial melt water.

The Inuit child is brought up with their father's dogs. But for how much longer?

An Inuit hunter and his team of sled dogs is a scene we all recognise. At one time his dogs helped him to hunt polar bears. His dogs transported him and his family or belongings across both sea ice and frozen wastelands from one seasonal hunting ground to another. They kept guard on his ice house during the dark winter nights and protected his children from fearsome predators. That was a way of life for both man and malamute for millennia, but now things are changing. The days of nomadic hunting over hundreds of miles of frozen wasteland are gone. Few of the Inuit alive today were born into that culture. Now that these indigenous people have taken to the sedentary way of the white man, with houses, regular jobs, (if available) and shops, the need to have a pack of ever hungry sled dogs has greatly diminished.

This move from nomadic hunter to sedentary house dweller has itself seen a decline in dog numbers, but now another factor has come into play - lack of ice on which to use the dogs. Unfortunately, in some of the settlements around Uummannaq, some of the hunters have shot their own dogs rather than continue keeping them as pets which have to be fed on food which would otherwise help feed their families. Hunting from a fixed base cannot give the kind of income that is needed to fund the new consumer society which has befallen the Inuit.

On a recent visit to Greenland I had a meeting with the curator of the museum in Sisimiut on Greenland's west coast north of the capital Nook. He informed me of the sad state of the Greenland Dog. Due to the lack of hunting opportunities due to climate change the number of dogs has dropped from around thirty thousand to nearer twelve. To try and save the breed the Greenlandic Government is subsidising the cost of dog food and only permits hunting by traditional sled teams rather than using skidoos. Whether this will save the breed remains to be seen as most of the dogs I saw at the 'Dog City' on Sisimuit's outskirts were lean and indeed underfed looking. In Northern Norway, where many dog sled racing events take place, the Siberian Huskies are always robust and well fed. This difference could well be attributed to the difference between keeping dogs as a hobby or pets than having them as a part of your culture of survival.

The traditional winter method of fishing by the inhabitants of Western Greenland was to cut a hole in the ice and lower a baited longline through the hole to drift along the bottom with the current. From the line, a haul of Greenland halibut would feed both dogs and man throughout the winter months. Now the winter season has shortened and ice fishing opportunities are less as the ice forming later and thinning earlier makes this type of fishing dangerous. Now most of the fishing, particularly in the settlements south of the Greenland capital of Nuuk, is from boats - often propelled by large outboard engines which use petrol which costs money. To pay for this, the Inuit fishermen - who for millennia were natural conservationists who only caught what fish they could use - now have to catch fish to sell to pay for boats and fuel. This also helps buy the hamburgers and other white man's goods of televisions and computers. What we need to ask ourselves is: 'Can this be good for a once very self -sufficient race or for the planet as a whole?'

To answer this is a difficult task. For the individual selling the fish and supporting a family it is of personal benefit. To the local economy it is of undoubted benefit. It also creates paid employment in other sectors of processing, chandlery, boat maintenance and exporting. However, in some of the more outlying settlements, it is difficult to keep the processing side of the fishing going as the population drops. One village in the Uummannaq Fjord came close to being abandoned when its fish processing plant was threatened with closure by the government-owned Royal Greenland. The locals in Niaqornat bought the plant. Otherwise, they would have to take their catch by boat to Uummannaq, 40 miles away, which would have been unviable. Greenland halibut is an expensive commodity by the time it reaches the upmarket restaurants in the EU or USA, but the prices paid to those that catch it are minimal. So much so that these same fish are fed to the sled dogs as that costs less than buying dog food!

How long small villages like Niaqornat (population around 50 and miles from any sizeable settlement) can hang on in a modern world is anyone's guess.

So, before donating to conservation charities that protect seals, ask yourself: 'Is my donation going to a group which is helping to destroy an ancient indigenous people's way of life or protecting predators which upset the ecological balance of the sea.

Greenland has a population of approximately fifty seven thousand of which around seven thousand are Danish citizens who have moved there to live and work among the indigenous people. Even the police constables who are responsible in patrolling the vast areas of sparsely populated coastline are on secondment from Denmark. Many of these Danes have married Greenlanders and have children. Back in 2014, while lecturing on a cruise ship, I was escorting a group of tourists in the town of Qaqortoq in the south of Greenland accompanied by a young guide who had been a student at the college in the town. This young lad was over six feet tall and blonde but born and bred in the area. He told me that the Danes in the town regarded him as Danish but when he visited Denmark as part of his university degree the Danes regarded him as an Inuit. As such the Danes in Denmark viewed him and his people almost as what might be termed as a 'charity case'. This has more than a passing similarity to the attitude I have found among certain factions of Norwegian society regarding the Sami people of Northern Norway.

So what is the reality of the situation? Are the Greenlanders really dependant on the benevolence of the Danish people? Or is there another totally different side to this situation?

Depending on whom you speak to and what their position in Greenlandic society is will give you very differing answers. Danish tourists have often a condescending attitude towards the locals and will tell you their taxes are what is keeping these indigenous people fed and housed. Others think that it is Denmark's duty to look after these people as, in their view, they are incapable of looking after themselves. These views differ greatly from the opinions of many of the honest, hard working locals I have met. Fishermen, seamen, tourism workers, all have told me that the Danes will happily inform anyone who will listen that Denmark finances Greenland to the tune of three billion kroner a year. What the locals say that the Danes fail to mention is that the Greenlanders have little choice but to spend six billion kroner per annum on goods shipped in from Denmark. Not only have Danish companies got an effective monopoly, through companies like Royal Danish, they also exploit the Greenlandic fisheries which are the biggest in Europe.

Across the whole spectrum of Inuit society there is always an air of cheerfulness accompanied with what may be described as a 'large dose of pragmatism'. Even as far back as the earliest days of the Scottish trappers and whalers there were comments about how the Inuit were cheerful yet seemed to accept hardship as an inevitable part of life. Today, in what is without doubt a worrying time regarding climate change, the modern inhabitants of Greenland have kept that tradition of 'cheerful pragmatism' alive.

Back north in Uummannaq the view of the local fishermen is that the climate has always changed. 'Didn't the Vikings leave when it got too cold for them?' was one comment. 'If it gets much warmer we can fish for a longer season.' was another. Such views are however interspaced with comments about the pollution of Greenland's waters by the industrialised nations. The view on this subject can make a very interesting topic of conversation, particularly with those of the younger generation who have had the benefit of a good education which has broadened their outlook much further than previous generations. These younger people feel that the industrial nations, who have the 'cheek to say the Inuit are untidy and dirty', dump their toxic filth in the air and in the sea so that it ends up in the Arctic. So maybe tourists from America and Europe should think before they make comments about old fishing boats and gear lying about Greenland's fishing ports. Disposal of modern materials is a problem in Greenland, but are the Inuit at the root of that problem? When one looks at what the litter is and its origins, one soon realizes that most of it comes from the white man. The Inuit for millennia only used what nature provided and what nature provides is invariably non toxic and biodegradable within an extremely short time on a geological timescale. What is supplied by industrial nations in terms of everything from consumer items, such as washing machines and televisions, through to the larger items that the tourists complain about, old fishing vessels and vehicles, are there for the long haul. In the case of plastics, which includes the derelict and abandoned GRP fishing vessels lying on quaysides, that biodegradation is going to be measured in millennia and has serious implications on both terrestrial and marine environments.

Another subject that the Greenlandic public are concerned about is independence from Denmark. Strangely it is the very opposite of the situation in Scotland. In Scotland it is the younger generation who think independence from the rest of the UK is a good idea. This is because many are young and idealistic without the wisdom of age. Many older Scots realise that Scotland is a small country on a small island that has limited resources. In Greenland it is the older generations where around seventy percent are in favour of independence from Denmark. The majority of the younger generation still want independence, but not to such an extent as the older generation. The current situation, where they have a devolved government of thirty one representatives, is one of limited power where all foreign affairs are controlled by the Danish

Parliament.

If independence were achieved, so locals in South West Greenland have said, climate change would enable mining of valuable minerals which are currently not being exploited. The value of these minerals could transform the lives of the indigenous Greenlanders, but only if mining revenues were retained in Greenland and not siphoned off by Denmark. What the actual value is, of course, currently an unknown but with an indigenous population of only fifty thousand it would not take much in overall financial terms to have a high per capita influence. There are large known deposits of iron ore which, due to the currently depressed steel prices, are not being exploited. Also as the Greenland Government has neither sufficient funds nor the Greenlandic people the technological expertise in mining the mining rights have been leased out to a foreign operator. If the Greenlandic government approached this 'lack of expertise' in the same way as Norway did back in the 1970's things would change. The Norwegians insisted that offshore supply vessels and oil production platforms that were to be used in the Norwegian Sector were to be built in Norway. Although they initially had to import the technology by employing non Norwegian engineers and designers, it only took a few years before the home grown talent were sufficiently trained to take over in the construction and operating of their oil installations. Greenland may not have as big a pool of potential labour but if the mining leases included terms that insisted on training local labour in both the manual and managerial skills it is feasible that within a generation they too could run their mining industry. A further benefit in such a move would be to slow down or even stop the departure of the younger generation to seek a better life elsewhere.

Although Greenland is deemed part of Denmark and Denmark part of the EU, Greenland is not part of the EU. This anomalous situation came about because the Greenlandic people decided to leave the EU rather than see European fishing fleets from Spain and Portugal plunder their fishing grounds. At the time of their departure from the EU, Spain and Portugal were about to join and the Common Fisheries Policy of the EU would have allowed these countries access to Greenland's prolific fisheries. The Greenlandic people are only too aware that, at that time, over ninety per cent of their gross national product was from the fishing industry. They had also witnessed in the not too distant past the collapse of the Canadian Grand Banks cod fishery. So it was of little surprise that they voted to leave the EU so that they could control their own waters albeit under the Danish flag and with other concessions to permit their access to the EU Single Market.

Greenland joined the EU back in 1973 along with Denmark but after a referendum in 1982, when 53% of the population decided to leave the EU, exit negotiations started. The only topic of discussion in the exit negotiations was that of fisheries. In fact it took three years of discussions before a deal was brokered and Greenland finally left.

If it took three years to discuss one topic it must make one wonder how the UK will manage to discuss and agree with the EU on the many complex issues that need to be settled before Britain's exit from the EU is concluded.

The Greenland withdrawal from the Common Fisheries Policy did not see an end to EU funding of the Greenlandic fishing fleet. The deal struck with the EU allowed limited access and fish quotas for EU vessels based on what was termed 'historic catch records'. In exchange for these quotas the EU continued to give the Greenlandic fishing industry payments worth around 43 million Euros per annum up until the year 2006. The EU fisheries commissioners then decided that the quotas that they were being allowed from the Greenlandic waters were too costly and the annual payments ceased. Much of this EU money went into the modernisation of the Greenland fleet. There is little doubt that this vastly increased the efficiency of the indigenous people's vessels in terms of catching capability and safety at sea. The downside is that it left lots of small ageing craft lying derelict on quaysides and shores. In some cases it allowed individuals to move away from the traditional small labour intensive vessels which concentrated on inshore fishing with lines and gillnets. This has led to the creation of a fleet of large highly efficient modern trawlers which have state of the art fishing technology but are capital intensive rather than labour intensive. A parallel can be drawn with the Scottish fishing fleet where the number of vessels has dramatically reduced in recent years but the actual catching capacity in terms of landing values and tonnages landed has not comparably declined. The biggest impact of this 'technological creep ', has been the drop in the number of people employed in the catching sector. This in turn has seen once thriving fishing ports no longer having fleets of inshore vessels or daily markets. It has also seen the decline in boat building and maintenance sectors with many once famous boatyards now condemned to history. Some of the small vessel owners in Greenland are concerned that their future may follow a similar path while those who invested heavily in large trawlers are lamenting the end of EU grant aid to finance the upgrading of their large trawlers, some of which are now beginning to show signs of ageing. Some of these owners clearly and openly state their view that rejoining the EU would be beneficial to them.

EU funding to Greenland did not totally dry up with the secession of payments to the fishing sector. Between 2007 and 2013 payments of 25 million Euros per annum were given out with the fishing industry for infrastructure projects. Further funding for the period from 2014 to 2020 has been set at 217.8 million Euros in total. This money has been allocated to development programmes with an emphasis on improving education. The views of many of the older generation, on spending this money on further education, clearly reflect their Inuit heritage. Often one will hear comments along the line of 'There are plenty of unemployed people who have university degrees but fishermen can always catch fish.' Usually said with a smile it is a classic example of Inuit 'cheerful pragmatism.'

Another point of discussion that arises with regularity in Inuit society is that of the EU banning the import of seal skins. As Pipaluk Hammekan so elegantly stated in 'Silent Snow', 'They expect us to eat hamburgers!'. The EU has not banned the hunting of seals but its effect on communities, particularly in the more northerly coastal settlements, where seal hunting has been an important part of the economy has been dire. The local Inuit hunters have hunted seals since long before the arrival of the Europeans. It is a central figure in all Inuit mythology. The seal was for millennia their main source of food, clothing and warmth. Its blubber gave light in the Arctic night long before organisations such as Greenpeace or Sea Shepherd ever saw the light of day. It was the European traders and whalers that changed the Inuit from hunter gatherers into a trading society. It was the Europeans who depleted the northern whale populations, not the Inuit.

Back in 2015, former Greenland Minister for Hunting and fishing made it quite clear to the EU that the overall ban on importing seal products to EU countries was seriously affecting the way if life for many Inuit settlements around Greenland. This despite the fact that the indigenous Inuit were still allowed to hunt seals and sell their skins to the EU. The scientific evidence clearly pointed out that the Inuit hunters were only killing 150,000 seals per annum when a cull of 500,000 seals per annum would be permissible without having detrimental effects on the environment. Even Greenpeace have started to rethink their views on culling seals and have acknowledged the fact that a growing seal population is impacting on fish stocks in the region. If this population growth is not stopped then ultimately the fish stocks will collapse and then the seals will starve. However before this point is reached the indigenous human population will need not only financial aid but also basic food to be imported. It is almost ironic that while sealskin products from a sustainable source are disdained that mink pelts from intensive farming is enjoying a revival in the fashion industry. The damage done to the Inuit culture was not of their making but by the images of Canadian seal hunters clubbing seal pups shown around the world's media in years gone by. The Inuit hunters do not club seal pups. For many years the Inuit have killed seals using high powered rifles and, unlike the farmed mink, the seals have had a natural and free life up until the moment the Inuit marksman pulls the trigger. Can we say that our meat, whether cattle sheep or pig, has had as stress free a life or compassionate ending? As a former farmer I know otherwise and yet the practices in the UK are preferable to many other countries which I will not name.

A parallel to the Greenlandic situation is that of the Grey Seal population in the North Sea. If the ecological system of the North Sea and its surrounding land masses had been left to nature there would not be a grey seal population of over a hundred thousand in that area. In that perfect 'natural state' the grey seal population may have been nearer one thousand. The reason behind this is that the grey seal weans its pup onshore for between two and three weeks. If man had not wiped out the large predators, the wolves and bears, the grey seal pups chance of survival would have been zero. That is without taking into account that the human predator also killed seals. The natural breeding habitat of the grey seal is islands or rock outcrops free from terrestrial predation and that was what kept their numbers regulated. Since habitat of this nature in the North Sea was limited to locations like the Farne Isles off Northumberland, this held the grey seal numbers stable up to the mid twentieth century. Up until then the wild salmon netsmen culled grey seals to protect their livelihood. Salmon angling interests then started to buy out netting rights along the Scottish East Coast and this altered the ecological balance. Once the nets were removed from an estuary the seals, now a protected species, moved in to the protection of the sheltered estuaries and started to multiply. The outcome was that far from increasing the numbers of salmon available to angler's rods the numbers started to tumble. It doesn't take a genius to figure out that having 'Scotland's indigenous netsmen' taking a couple of thousand Salmon in a regulated fishery is preferable to having a thousand grey seals in a river estuary. Yet the salmon angling organisations and would be conservationists think it is. The situation regarding the Inuit seal hunt is no different. Where the answer lies is with the media. Instead of showing presenters announcing that 'these lovely seals have had a wonderful breeding season' they should be telling the public that these 'now out of control ferocious killers are on the increase and above sustainable levels'.

If the media took that approach the Inuit would soon be able to run a sustainable and profitable business in supplying skins for leather and clothing. The seal meat could be dried and exported to poor countries as a cheap source of quality protein. If African countries are willing to take dried cod heads they would most certainly take dried seal meat. The issue of the chemical content in the meat would not be of great concern as most of the POPs and PCBs are concentrated in the blubber rather than the meat. It is the fact that the Inuit diet consists mainly of seals, fish and cetaceans that causes the accumulation in their bodies. They also eat the blubber in the Inuit favourite 'muktuk' which would not be part of a seal meat trade.

Surely, if even Greenpeace sees that there is a case for lifting the sealskin ban, it is time our governments had a rethink without being influenced by fanatical factions like Sea Shepherd. These 'ignorant of the facts' types are doing more damage than good to our marine ecosystems despite all their good intentions.

A further point that has recently caused concern among the inhabitants of Greenland is the manner in which the American base at Thule in North West Greenland is being run. In the past this American base was part of what was known as the DEW (Distant Early Warning) line of early warning monitoring bases during the 'cold war era'. Since the end of the cold war its function has remained under the control of the US. The reason it has been able to do so is because of a contract agreed between Denmark and the US during WW2. In this contract there is a clause that states that the US has the use of the base as long as there is a threat to the US.

The current perceived threat is that of North Korea's missile capability development and the ongoing distrust of Russia.

Up until 2014 three major contracts involving maintenance and transport at the base were held by Greenland based companies. More recently two of these contracts have been given to US companies despite in the second case of the Greenlandic tender being around half that of the US company, Schuyler Line. In this case it was Greenland's Royal Arctic Line that lost out to the tune of $8.5M. Although this is not a massive sum of money, and Royal Arctic say they are not too upset, it is not being seen by the majority of the Greenlanders as a good way to treat a host country. The general view regarding this is that if Royal Arctic had been a US based company it would undoubtedly have been retained for the marine transport work it had done in previous years. What was regarded as a much more serious loss was that of the Thule Base Maintenance Contract in 2014 which had for many years been run by Greenland Contractors. This company is part owned by the Self Rule Authority and employs indigenous people. The contract which was awarded to Excelis was worth over $400m over the eight year contract. What really annoyed many Greenlanders was that Excelis is a company which is registered in Denmark but in turn has an American parent company. The original agreement stated that work at the base would be awarded to Danish companies, but this was before Greenland had its own autonomous government. Using an ostensibly Danish company to comply with the treaty agreement is rightly viewed by the members of the Naalakkersuisut, the elected Greenland Government, as totally underhand and unacceptable.

Currently the US do not pay for the lease of the Thule base and many Greenlanders see it as time to scrap the old agreement which they had little part in setting up in the first place. If the US sees Thule Air Base as an important part of their national defence system then they should be rethinking how they treat the indigenous population.

A final problem faced by the Inuit of Greenland is that of maintaining family ties with relatives on the west side of Baffin Bay. Before the effects of climate change it was possible to cross the waters of the Smith Strait by dogsled during the months of the winter freeze. This is no longer safe to do and now the only way to reach their Canadian family members is via Copenhagen. The cost of which is prohibitive.

Inuit Canada.
Inuit Nunangat—the Inuit Regions.

It is estimated that the northern territories of Canada have a population of over sixty thousand indigenous people who can rightfully claim to be of Inuit origins. The majority of whom now live in just over fifty settlements spread across the north from the Alaskan- Canadian border in the west to the coast of Labrador in the east.

These Inuit represent around 4.3 per cent of the indigenous people resident in Canada. The largest group of indigenous people are what were previously known as Red Indians, now better known as the First Nations People. Since the second half of the twentieth century attitudes towards Canada's indigenous people have vastly improved. Land settlement agreements have led to a better relationship between all concerned and it is hoped that these agreements will be beneficial not only to the human inhabitants of Canada's wildest regions but also to both flora and fauna. In some of these land settlement agreements mineral rights, including both gas and oil have been included. Where this is the case companies have been set up to ensure that the indigenous people are beneficiaries of any forthcoming development or exploitation of these assets. This will hopefully help alleviate some of the current issues being faced by both First Nations and Inuit Society.

From the North West Arctic region across to the Labrador Coast in the east, four semi- autonomous areas are now designated as Inuit Land Claim Regions.

Inuvialuit.

Furthest west of the Land Claim Regions is the Inuvialuit Settlement Region in the North West Territories. This area is home to the Inupiat Inuit who are also native to the area further west in Alaska. The Inuvialuit Land Claim was settled in June 1984 and is referred to as the Inuvialuit Final Agreement which is protected under the Canadian Constitution. Covering an area of 91,000 square kilometres it gives all the mineral rights, including oil and gas, to the people resident within the settlement area. To ensure that these rights would only be operated to the benefit of those whom they were intended the Inuvialuit Regional Corporation was established. Within its remit are the protection of both the culture of the Inupiat people and the protection of all Arctic flora and fauna. This includes both terrestrial and marine ecosystems. The corporation is also responsible for protecting its beneficiaries rights in all negotiations with either government or industry. Its current negotiations with the Central Canadian Government include seeking self rule for the area.

Nunavut.

Lying between the Inuvialuit Settlement Region and Baffin Bay is the land claim region of Nunavut. By far the largest of the four regions it covers an area of approximately two million square kilometres. To get an idea of how large this area is, it is two thirds the size of India or the size of France, Spain, Norway and Sweden stuck together. Yet it only has a population of fewer than thirty eight thousand. The Land Claim Agreement was reached in 1995 and by 1999 a government had been formed to represent all Nunavut citizens, including non indigenous Canadians. To protect the rights of the Inuit beneficiaries of the agreement a company was set up with power of attorney over both the land and marine assets assigned to the Inuit. This company, Nunavut Tunngavik Inc., operates across the region and has the responsibility over the most northern parts of Canada's Arctic Archipelago. Much of this area is uninhabited islands which up until recently were icebound throughout the year. Its 'capital city' is Iqaluit on Baffin Island, which was previously known as Frobisher. Part of the area consists of the northern regions of the mineral rich Canadian Shield. Forming a horseshoe around Hudson Bay, the Shield is a granite plateau rising to over two thousand metres in height above sea level. It covers over 4.6 million square kilometres, nearly half of Canada's landmass. Its Precambrian rocks are more than 600 million years old, making it one of the world's oldest landmasses. Aeons of erosion have stripped most of its soil except in low lying areas of saturated bog. Stretches of forest are interspaced with countless lakes, many of which hold pre-glacial coregonids, a primitive ancestor of modern day salmonids. Across the Shield human settlements have always been few and far between and are concentrated only where rich mineral deposits have been found. It is these deposits of gold, silver and nickel that are the hidden wealth of the Shield and led to its exploration by prospectors in the 19th century and into the 20th century. Hopefully any new discoveries of noble metals or other valuable minerals within the new Inuit region of Nunavut will improve the lives of the indigenous people.

Nunavik.

South of Nunavut on the East coast of Hudson Bay one finds the Nunavik Settlement region. Stretching from its southern most point on the north east corner of James Bay it s north coast is the Hudson Straits from the Ungava peninsula west to the northern end of Labrador where the Torngat Mountains tumble into the freezing waters to mark the exit from the Hudson Strait into the Labrador Sea between Canada and Greenland. Originally this land area was part of the Province of Quebec but became incorporated into Nunavik as part of the 1975 James Bay and North Quebec Agreement. The southern boundary lies along the 55th parallel and the land north of this equates to a third of the total land mass of Quebec Province. The area covered by this agreement extends to 550,000sq kilometres and is administration on behalf of its Inuit beneficiaries is carried out by the Makivik Corporation.

The word 'Nunavik' means 'great land' in the Inuktitut language. The Inuit people of the region call themselves 'Nunavimmiut', people of the great land. The 2011 census put the overall population at just over twelve thousand, of whom ninety per cent were deemed to be Inuit. With a total of fourteen registered villages its capital is Kuujjuaq. This settlement lies at the southern end of Ungava Bay across the river from the original Fort Chimo which was the site of Scottish author R.M. Ballantine's book 'Ungava'. The current settlement is built around a former US airbase which was returned to Canada after WW2. Due to the lack of a road infrastructure travel is difficult within the region, in particular the only practical way to get to the cities of

Southern Quebec is by plane.

The area has extensive mineral deposits including large nickel deposits currently being mined by mining giant Glencore at their Raglan Mine near the north end of the Ungava Peninsula. As there are no roads south the ore is milled on site before being shipped south by freighter to Quebec. Currently the workforce is predominantly French Canadian from South Quebec with less than twenty per cent being local Inuit. Although Glencore are striving to increase this figure there are still perceived to be problems with ethnic and racial issues on site.

Politically, negotiations are ongoing to form an inclusive Katavik Government to include all inhabitants of the region but this has, in the past, run into opposition. The current situation is that regional funding is raised from three sources. Quebec Regional Government is the largest, supplying fifty percent of the revenue. The Canadian Government and local taxation account for the rest on an equal basis.

Nunatsiavut.

The Inuit Region of Nunatsiavut is the most easterly of Canada's four Inuit Regions.

It is part of the Province of Newfoundland and Labrador and is the smallest of the Inuit Regions and consists of two separate areas. Sandwiched between Nunavik and the Labrador coast, the Northern area extends from the administrative capital of Nain to the north tip of the Torngat mountains. This area includes the Torngat National Park. The southern area extends inland around the Hamilton Inlet with the legislative capital of Hopedale being the main settlement. The total area of the region is 77,520 square kilometres of land area and an additional marine zone of 44,030 square kilometres. The total population in the 2006 census was 2,160 of whom the majority lived in the southern area. The population of the Hopedale area was stated to be 1403 in 2011. Most of region is completely isolated and has neither road nor rail infrastructures with the settlements being built on what were previously Moravian Church Missions. Currently the five main settlements and some of the smaller settlements are served by a ferry run by Nunatsiavut Marine Inc. The only other means of reaching these settlements is by air and two companies provide such a service, Air Labrador and Provincial Airlines.

In recent years the idea of connecting Nunatsiavut with the Trans Labrador Highway has been put forward and is under consideration.

The formation of the Nunatsiavut Region, which means 'Our Beautiful Land' in the Inuktitut language, has not been without its share of problems. One problem was that of the Metis people. The Metis are not indigenous as such but the result of the mixing of the original French trappers and settlers with local tribes. The Labrador Metis Nation challenged the formation of Nunatsiavut in the Supreme Court of Newfoundland. Their own claim being all of Labrador south of Nain. This would have included all of the Southern Region of Nunatsiavut around the Hamilton Inlet including what is now the legislative capital of Hopedale. The Canadian Federal Government suggested that the Labrador Metis Nation should join with the Inuit community of Nunatsiavut to form a strong Inuit semi-autonomous region. This in many ways recognises the fact that the Metis of Labrador were indeed an Inuit Culture. This resulted in the Labrador Metis Nation changing their name to Nunatukavut in 2010. Nunatukavut means 'Our Ancient Land' in the Inuktituk language and is much in keeping with the overall naming of the region

Another problem that was encountered during the three decade long process of attaining a ratified constitution was surprisingly from another Inuit region. The Makavik Corporation, who are responsible for protecting Inuit rights in neighbouring Nunavik, had claimed territorial rights over Killiniq Island on the extreme northern point of the Torngat Peninsula. Geologically this island is where the Torngat Mountains continue into the sea and could therefore be reasonably claimed as part of that mountain range. The now uninhabited island, which means 'ice floes' is now part of neither Nunavik nor Nunatsiavut but under the jurisdiction of Nunavut.

After three decades of claims, arguments and negotiations a final agreement was reached and on 1ˢᵗ Dec 2005 the Constitution of Nunatsiavut was ratified. This gave the Inuit responsibility for all issues relating to health, education, preservation of the Inuit Culture and language. It also gave them the responsibility of maintaining the environment and wildlife, both terrestrial and marine, including the Torngat National Park. Also as part of the agreement was the rectification of a long standing injustice that was imposed on the Labrador Inuit in the 1950s. A payment of $130 million was made as compensation to the Inuit people for the forced relocation that the Canadian government had instigated. This plus another $120million, which was paid by the Provincial Government of Newfoundland and Labrador, as royalty payment for minerals which had extracted from the appropriated land, were included in the settlement agreement. Once the constitution had been ratified the first election for a Regional Government soon followed and in October 2006 that government became a reality.

Baffin Island.

Lying due west of Greenland across Baffin Bay is Baffin Island, the world's fifth largest island with an area of 507,451sq.km. It has a population of approximately 11,000 people, of which over 80% are Inuit. Its largest settlement is Iqaluit, with a population of around 7,000 people. Iqaluit is also the capital of Nunavut, one of the homeland territories of Canada's Inuit.

Interesting as these statistics are, they fail to have the impact of one single statistic that Nunavut is not so pleased to publicise.

Nunavut is possibly the suicide capital of the world.

With a suicide rate of 120 per 100,000, nowhere else comes close (with a current population of around 32,000 this means around 40 suicides per annum).

Most of these suicides are young Inuit males. Suicide among young Inuit males is also a problem in Greenland but there it is not quite so severe, although it is still cause for serious concern. As a Scot whose ancestors were involved in whaling I almost felt ashamed when I saw the effects that alcohol had on both male and female Inuit in some of the Inuit settlements I visited on my last two visits to Greenland and yet, bad as the alcohol situation is in Greenland, things are even more serious on Baffin Island.

The root cause of many of these young people taking their own lives is, in many cases, alcohol and drug abuse. Despite the restrictions on alcohol sales throughout Nunavut - where it is often easier to buy a rifle than a beer - alcohol is also a contributing factor to the high rates of violence and homicide throughout the territory. It is also estimated that 95% of police call-outs are alcohol-related. Bootleg liquor is currently estimated by the RCMP to be a $10 million a year business that any self-respecting 1930s Chicago mobster would be proud off. Many sociologists think that the restrictive regime of prohibition is the cause of the alcohol abuse problem; others think that liberalisation of liquor sales would only make the situation worse. The only certainty is that, as long as the young Inuit males are under-employed and feel that they have little to offer to society, suicides will continue.

In 2013, when there were 45 suicides in the territory, the suicide rate among Nunavut's Inuit population was 13 times higher than the Canadian average. The suicide rate among young Inuit men was 40 times greater than that of their peer group in Southern Canada. Unable to live their traditional hunter existence and yet feeling that they don't fit into 21st century Canadian society, the future for many young Inuit in Canada looks bleak.

The general opinion among many Canadians is that the Inuit are happy to live on welfare handouts, get drunk and die young. This is not the case. The white man took away their nomadic lifestyle and, although many at the time thought they were helping these people by giving them a new and better existence, the outcome has been less than successful.

Hopefully, the opening of a new deep water port at Iqaluit may help create employment - not only in freight handling but possibly in the tourism sector if cruise companies decide to use the facility.

As climate change warms the Arctic, easier access to ports in both Baffin Island and Greenland should enable better and more reliable mobility among its people. Tourism, hopefully, may replace some of the jobs lost in the hunting sector. Hunters make exceptional guides as their natural stealth and knowledge of their quarry far exceeds that of a town-dwelling tourist. Whereas you can only shoot a seal or bear once with a gun you can get lots of shots with a camera.

It was the 'civilised' world that introduced the Inuit to alcohol, drugs and consumerism. Now, it appears, we will not accept the same products that we initially exploited these people to obtain.

Inuit Whaling and Hunting Practices in the 21st Century. After the devastating slaughter of whales by the commercial whaling fleets from many nations it became evident that something had to be done. If not the extinction of these magnificent creatures would have been inevitable. By the time the International Whaling Commission (IWC) had been set up the populations of baleen whales in both North Atlantic and North Pacific had been reduced to a fraction of their former numbers. The initial intention, when in December 1946 the IWC was formed, was "To provide for the proper conservation of whale stocks and thus make possible the orderly development of the whaling industry."

Whether there is need for a whaling industry at all in the 21st century is very debateable but, whether it is or isn't, is of little importance to the indigenous people of the Arctic. For millennia the whale has been not only of cultural importance to the Inuit but also of nutritional necessity. This fact has not gone unnoticed by the IWC and it has always looked upon the hunting of whales by the Inuit as a necessity rather than as "for profit" venture. This view is now shared by the world's best known conservation body, 'Greenpeace', who now have acknowledged both the cultural and nutritional significance that whaling has to the Inuit. The fact that the overall numbers taken by the Inuit is actually very sustainable and as the amount of waste generated is minimal has not prevented other less reputable 'conservation organisations' from contesting the right of the Inuit to hunt.

Due to the pressure from these "would be conservationists" many Inuit communities gave up their right to continue hunting whales as a means of supporting their families. However in recent years there has been a return to what has been described as 'Our culture of whaling' by a number of Inuit communities across the whole of the Arctic. From the Inupiat in Alaska to the Baffin Island Inuit of Clyde River the hunting of the large baleen whales has returned. The level of hunting is low and controlled so that its impact will not impede the recovery of populations of the species being hunted. The three species which are being taken are Grey, Humpback and Bowhead. In all three species there has been a remarkable recovery in numbers since the IWC moratorium on whaling was implemented back in 1982. The main difference between the Inuit whale hunters of the twentieth century and those of the twenty first century is that of equipment being used although some places still hang on to the traditional methods. Sticking out into the Chukchi Sea on Alaska's North West shore is the Inupiat Inuit settlement of Point Hope. With around ninety percent of the population of around seven hundred being indigenous Inupiat Inuit it is one of the largest settlements on the North Slope of Alaska and is highly dependent on subsistence hunting and gathering. With food prices in the local shops often being double that found in Anchorage, seven hundred kilometres south, it is no surprise that more than fifty percent of the food consumed locally is either hunted or foraged during the short arctic summer. It is estimated that the average consumption of wild hunted meat in the area is around two hundred kilos per person annually. According to the US Alaskan State Census fifteen percent of local households live below the poverty line so the hunting of bowhead whales is a necessity to prevent starvation and malnutrition among the population, particularly among the elderly. When questioned about the local whale hunting former mayor, Steve Oomittuk, very concisely stated, "Without the whale we wouldn't be who we are." The relative poverty of this community may be one reason that they still hunt the mighty bowhead using traditional Inuit Umiaks and hand harpoons launched at close range. The only concession to modernity being that the harpoon has an explosive head that helps to kill the whale swiftly. In years gone by the whale would be dragged on to the ice to be butchered. This was achieved by the community turning out at the sound of the local church bell to pull the beast up using block and tackle. When one realises that a large bowhead can weigh up to a hundred tonnes, this was no mean feat. Nowadays the locals say that the spring ice is too unstable to do this and so a channel is cut to drag the whale ashore where butchering can be done in a safer fashion. Once butchered the locals have a feast of fresh muktuk while scientists collect the lenses from the whale's eyes to enable age and growth rates to be recorded. Another feature of the feast is that of the Inupiat women preparing 'Akutuq' for the hunters. Akutuq, otherwise known as "Eskimo Ice Cream" is made by melting caribou fat in a pot and leaving it to cool. Once it is cool enough to stir with bare hands it is whipped to mix air into it and then flavoured with either berries or sometimes shredded meat.

It is not only the landing of the whale that has been compromised by climate change. The whale meat has for more than two millennia been stored in cellars cut directly into the permafrost below the level of the Inupiat dwellings. In recent years the meat has been thawing during the warmer months causing it to spoil. Since all members of the community get a share in the bounty of a whale kill the problem of thawing affects the entire community, but for those deemed below the poverty line it creates the greatest hardship. The settlement of

Point Hope is famous for its archaeological remains of Inupiat semi subterranean houses dating back over two thousand years. Remains found in these dwellings confirm that hunting bowhead whales has gone on at this location since the ancestors of our modern Inupiat first inhabited the area. The area does receive large subsidies via various government agencies but the withdrawal of multinational oil giant Shell has meant that much anticipated funds from oil revenues and jobs will not be realised.

Four hundred kilometres east along Alaska's North Slope is

the settlement of Barrow. Since December 1st 2016, this settlement has been officially renamed "Utqiagvik", an Inupiat name meaning "Place where snowy owls were hunted". With a population of around four thousand four hundred it is the largest town on Alaska's North Slope. It is also the most prosperous due to both funds from an indigenous people settlement agreement with the government and oil revenues. Of the local population around sixty percent are indigenous, the other forty percent being of a wide mix, most being involved in the oil business.

On first being viewed it gives the impression of being a 'new frontier town' but that is certainly an illusion. The original settlement by the Inupiat has been dated at around AD500 as the remains of seventeen semi-subterranean sod houses have revealed. Most of this type of dwelling across the region incorporated whale bones in their construction. As timber was not available, roof beams were made from ribs and jawbones of large baleen whales, either grey or bowhead. Evidence like this makes it clear that the hunting of large whales is part of the genetic heritage of the North Slope's indigenous people and no-one should have the audacity to say that these people should refrain from hunting. However, unlike Point Hope where the percentage of people living in poverty is quite high, the poverty rate in Utqiagvik is stated to be around 8.6 %. This relative opulence has enabled the whale hunters of Utqiagvik to use twenty first century technology. This includes what one local cynic refers to as the traditional speedboat and traditional loader.

As the bowhead whales head west then south through the Bering Straits to escape the Arctic winter they pass close by Point Barrow. At the first sight of a whale blowing the hunters launch their outboard powered speedboat and head toward the giant creature. On board they are armed with a harpoon gun with an exploding harpoon ready to fire. This modern weapon reduces the danger associated with using a hand thrown harpoon at close quarters as used by those brave souls at Point Barrow. The power of the massive outboard also means that the hours of exhausting paddling by crews of skin covered Umiaks is a thing of the past for the high tech whalers of Utqiagvik. Towing the whale home is now a much easier job requiring fewer men and much less time as engine horse power replaces Inuit man power.

Once ashore the whale is hauled up a slipway by a large Diesel Caterpillar loading machine. This also helps in the dismembering of the animal. Each whale kill is greeted with a party where Muktuk is handed out to all present and although the local indigenous people are still very much fed on a hunter gatherer diet there are often unclaimed quantities of blubber. No longer is this once precious commodity the fuel that supplies light to the Inuit sod house in the long dark winter, this has been replaced by cheap natural gas from the nearby oil fields.

Despite the positive benefits of an increase in the bowhead population there are other factors coming into play that are causing concern to both ecologists and the Inuit hunters of Alaska. Orcas, which in the past have avoided this area are now appearing and hunting young bowhead and grey whales. Lack of sea ice has meant that walrus are now hauling up on shore where they are easily panicked. This causes stampeding adults to injure the juveniles leading to high mortality rates. What effect this is having on the overall population is very difficult to assess as walrus are extremely difficult to accurately count. The fact that the colonies are on shore also means they are further from their feeding grounds. Each year the timing of traditional hunting seasons seem to be changing but the Inupiat will try to cope with the changes as they have always done. But it must be realised that unlike the view held by most people of Inuit being nomadic people travelling thousands of kilometres each year in search of food, those of Alaska's North Slope have always played a waiting game. For millennia the whales came to them each spring and autumn. The question of for how much longer and in what numbers goes unanswered. One tradition that will go on is the "Naluktaq" or "blanket toss", which reputedly had its origins of throwing a lightweight person as high as they could to see further out across the waters of the Beaufort Sea to spot whales. The Naluktaq may continue and may even entertain tourists from the increasing number of vessels traversing the once fabled, now open, North West Passage, but the whale spotting aspect may fade into Inupiat history.

Arctic Canada.
Thousands of kilometres east of Point Barrow, on Nunavut's Baffin Island, is the home the Clyde River Inuit. Unlike the Inupiat of Alaska, the Inuit of Clyde River were the descendants of the nomadic Inuit who had replaced the Thule Culture Inuit around the eighteenth and nineteenth centuries. In reality the Clyde River Settlement was only created by the coming of the Scottish whalers and companies such as Sabellum and Hudson Bay Company in the early twentieth century. It is difficult to establish whether the Clyde River Inuit, or Kangiqtugaapingmuit as they are named in Inuktitut, could really claim to have had a culture of hunting large whales on a regular basis. But the fact that they hunted them once the commercial world was thrust upon them is in little doubt. The current inhabitants of the settlement, which has a population of around nine hundred proudly and vociferously, declare "Our ancestors were whalers!" However for many years they had not hunted the whale. The reason behind this was that back in nineteen seventy one a group of people opposed to sealing and whaling was set up in Vancouver, on the far side of the continent, thousands of kilometres from the subsistence hunters of Clyde River. This group grew into what we all now know as "Greenpeace". The establishment of this organisation was to bring hardship, misery and even death to the people of the North for decades to come. Within a year of Greenpeace being founded the Federal Government had imposed a ban on all commercial whaling and although this did not include the subsistence hunting it did impact on Inuit settlements.

Open condemnation by Greenpeace and its members of the Inuit killing marine mammals had a devastating effect on Inuit society. Throughout the nineteen seventies suicide rates soared among young Inuit males. Many of these were young men with families who suddenly felt that their personal worth was so diminished that they could no longer continue. The law and the view of the outside world regarding their hunting made it impossible for them to feed their families without the aid of government handouts and this was too much for many once proud providers to bear. No arctic settlement has a graveyard devoid of young Inuit who have taken their own life. Others turned to the white man's poison of alcohol. Even after the Federal Government introduced quotas to allow the Inuit to resume hunting in nineteen ninety one the pressure from the outside world was so great that the Inuit harpoons were left unused.

In August 2014 things changed.

Across the frigid waters of Patricia Bay a fleet of six umiaks paddled toward a bowhead whale. From the bow of one of the umiaks an Inuit woman thrust her explosive tipped harpoon into the sixteen metre long giant. The monster replied by thrashing its flukes and sending one of the umiaks' crew into the air. Luckily they fell back into the boat but their boat was so damaged that they were forced to retreat to safety. The other umiaks moved in and continued to thrust harpoons into the whale. Then after nearly an hour and a half the giant was lying dead on the surface. This was the first bowhead killed by the Kangiqtugaapingmuit for a hundred years.

Once hauled ashore, amidst a swarm of photographers and newspaper men, the task of cutting the whale into the traditional muktuq began. Both muktuq and the whale meat were distributed among the people of both Clyde River and the surrounding area. The actual butchering was carried out over fifteen kilometres away from the settlement so that the problem of marauding polar bears scavenging on the remains would pose no risk to Clyde River inhabitants. While the hunters and all the other assembled parties were taking part in the festivities a strange and unexpected message arrived. Greenpeace were congratulating the Kangiqtugaapingmuit on their successful hunt. Some people at first thought it must be a hoax, but it was not. The actual Greenpeace statement read as follows:-

"Greenpeace respects the rights of Clyde River and other

indigenous communities to sustainable, traditional hunting and fishing."

This, needless to say, was viewed by many with extreme contempt. Why, many were asking, would an organisation that had contributed to the hardships and to the suicides of Inuit across the Arctic be acknowledging that these people actually had the right to hunt in the manner that their ancestors had for millennia? The answer was clear to many and was easily found in another part of the Greenpeace statement:-

" Baffin Bay is a critical habitat for bowhead whales, which brings into question the National Energy Board's recent approval of seismic testing for oil and gas in those same waters.----
---- If seismic testing is permitted , marine mammals, including bowhead whales, could suffer permanent damage and a disruption of their migration patterns, which could have adverse effects on the population and on the Inuit people's ability to carry out their sustainable, traditional hunt."

Farrah Khan, Greenpeace Spokesperson.

This acknowledgement that the Inuit had the right to hunt sustainably allied to the need of Greenpeace to have the backing of the Inuit to fight Arctic development surely marks a turning point in the field of ecosystem conservation. The feeling that times and attitudes are changing was reflected in a statement that day by Clyde River's mayor Jerry Natanine who said:-

"The times are a changing and I'm glad to be part of it."

If the generation of Inuit children can forgive those who brought on their loss of fathers and the new generation of Greenpeace activists, many of whom were not even born during these darker times, work together to preserve both the wildlife and way of life in the Arctic things might get better.

The three regions of Nunavut now have annual hunts for bowhead whale. As well as the Clyde River hunt there are hunts conducted from Chesterfield Inlet in Kivalliq and Kugaaruk in Kitikmeot.

The bowhead is not the only species hunted by the Inuit. Whether the current levels of exploitation of these other species are sustainable is subject of debate among all concerned parties in the region and beyond. The two species that, I think, warrant most concern are the Beluga and the Narwhal.
Estimates vary as to the overall numbers of beluga. This is not surprising as this species is highly mobile and individuals frequently move from one pod to another and therefore can either be missed in a count or, more likely, counted more than once. Most estimates seem to be averaging around one hundred and fifty thousand. Scientific studies, using the latest DNA technology has established that the overall population is made up of many individually unique genotypes, which inhabit well defined territorial zones. Occasionally these territories may overlap but in general they are isolated from each other. A parallel may be drawn with the unique genotypes of Atlantic salmon, where each population is unique to its natal river. This leaves the whole population at risk if pollution or access to the spawning grounds becomes an issue. If pollution causes a total wipe out of in-river juvenile stock over a period of years salmon will no longer return to that river to spawn. Even stocking non-indigenous stock is difficult unless a genotype very similar to that of the original stock can be found. The situation with Beluga is very similar. The one benefit of having separate stocks is that they are easier to monitor and this makes assessment of conservation status more accurate. It also makes it easier to spot problematic trends before they become irreversible.

In the case of the unique beluga population of the Gulf of St Lawrence studies have indicated some worrying problems which could lead to serious depletion of beluga numbers in the future. This, considering that there is no hunting of the species in that area, is worrying. The St. Lawrence stock is the only beluga stock considered to be outside "Arctic" waters. The reason that this population exists is that it colonised the Gulf of St. Lawrence just after the last glacial period ended about ten thousand years ago. The flow of cold water coming down from the Labrador Coast flows up the gulf hugging the depths before hitting the sill between the Gaspe Peninsula and the North Shore east of the Saguenay Fjord. This causes an upwelling of nutrient rich water from the depths to mix with the warmer surface waters, which in turn triggers a massive plankton bloom. From this plankton bloom a whole food chain is established, including food to sustain both baleen whales and toothed cetaceans. Back at the start of the twentieth century it was estimated that the beluga population of the St. Lawrence numbered around ten thousand. This did not please either commercial fishermen or salmon anglers who fished the world famous salmon rivers of both the Gaspe Peninsula or the rivers on the Quebec North Shore. From eighteen eighty to nineteen fifty an estimated fifteen thousand beluga were killed. What may be partially responsible for this large and unsustainable cull was that in nineteen twenty eight the Government of Quebec offered a $15 (Canadian) for every beluga carcass landed. Culling ceased in nineteen seventy nine, but full legal protection for the St. Lawrence beluga was not implemented until nineteen eighty three. When one considers that it is over thirty years since hunting ceased it would be reasonable to assume that the St. Lawrence population would be showing signs of recovery, but that is not the case. At the time culling ceased the population was estimated at between six and seven hundred. Up until the year two thousand increasing numbers were noted with the population peaking in the early years of the new millennia at around one thousand. Since then a decline in the overall population was noted, this was across all age components of the stock.

At one time it was thought that beluga lived for between thirty five and fifty years. More recent research has now put it at nearer our own human life expectancy at seventy to eighty years and similar to humans they do not breed much over forty years of age. This means that of the estimated two thousand and twelve population of eight hundred and eighty nine only about three hundred could be regarded as of breeding age. If numbers of male and females are equal, as is common in many mammalian species, this reduces the potential of breeding females to around one hundred and fifty. If these females were to produce a calf every year population recovery might be rapid, but that is not the case. At best a healthy female beluga can produce a calf every three years, reducing the potential annual recruitment to around fifty calves. Even this figure is over optimistic as, although the average age of female first calving is between eight and nine years, fertility starts to reduce at around twenty five years with menopause being no later than forty one years of age. Taking all these factors into account it does not leave much optimism for recovery. All of this is without the factors of habitat pollution, climate change and human interference.

Looking at the problems faced by the beluga which are thought to be associated with pollution and one sees parallels with some which are similar amongst the human populations who live in areas where environmental pollution is rife.

When humans live in an environment where carcinogenic chemicals are rife we expect to see high rates of cancers, whales living in polluted waters are no different. From nineteen thirty three through to nineteen ninety eight autopsies carried out on one hundred and nineteen beluga revealed that eighteen percent had died of cancer. Of nine beluga found dead in the St. Lawrence in nineteen ninety nine, three were found to have cancerous tumours. Despite modern laws to control pollution and marine dumping the seabed will take centuries to recover from over a century of uncontrolled dumping from industries upstream on both sides of the St. Lawrence River.

Human interference, not including hunting, is in the main the destruction of marine habitat. But this is not the major cause for concern in the St. Lawrence. Since 2008 numbers of dead beluga calves have turned up on the beaches. Most of these calves were emaciated, showing signs of starvation and yet food for the adult beluga was still plentiful. So why would calves be going unfed if the mothers were able to obtain plenty of food to produce milk? This enigma is thought to be caused by the manner in which mother and calf communicate. Belugas are also known as "sea canaries" and use a wide range of sounds for both echolocation of food and for communication among members of the pod, including calves. If the frequency of the sounds used, to either summon the calf for feeding or the calves to find their mothers, is interrupted the calves may get separated from the mothers. Since the waters of the St. Lawrence are particularly turbid and belugas sight is poor the chances of finding by sight are approaching zero. The problem of this interruption of sound interference is thought to be caused by the vibration frequency of outboard motors overlapping that of the belugas. One of the main areas of this happening may be where "whale watching" trips in large outboard powered rigid inflatable boats, otherwise known as Ribs, are used. In 2012 the number of dead calves found was sixteen, but there may have been others that did not get washed ashore and counted. This is more than a significant percentage of the juvenile population. If losses on this scale were to continue the future for this unique sub-arctic population of this most charismatic of cetaceans would be really bleak. Since the 3rd May 2016 the St. Lawrence beluga have been classified as endangered.

Elsewhere in the Arctic, other beluga populations are also causing concern. In 2006 the beluga of Alaska's southern shore around the Cook Inlet were designated as "Critically Endangered" under the Endangered Species Act. To understand just how a collapse in an isolated stock can happen in a relatively short time one only needs to look at the Cook Inlet population figures since 1979 as published by the National Oceanic & Atmospheric Administration (NOAA). The NOAA aerial surveys taken between 1979 and 1989 indicated a resident beluga population in the order of 1,300. By 1994 this had declined to 653, a fifty percent reduction in just five years. Things only got worse when in 1998 the population was counted at 347. At this time the indigenous Alaskans were not subject to any restrictions on numbers of animals killed as their activities were classed as an "Unregulated Subsistence Hunt". This triggered a reduction in beluga hunting in 1999, but despite this the population has continued to decline. In 2014 it was counted at 340, which indicated that although still in decline this was not as rapid as previous years. If declines like this can happen in the Cook Inlet are they likely to happen elsewhere across the north where indigenous hunting still carries on?

Canada have for a number of years controlled indigenous subsistence hunts by using a quota system which allows, in theory at least, the hunting of species otherwise covered by the Endangered Species Act in a sustainable manner. In the case of beluga this has been since 1980. The only problem with such a system is that it relies on not only nature to remain stable but also for those covered by the quota system to adhere strictly to that system. Occasionally these requirements do not hold and the outcome is that no-one benefits in the long run, including the protected species. So what happens when nature decides it is time to throw a curved ball? This is exactly what happened to one Inuit community in February 2013. Sanikiluaq, which is the semi-autonomous Inuit Region of Nunavut's most southern community, lies on the Belcher Islands in Hudson Bay. With a population of 882 (2016) it is a very poor area where subsistence hunting is almost essential for not only cultural survival but also a buffer against starvation and malnutrition. What happened in February 2013 may have been viewed by the local Inuit as a gift from whatever god they worshipped, but was certainly not of benefit to the welfare of the East Hudson Bay beluga. This component of the Hudson Bay stock is currently viewed as threatened while the nearby James Bay component is in a much healthier state. Which of the two stocks were involved in the following incident is still unclear. What actually happened was due to weather conditions a large pod of belugas were trapped under the ice with only limited access to open water as breathing holes. Initially the Inuit thought that there were about twenty belugas trapped under the ice and these were being mauled by polar bears every time they came up to breath. A communal decision was made to catch all the trapped whales rather than let the bears kill or main them. This figure proved to be a severe underestimate as the final tally amounted to over seventy being killed of which the bears killed and ate twenty. During the time the Inuit were catching the belugas two marauding polar bears were also shot as they were becoming aggressive and a danger to the Inuit hunters. Many of the whales caught by the Inuit had already been mauled by the bears. In some cases they had potentially fatal wounds and if they had not been culled by the hunters may have died in any case and not have been counted. How many others succumbed to injuries and died under the ice will never be known.

Was it better that the Inuit culled the pod or leave them to be mauled and either eaten by bears or die under the ice? My own view is that the decision taken by the Inuit of Sanikiluaq was the correct one – even if it did exceed their given annual quota. More recently, in the Semi-Autonomous Inuit Region of Nunavik, a new quota system has been set up to protect beluga stocks in the region. In theory this complex quota system has been set up to prevent the over exploitation of the East Hudson Bay component of beluga. Again, theoretically there are four component stocks in the region, all of which are genetically unique. These are the East Hudson Bay, James Bay/Long Island, West Hudson Bay and the Ungava Bay. The latter of which is thought to no longer exist. Scientifically speaking the Ungava component cannot officially be termed extinct as it is not a unique species. The term used by the scientific community for this type of "extinction from an area of natural habitat" is "extirpation". So the object of the latest quota system is to prevent not the "extinction" of the East Hudson Bay beluga, but their "extirpation". How this is to be achieved has obviously been worked out by a politician with the mindset of a Mississippi river boat gambler for calculating gambling odds. The official figure of beluga allowed to be taken in the three

years up to 31st January 2020 is 187. This figure is somewhat misleading as the actual figure that will be taken could be as high as 387, according to the Makivik Corporation who look after Inuit affairs in the region. How this figure has been arrived at is that depending on where and when a beluga is killed it might not be counted as a "whole" beluga. If, for example, a beluga is killed up in the Hudson Strait and is proven by DNA samples to be a West Hudson Bay beluga it doesn't count toward the quota. If a beluga from one of the other listed stocks is killed, but is not, by DNA samples, an East Hudson Bay beluga, it may count as little as one tenth of a beluga toward the quota. It is hoped that by doing this the Inuit hunters will send in samples with the view to increasing their own local quota, as the total quota has been divided up among the various Inuit communities in the area.

One problem that hasn't been taken into account is that of bioaccumulation of toxins. This applies to both Beluga and Narwhal. Bioaccumulation is the effect of toxins such as POPs, (persistent organophosphates), and PCB's, (poly-chlorinated bi-phenols) building up in an organism which is then consumed by another creature where it again becomes even more concentrated. With each stage up the food chain it increases the level of toxicity until it reaches lethal levels.

If the levels of bio- accumulated toxins in the Canadian Belugas are even approaching those of the seals and narwhals that are causing problems with breast feeding Inuit children across the sea in Greenland should the Inuit be eating them? This question is really difficult to answer as hunting beluga is part of Inuit culture as well as a significant part of these indigenous people's diet. If beluga hunting were totally banned it might enable the beluga populations to regenerate to a sustainable level well above the current levels of concern. That then would leave the problem of feeding the Inuit population. If the numbers of larger baleen whales were such that they could sustain a larger cull, this might be an answer. As baleen whales, despite their massive size, are placed lower in terms of the biotic pyramid the chances are they will be a degree of toxicity lower.

The comparison in terms of position in the number of stages up the food web of Baleen Whales versus Toothed Cetaceans is as follows:-

Baleen Whales:- Phytoplankton—Zooplanktons—Krill—Baleen Whale = 4 stages

Toothed Cetaceans:- Phytoplankton—Zooplanktons—Krill—Fish—Beluga = 5stages.

Although this looks like eating Baleen Whales may be only twenty percent less toxic than eating Beluga that is not how it works. The higher up the food chain the greater the concentration becomes as the larger a creature is the more it has to consume to maintain its energy levels. By consuming a greater weight of these toxins, which it can only dispose of through faecal waste or in the case of mammals and birds via egg yolk or breast milk, each stage up the chain is proportionately higher.

In general the toxin levels accumulated in invertebrates and fish are much lower than those found in birds and mammals. Mammals are warm blooded creatures and require much higher calorific intake to maintain their body temperature and also to grow. Since this requires a higher food intake they ingest more toxins. Fish and a variety of other marine organism are very different as they are able to rid themselves of a proportion of the pollutants. In the case of fish this is achieved via the gills.

If the accumulated toxins found in the St. Lawrence beluga are responsible for the cancerous tumours found during the autopsies is there not a case for closing the beluga hunting and giving the Inuit greater quotas of baleen whales? Surely this is preferable to exposing the indigenous people of the Arctic to potential cancer risks emanating from the industrialised societies.

Narwhal Hunting.

The narwhal and its close relative the beluga are the only two members of the Monodontidae family. Unlike the beluga which is frequently found inshore in shallow estuaries the narwhal is a creature of the deep waters. The name narwhal means the "corpse whale" being derived from the "Old Norse" words Nar, meaning corpse and Kval, meaning whale. Whether it was so named as the Vikings thought it looked like a bloated drowned corpse or because it often would lie still on the surface is still under discussion.

The total number of the Narwhal population also seems uncertain with estimates varying from fifty thousand to almost treble that number. The WWF puts its current overall population at around 80,000. However, one Canadian source puts the Canadian population at that same number and reckons that is about 75% of the overall worldwide population. Whereas the accepted conservation status is that of "Near Threatened" the Canadian authorities list it as of "Special Concern". Whatever status you accept there is little doubt that this species is going to be affected by climate change. Neither narwhal nor beluga has a dorsal fin. This evolutionary adaption enables them to hunt close under the icepack without the risk of damaging such an appendage. The Orca, otherwise known as the "killer whale", does have a dorsal. This fin, which can be over 1.5 metres high in the case of large bulls, prevents the orcas from hunting under all but loose ice floes. This inability to hunt in the northern ice pack has prevented the orcas from actively pursuing the much slower moving narwhals in the icebound areas of the Canadian Arctic Archipelago. How long this will remain the

case is a real cause for concern as the earlier breakup and later formation of the winter ice has seen packs of orcas move further north. In the case of the Pacific the orcas have gone through the Bering Straits and have been seen hunting of the North Slope of Alaska in areas where they had previously been absent.

With problems of climate change looming it is hardly surprising that some conservation organisations are less than happy about the Inuit hunting that they perceive to be unsustainable.

The narwhal has a lifespan of around fifty years and with breeding and stock recruitment similar to that of its nearest relative, the beluga, faces the same problems. Large males weigh around 1900kg with the smaller females being about 1550kg maximum. Due to their size and habitat their only serious predator up to now has been man. Polar bears do take narwhal but this is usually confined to juveniles.

A further problem that faces this species is that of chemical and metallic contamination. Cadmium and zinc were found at high levels in the kidney while the liver showed elevated levels of both lead and copper. As climate change will enable the increase of mining in the Canadian Arctic it is likely that this problem will get worse. In the case of chemical pollution, the narwhals' diet is the primary source of both persistent organophosphates and poly-chloronated-byphenols, (POP's and PCB's). The Greenland halibut makes up a large percentage of narwhal food and as it is already high up in the biotic pyramid it contributes greatly to the bioaccumulation of chemical contaminants in narwhals. Narwhals are a major source of food for the Inuit in the Disko Island/ Uummannaq area of Greenland where young Inuit girls are advised not to breastfeed because of chemical bio-accumulation. So for this reason alone a case may be made to encourage a reduction in consumption of narwhal meat across the whole Arctic region.

Both Canadian and Greenlandic Inuit hunt narwhal and although many countries have banned the import of the narwhal tusks they are still regarded as a valuable source of revenue to many Inuit hunters. In some parts of both Canada and Greenland hunting of narwhal, or "tuugaalik", is done in the traditional method of harpooning from kayaks. With this method once a narwhal is harpooned it rarely can escape and will become part of the counted annual harvest. A problem arises when modern speedboats and high powered rifles replace the traditional harpoon. Often when shooting from either boat or from the ice along open leads the narwhal will dive under ice if not killed outright. This not only causes prolonged suffering to the animal but also means that the number killed will be very different to the number recorded as harvested. On one documented hunt a hunter admitted to shooting fourteen narwhal but only harvested two. His main concern was not that twelve wounded creatures would needlessly die under the ice but that thousands of dollars worth of tusk was lying on the seabed. I know from personal experience that this is not the general attitude of indigenous hunters but it only takes a few on this scale to cause damage to both the species hunted and the general perception of the public worldwide regarding a sympathetic view of subsistence hunters.

Much of what has been said about the beluga also applies to the narwhal and similar incidents to that of the beluga being trapped under the ice have occurred with narwhal. Needless to say when this does happen the actions and comments of both the hunters and the anti-hunting "conservation lobby" are similar to the beluga case.

One such incident occurred in December 2015 near Pond Inlet at the north end of Baffin Island. A large pod of narwhal became trapped under ice and were unable to either escape or find enough open water in which to use as breathing stations. As it was obvious to both the Inuit hunters and the Canadian officials at the Federal Fisheries and Oceans Ministry that these creatures would either die of hunger or drown the decision was made to harvest them. The Nunavut Wildlife Management also sanctioned this action. Two hundred and thirty animals trapped under the ice were harvested by the Inuit, eighteen were taken by polar bears and fifteen were lost. The Canadian Government were severely criticised for not sending an icebreaker to free the trapped narwhals. The fact that the nearest available ice breaker would have taken a week to get there didn't seem to register with the anti-hunt supporters. If the Government had sent the icebreakers it would not have made any difference as the narwhals could not have survived that length of time.

The food and financial value of the tusks were of great benefit to the local community and to the polar bears. Dead narwhals under the ice are of little benefit to anyone or to the arctic ecosystem overall. This incident is not the only mass entrapment of narwhal in the Pond Inlet area in recent years. Back in December 2008 the local hunters harvested around six hundred animals under similar circumstances.

It has to be noted that these cases of narwhal and beluga being trapped are not being seen as directly caused by the current situation regarding climate change as these types of incident have occurred and been documented over the past decades as far back as the eighteenth century. But we cannot be complacent about climate change as its effects in the Arctic are occurring at approximately double the speed of elsewhere on the planet.

Walrus Hunting.

Walrus have always been part of Inuit culture and mythology as well as one of the main species on which survival depended. Although there is only one species of walrus, Odobenus rosmarus, the population throughout the Arctic region is regarded as three different subspecies.

The largest component of the overall stock, which is estimated at around 230,000, is that of the Pacific Walrus, O.r . divergens, which was estimated at 200,000 in 1990. It is also the largest physically with large bulls weighing in excess of 2,000kg. The range of this component is from the Wrangle Islands north of Russia in the Chukchi Sea east to the Canadian Arctic in the Beaufort Sea. The hunting of this stock in the was never as intense as that of the walrus in the Atlantic and hence its numbers can withstand a controlled hunt without creating conservation issues. The Eskimo Walrus Commission (EWC) was set up in Alaska in 1978 by Kawarak Inc. To represent the walrus hunting interests of the nineteen Inuipiat communities between Bristol Bay and point Barrow. This protected both the indigenous people's hunting rights and the overall Pacific Walrus population within US waters. It did not, however, cover the stock to the west which was in waters controlled by the Chuckota Autonomous Okrug in Arctic Russia. This problem has been resolved by the US. Fish and Wildlife Service working closely with the authorities in Chuckota. Both regions now carry out annual walrus hunts in a sustainable manner.

The Atlantic Walrus, O.r.rosmarus, was the subject of excessive hunting pressure from the seventeenth century onward. With its range at one time covering as far south as the Gulf of St. Lawrence, east beyond Russia's Kola Peninsula and west to the islands of the Canadian Arctic Archipelago, it has now been extirpated from much of that range. Only the occasional stray walrus is found in the Barents Sea area of Northern Norway where once the ancient Komsa people would have regularly hunted it as a food source. Even in the northern Islands of

Svalbard it was almost hunted to the point of no return. Thankfully it appears to be re-establishing colonies on the shingle bars of the Nordaust Svalbard Nature Reserve where the Norwegian Authorities have imposed strict rules on both scientists and cruise ship tourists. After a period of absence returning walrus tended to be mainly groups of bulls but in more recent years cows and calves have reappeared. This gives one hope that elsewhere in their historic territories they may be re-established.

The mid-eighteenth century to the early twentieth century saw the near extinction of the large baleen whales in the North Atlantic from the hunting activities of European and American whaling fleets. As the number of whales reduced attention was turned to both seals and walrus as alternative sources of "whale oil". The skins were also used to produce leather. This wholesale slaughter, prior to WW1, drastically reduced the number of walrus in Canadian and Greenlandic waters. The once prolific walrus of the Magdalen Islands in the Gulf of St. Lawrence were extirpated once the white man arrived. Previously the local Micmaw Indians of Quebec hunted them in the winter months when herds of eight to ten thousand walrus would come ashore. Occasionally a walrus is sighted west of Newfoundland in the Gulf of St. Lawrence but, as of now, no positive signs of any recolonisation have been noted. The situation elsewhere in the North West Atlantic, in both Canadian and Greenlandic waters, is that of isolated colonies with stable numbers due to quota controls on numbers of animals harvested. The most recent estimate of Atlantic Walrus numbers is a figure of around twenty thousand.

In some areas the walrus meat and blubber is only seen as being good for dog food. There is little doubt that dogs thrive on this better than on caribou meat which in comparison is deficient in calorific content. Elsewhere the situation is very different.

On Baffin Island and across on the west side of Nunavut and

Alaska the Inuit delicacy of "Igunaq" is highly valued food. Basically it is fermented walrus blubber and meat. Believed to be an excellent body building food the Inuit insist that in areas where Igunaq is eaten the men are more muscular. The reputation of its fragrance, more often referred to as "gut wrenching stench" by non –Inuit, is widespread. Rolls of walrus blubber and meat are buried in shore gravel for around five months and allowed to ferment. Not only is the quality of the meat important the gravel in which it is buried is also crucial to the quality of the finished product. That is presuming that whoever buries the stuff is fortunate enough to be able to dig it up before the polar bears get there. Quite often the bears with their super sense of smell will locate the cashed meat and dig it up with amazing enthusiasm. This despite the Inuit having placed massive boulders and flat rocks over it as a deterrent. Two areas which are famed among the Inuit for the high quality of their Igunaq are Igloolik and Hall Beach on Baffin Island which are said to have the perfect gravel for Igunaq production. Eating walrus meat is not without its dangers. Two particularly problematic health risks associated with eating walrus are those of botulism toxins and the parasitical worm which causes Trichinosis. The latter of these two problems, Trichinella parasites, is often found in both walrus and (more often) in the meat of polar bears. Where walrus meat is being used to make iguaq it is important to ensure that the animal from which the meat is sourced is free of this parasite. The reason this is so important is that the trichonella can readily survive the process of fermentation required to make this Inuit delicacy. To ensure that the meat is free of the parasitical infection the Nunavik Research Centre in Kuujjuaq supplies the hunters in both Nunavik and Nunavut with sampling kits. Once the laboratories receive the samples they have them processed within twenty four hours and the results sent back to the hunter. While they await the results the meat is frozen and only if the tests give the all clear is the igunak buried. In the case of botulism, this is spotted using the colour of the blubber, if it is dark don't eat it. Another point raised is that Botulism thrives in anaerobic conditions, so it has never to be stored in air tight plastic containers. Problems with both these health risks have reduced in recent years but nevertheless caution is required whenever walrus meat is to be eaten.

The third and smallest component of the walrus stock is that of the Laptev Sea Walrus, O. r. laptevi, which is thought to number between five and ten thousand. This sub-species is thought to be more closely related to the Pacific Walrus than the Atlantic Walrus. So close genetically that some scientists think it should be deemed part of the Pacific stock. The Laptev Sea lies between the Taymyr Peninsula, to the west, and the New Siberian Islands, to the east, on the north coast of Siberia. The Laptev walrus are known to be contaminated due to pollution from the industries which surround Lena River which drains into the Laptev Basin and for this reason they would not be advised as a food source. Despite the fact that these walrus are not hunted their conservation status is of greater concern than that of the other two subspecies.

One serious cause for concern to all the Inuit people, from Chukota east to Greenland is that walrus of all three sub-species are vulnerable to the effects of climate change. The problem of having less ice enabling orcas into hitherto inaccessible regions will make them subject to predation, but a more serious problem is that of suitable haul out zones. All walrus use the ice as a base for both nursery and hunting activities. As their main food is clams the ideal haul out is where the ice is over relatively shallow water. As the main Arctic Icepack retreats further from shore the animals will have to travel further towards the shore to feed. This will leave the calves unattended for a longer period as well as create less feeding opportunities for the calf. In recent years this has led to many walrus colonies hauling out on gravel banks where they are then exposed to polar bear attacks. When bears attack and stampede the walrus, many young calves or older infirm animals can and do get injured. In the case where a colony of cows is rearing very young calves it often leads to high mortality rates among juveniles. This problem allied to all the other problems faced by the species make many Inuit Hunters, particularly in Alaska and Nunavut, worry that within a few years the hunting of walrus may cease. If this was to be the case then the current situation of many Arctic dwellers food "insecurity" would only become worse.

Caribou.

From the very first Inuit set foot on North America their survival was intertwined inextricably with that of the caribou. Just like the Sami of the "Warm Arctic" the Inuit people used the skin of the caribou for a multitude of purposes. Clothes, bedding, tent coverings being the main uses. Sinews from the animal were the Inuit's thread. The bones were used for making many household implements before the arrival of the white man and his metal. All this is before we even consider the value of its meat. Where the meat was concerned every bit of the beast was used, even the stomach contents and hooves. The stomach contents invariably contain lichens and mosses that under normal conditions would be toxic if consumed by humans. However, once they have undergone partial digestion and fermentation in the caribou's gut they no longer constitute a danger and become a sought after food. The hooves are allowed to partially ferment to become the Inuit delicacy know as "isigaich", which is sucked from the bone in a semi frozen state.

In many Inuit regions the caribou were hunted by not only the Inuit but by other indigenous people such as the Yupik and Dene people in Alaska and the Innu of Labrador. For centuries, before the Hudson Bay Company helped defuse the situation, it was the hunting of migrating caribou that caused friction between the Iroquois and Inuit in the James Bay area at the south of Hudson Bay. What made the caribou so important to the Inuit was that the hollow hairs of its coat were the perfect insulation for those who lived in temperatures that could regularly drop to below minus forty degrees Celsius. As the quality of the coat varies according to the time of year the Inuit hunters would hunt caribou in late summer or autumn. At this time, when the Antlers were in "velvet", the old coat would have moulted and the new coat would not yet be soiled by either weather or, in the case of the bulls, rutting activities. Much of the meat from animals taken at this time was cashed in a similar manner to that of walrus and seal meat. Buried in shingle with large stones placed on top, to protect it from both wolves and foxes, it was not long before the encroaching winter froze the meat into a rock solid state. The period of time prior to it being thoroughly frozen was little different from the white man's practice of hanging beef or venison for a time to allow it to lose some moisture and 'mature'.

The current situation across Arctic Canada and Alaska is that of drastically low numbers of caribou across the zone north of the tree line. Even in the more sheltered regions of the Boreal Forest numbers have seriously declined. This is not the first occasion in recent times that the caribou numbers have collapsed. Back in the early part of the twentieth century many of the large caribou herds became victims of over exploitation for both meat and more significantly their skins. The sudden availability of guns among the indigenous peoples, not only Inuit but also Innu, Dene and Yupik, to name but a few, meant that hunting as a source of trade goods became common. Although the meat and supply of skins for clothing was still the initial motivation for Inuit hunters any surplus was used to buy goods from the white man. This in turn encouraged the unsustainable killing of thousands of caribou until it reached a point where declining deer numbers made the enterprise uneconomic. Once the hunting returned to sustainable levels, and restraints were put on the culling, numbers improved. Hunting is not regarded as the prime cause of the current decline in caribou stocks. It is thought that the current decline is the accumulated effect of climate change related problems and increased human activities such as mining, road construction and general disturbance of their environment.

As previously stated it is not only the caribou of the tundra that have seen serious decline in numbers but also of those herds which inhabit the Boreal Forest. One herd, the Bathurst Herd, has a range which covers both types of ecosystems. The range covered by this herd is very extensive. Stretching from the shores of the Arctic Ocean in the vicinity of Coronation Gulf in the North, its western flank is roughly from the east end of the Great Bear Lake, through the Great Slave Lake in the North West Territories, to a point south of the Saskatchewan Border. Its most eastern limit is a wavering line from Umingmaktok on the Bathurst inlet in the north, in Nunavut, to just north east of Stony Rapids, in Saskatchewan, in the south. Despite having this enormous range the herd has seen a decline from high of an estimated 450,000 in 1986 to an estimated 20,000 in 2017. A decline of over 90% in thirty years.

Back in 2013 the Boreal Caribou were declared as endangered under the Species at Risk Act (SARA). A following report by two influential groups involved in conservation declared that despite the species now being designated as endangered there was a lack of political will to implement a recovery plan. This report titled "Population Critical: How are Caribou Faring?" was prepared jointly by the David Suzuki Foundation, which is based in Vancouver, British Columbia, and the Canadian Parks and Wildlife Society (CPAWS) which was founded in 1963 with the object of protecting Canada's wilderness areas. The highly critical report which was published in December 2013 looked at the overall situation regarding Canada's caribou.

The initial reasons which were stated as being contributory causes of the Bathurst Caribou Herd decline were as follows:-

Mining operations with their associated disturbance, the noise of which would be totally alien to these animals.

Roads, these cross the paths of the migrating caribou and as they are not a natural feature the deer are wary of crossing them.

Habitat destruction, whether from construction of mines or timber extraction in the Boreal Forest itself reduces the areas in which the herds feel secure.

Other reasons associated with climate change included:-

Increases in both biting flies such as Black-fly, Mosquito and Horseflies, all of which can cause blood loss to an extent that the animal can die. In Scotland, the red deer herds move up the mountains in the summer months to avoid the notorious Scottish midges. On both the Tundra and the in the Boreal Forest the caribou are unable to seek such a refuge. In Labrador, where insect problems are severe, there have been numerous cases of caribou jumping into fast flowing rivers and drowning while trying to avoid swarms of biting insects. In southern areas ticks can carry serious infections that can also be transferred to humans. Other parasitical infections are also becoming more prevalent as winters become milder.

Difficulties in feeding. In the past, the normally extremely cold weather meant that no rain was encountered only snow. Since the nineteen nineties increasingly warmer winters have seen temperatures in both the Boreal Forest and the lower tundra rise above freezing. When this occurs, what would previously have fallen as snow falls as rain. This rain then freezes to form a hard ice barrier on top of the normally soft snow. This hard barrier often prevents the caribou from scraping away the covering of snow to access the lichens which form the main constituent of its winter diet. When this occurs weak and old animals can easily succumb to starvation.

What has annoyed many Inuit in the North West Territories is that while they are now barred from taking caribou from the Bathurst Herd the government are allowing further developments in the mining sector. A further problem is that while there is an enforced ban in the North West Territories, which many Inuit leaders agree is needed, the Government of Nunavut has not agreed to such a ban. This has caused discord among neighbouring Inuit communities either side of the border. Inuit leaders in the North West Territories are saying that without a similar ban in Nunavut their sacrifice of a food source in the name of conservation is pointless.

Over to the east in the semi autonomous Inuit Regions of Nunavik and Nunatsiavut another caribou herd is in serious trouble.

The George River Caribou Herd was at one time regarded as the biggest in the world when in the early 1990's its numbers peaked at over 800,000. Now, less than thirty years later its numbers have crashed to fewer than 30,000, a decrease of over 96%.

This is not the first time this herd has had a catastrophic collapse in numbers. Back in 1958 it dropped to an all time low of around 15,000 before recovering over three decades to reach its record high. The fact that it did recover shows that the natural cycle of species having numerical peaks and troughs applies to the caribou. The main causes of species collapse in the past were in the main natural causes. When the population of a single species becomes too great for the resources within in its natural range it either has a population collapse or increases its range. In the case of the George River Caribou it has done both. During the period before it grew to its maximum the normal annual migration route was a distance of around 3000 kilometres. When it peaked in the early 1990's the annual migration covered a distance of roughly double that at nearly 6,000 kilometres. As the recent collapse was becoming obvious in 2013 the Newfoundland and Labrador Government decided to impose a five year ban on the hunting of George River Caribou. The Inuit in Labrador followed suit when the following year they decided through their own hunting groups to impose a moratorium. Unfortunately the neighbouring Innu people refused to accept these decisions and wanted to carry on hunting but stated that they would reduce their annual cull by 75% from 1200 to 300. Many of the other indigenous groups were unsurprisingly disappointed in this outcome as both the Innu and the Inuit of the Nunatukavut Community Council are members of the Ungava Caribou Aboriginal Round Table which had been set up specifically to protect the number of caribou herds in the district. These herds included the George River Caribou Herd.

Again there were many reasons for the collapse of the herd but one that must seriously be considered is that it was allowed to grow to such an extent that the food pyramid below it had collapsed. When this happens it is the top of the pyramid which shows the greatest reduction, particularly in reproducing. Two similar sort of collapse scenarios are that of the Arctic Lemmings and the European Eagle Owls. Some years, when snow conditions are perfect, lemmings will have much higher than normal survival rates when breeding. When the thaw comes in the spring the numbers of lemmings looking for food vastly outstrips the availability of edible vegetation. This then triggers a mass migration of the tiny rodents in search of new feeding grounds. Often when they reach either wide rivers or lakes the poor sighted little creatures strike out en mass for the other side. Failing to realize the distance causes many of them to drown due to exhaustion and becoming waterlogged. This phenomenon led to the myth that lemmings committed mass suicide. This was aided and abetted by a film supposedly showing thousands of the unfortunate little creatures jumping to their deaths from a cliff overlooking the sea. The film was taken in completely by the public and even today many people are convinced of its authenticity, despite it being a total fraud.

In the case of the European Eagle Owl, its main prey is voles, a relative of the aforementioned lemmings. Like the lemmings the voles will continue to multiply in number until the food source collapses. In the years that they are increasing the number of eagle owl chicks being successfully reared by the parent birds is high. This is fine as long as the vole population is increasing but when it collapses the owls fail to raise young which leads to a collapse in owl numbers. Being large and visible this is very noticeable.

With the caribou the amount of 'deer moss', which is actually a lichen, needed to support the herd is finite, it is also not the fastest growing organism due to where it grows. So when deer numbers go up the foraging area also needs to grow, hence the longer migration taken in the annual cycle. When the migration reaches a point where bare ground is encountered, where previously the lichen was found, the stock collapses due to starvation.

Now that both climate change and human activities are impeding the recovery of lichen cover the availability of caribou as a primary food source in the future is very uncertain throughout the Arctic regions of North America. (see also Appendix 3, Peary Caribou)

Polar Bears.

It would be difficult to write anything about the Arctic in the 21st century without including the current plight of its most "iconic species". Although it is often stated to be the "Apex Predator" anyone who has studied the Arctic in any meaningful form would have to put this magnificent animal in second place behind the resourceful indigenous people of this bleak but fascinating ecosystem. Just draw a diagram of the food web of the Arctic and see what sits at the top.

The Inuit have hunted the polar bear for millennia. They ate its flesh and used its fur to make clothing. The only parts discarded were those, like the liver, which were toxic. In the days before the white man they hunted it using their dogs and spears. After the coming of the white man the spear was replaced with the rifle. Now even the faithful malamute dogs have in many places been replaced by motor driven ski-mobiles and the deliberate and targeted hunting of the bears has all but gone from most of the frozen wilderness that constitutes its home.

One of the few areas where the tradition of polar bear hunting is still carried on is Greenland. Where polar bears are hunted the usual method employed is a high powered rifle complete with telescopic sights poking through a white screen. The screen is mounted on a small sledge which the hunter pushes in front of himself until within range. The screen is just large enough to conceal the hunter from the bear. It is only at the last minute that the barrel of the gun is pushed though the opening in the screen and allow the hunter to make a clean kill. The meat is still eaten, but unlike whale meat it is never eaten raw due to its parasitical infestations which would invariably lead to trichinosis. The use of either ski-mobiles or large powered boats in hunting bears is prohibited and this ensures that the numbers killed are kept to an acceptable and hopefully sustainable level.

Elsewhere, in Canada, where sixty percent of the world's polar bears reside, bears are still hunted but with a quota system that is allocated to the indigenous people. The manner in which this quota is managed in Nunavut is by a lottery system where if a hunter is allocated a tag he has forty eight hours in which to kill a bear. If, within this time, he fails to find and kill a bear his tag is given to another hunter. A hunter may choose to sell his tag to a trophy hunter from out with the Inuit people. In this case the Canadian Government charges a trophy fee of $750C. The hunter keeps the meat and with polar bear skins fetching around $10,000 US the income to an Inuit family is considerable. However, if he sells his tag to a non-Inuit trophy hunter that could see his profit double, or even treble.

In Alaska the situation is different. Only indigenous people with at least one grandparent being classed as indigenous are permitted to hunt polar bears. These indigenous people are not only the Inupiat Inuit but other indigenous people including the Aleuts and Yupik. In the Alaskan case no limit has been imposed on numbers of bears being hunted but it is illegal to sell either the right to hunt the bears or sell its pelt or other body parts to other than another indigenous person. Removing the ability to access hard cash from bear hunting has the effect of keeping the numbers of bears killed down to a sustainable level.

The overall situation regarding polar bears has been the subject of many magazine articles and television programmes in recent years but rarely is the full scenario explained to the public at large. One of the points raised is that of the increasing temperatures leading to habitat loss. This decrease in the overall area covered by snow on the land has seen the range of the grizzly bear moving north. This has meant that the ranges of both polar bear and grizzly bear having a considerable area of overlap. When this happens where two very similar species interface the inevitability of hybridisation occurs. For many years some ecologists have believed that Grizzly bear and polar bear were merely variations of the same species.

The overall picture doesn't look good for the polar bear. As the climate is warming the increased seasonal loss of ice is dramatically reducing the habitat of the remaining bears. The bears of Bear Island, or Bjornoya as it is called in Norwegian, are already confined to the history books. That island is now bereft of the permanent ice habitat required to sustain the polar bear. The future of Svalbard's bears is also uncertain with the accelerating loss of habitat and with it less opportunity for the bears to hunt seals effectively.

However in Alaska and the Northern Territories of Canada, particularly those occupied by the Inuit in the semi-autonomous region of Inuvialuit, a different scenario is emerging.

As already stated, many ecologists have long believed that polar bears and grizzlies are variations of a single species. There is an increasing body of scientific knowledge to support this theory. Where the grizzlies move north and their territories interface with the polar bears there is an increasing incidence of polar bear/grizzly hybrids. These hybrids are not a new discovery as they have been known for many years.

There is an example of one in the Rothschild Museum at Tring in England. This example of polar/ grizzly hybrid was one of many that were bred in zoos in the nineteenth century. The outstanding feature of these hybrids was that they were fertile and able to breed both among themselves and also with both parent species. This clearly indicates that the division between polar and brown bear was not that far in the distant past. The Canadian Broadcasting Company have regularly referred to these hybrids as Grolars, where the male is a grizzly, and Pizzlies, where the male is a polar bear. Another proposed name for the hybrids is that of 'Nanuiak' a combination of the two Inuit names of the bears. Nanuk is Inuitituk for polar bear and Akiak for grizzly bear. The hybrids are not just the result of zoo breeding but have been noted in the wild for many years. As far back as 1864 a hybrid bear was shot at Rendevous Lake in the Barren Lands area of the North West Territories. This bear was described as being 'buffish white with a golden brown muzzle'. More recently a sport hunter shot a hybrid bear on Banks Island, in the North West Territories. This hunter was only spared the prospect of both a fine of C\$ 1,000 and a year in prison when modern DNA technology confirmed that it was indeed a hybrid and not a pale coloured grizzly bear. He had a license to shoot a polar bear but not a grizzly.

Incidents such as these certainly give hope that in the event of our present race of polar bears vanishing that in a future 'ice age', or global cooling event, a new race of white polar bears would emerge. Fossil remain of proto-polar bears in Himalayan regions give support to this hypothesis. Up to a few years ago it was thought that the species diverged as much as five million years ago. More recently scientific sources have estimated that the two species diverged as recently as three hundred and fifty thousand years ago, possibly even less. So although it would be terribly sad if our immediate future was bereft of polar bears there is still the hope they would re-emerge.

One area casing serious concern is that of the increasing

conflict between the polar bears and the humans who inhabit their arctic ecosystem. Increasingly bears are entering the realm of human settlements. In Manitoba this phenomenon has led to the highly publicised polar bear tourist industry in the town of Churchill on the western shore of Hudson Bay. Since the nineteen nineties a fleet of eighteen tundra buggies have transported tourists to watch the migrating bears. The peak time of October and November sees thousands of tourists on bear watching trips contribute to the local economy. In this case the watchers are safely positioned high above the bears in the elevated vehicles, elsewhere encounters with polar bears are not so regulated or nearly as safe. The case on Svalbard in August 2011, where a schoolboy from England's famous Eton College was killed by a polar bear, shocked the world. Yet when one looks at the statistics it should not really have happened nor should it have been such a surprise when it did. Statistics regarding bear attacks on humans in Russia, Canada, Greenland, Norway (including Svalbard) and USA covering a period of one hundred and fifty years have revealed some interesting facts. Of seventy three cases of polar bear attacks sixty three people were injured and twenty people were killed. In most cases the bears were assumed to be in hunting mode rather than in defensive mode. It was also noted that the bears involved in the attacks were observed to be mainly male bears that were presumably hungry. Over the period studied attacks by polar bears averaged around eight per decade up until 2010.

What is now causing increasing concern is that from 2010 onward the number of polar bear attacks appears to have increased significantly, with the 2010 to 2014 period having fifteen confirmed attacks. It was around this time that Arctic ice melt started to accelerate creating less hunting opportunities for the polar bear population. Currently the situation regarding polar bear attacks compared to both brown and black bear attacks is that polar bear attacks can still be viewed as rare. However one must take into account that the areas frequented by both brown and black bears are much more likely to be frequented by humans than the frozen realm of Ursus maritimus.

FOOD INSECURITY.

In recent years we have heard the phrase 'food security' being used as what the media describe as a 'sound bite'. What they actually mean is that we need to produce enough food within our own economic zone, whether that is a country, an island or even a locality which can be isolated, to feed our people in the event of imported food being no longer available. The situation in the Arctic and among the indigenous people of the Arctic is somewhat a different case. Here it is a case of "food insecurity". Since prehistoric times the people of the Arctic have had to deal with issues of food security. Their cultures evolved in a manner that in general was able to resolve many of the problems faced by the hunter gatherer. Methods of preserving food during times of plenty developed over many generations of both the Inuit and the Sami.

Fish were air dried by both cultures. In the Sami regions cod and saithe were hung up to dry in the winter and spring when the frigid air was still too cold for emerging flies to lay their eggs. Once dry these fish would keep for years, only requiring to be rehydrated to become a high protein food source in times of scarcity. It was this practice that helped found the famous Hanseatic trade of the fourteenth century. Although the Hanseatic League was based in Lubeck in Germany, its outposts such as Bergen were dependant on the dried cod of the Sami regions to be profitable. This trade is still going on with the dried cod, or Bacalhau , from the Lofoten Islands annually going south to Portugal and Mediterranean countries. Meat from surplus sheep was also air dried with a minimal addition of salt to help preserve it for the winter months. But as most of the farmed livestock needed for future breeding was kept indoors it was hay that was stored as winter

fodder for the animals. The same system still operates today.
The Inuit traditionally caught Arctic Char and hung it up to dry; this also allowed the oil from its flesh to ooze out. This oil had a high calorific value and was often collected and used in many different ways from food and fuel to preserving harnesses. Caches of dried arctic char were an essential part of the Inuit survival strategy. If the caribou hunt had been poor these caches were of even more significance as they gave the whole population a safety net of both vitamins and protein until the sea ice was thick enough to allow the 'breathing hole' hunting of seals to resume. Although the caribou harvest was always variable the char were usually more reliable and this was a feature of which the Inuit were well aware. They were also wise enough not to over exploit this resource. As the char were hung out in the Arctic sun to dry the vitamin rich oil would drip from the blood red flesh. Drying the fish was the preferred way to preserve it as wood was too precious a commodity to use for smoking. Wood was more wisely used in the building of kayaks, sleds and as harpoon shafts. All of these items were ultimately used in the securing of food.

During the brief Arctic summer both Sami and Inuit would take advantage of the abundance of berries which were available on the tundra. Berries which, thanks to the twenty-four hour daylight with clear blue skies; ripen much faster than the same or similar species which are found further south in temperate climes.

In Arctic Norway the children gathered cloudberries and blueberries, which were preserved in jars, as a rich source of vitamin C to be used throughout the long Arctic night. In the summer months they would have regularly dined on the sweet strawberries which thrive in the fertile soils of the Dalen, or valleys, as far north as North Troms. The twenty four hours of daylight ensured that these berries ripened fast and successions of fruit were available throughout the brief summer to boost the health of the people before winter arrived. From the time the potato was introduced to Arctic

Norway the Sea Sami on the coast cultivated the tubers and stored them in their cellars for winter use and over the years have created their own local varieties which are both disease free and delicious. Other vegetables that could be stored such as carrots were, where possible, grown and stored in the cellars of the Sami dwellings as a short term measure until the winter cod arrived from the offshore waters of the Barents Sea.

On the other side of the Atlantic, the Inuit also made use of the brief summer where and when possible so as to vary their meat based diet. By including the plants and berries found near the coast they were able to attain sufficient levels of essential trace elements and vitamins which were absent or in their main diet of marine based meats and caribou.

Some of the berries which were eaten were found in profusion in areas such as Nunavut's Baffin Island and on the Ungava Peninsula in Nunavik. In other areas like the far north Ellesmere Island berries were not so prolific. But whenever the opportunity arose the Inuit would utilise the resource. Baffin berries, a bit like raspberries, were obviously found on Baffin Island and were one of the many types of berry foraged by Inuit of all ages. Other sought after fruits included cloudberries and blueberries similar to those picked by the Sami children in Norway. Crowberries and wild gooseberries added variety to the selection of fruit which was either eaten fresh or dried to supplement winter stores. One uniquely Inuit way of eating berries was in what is known as Eskimo Icecream.

This Inuit speciality, which is found from Alaska east across Arctic Canada, is known as Akutaq or Agutak in the Inuit language. The name is actually a Yupik word meaning 'something mixed'. The basic ingredients are quite simple, whipped fat or oil from seals to which the berries are added. Like all good ice-cream it can come in different flavours. By varying the source of the fat, to use caribou or moose tallow, and by replacing the berries with leaves of tundra plants or even fish, (freshwater whitefish of the Coregonid genus is a favourite) a whole new world of culinary delight is opened up. Among the tundra plants which were not only used as 'ice-cream' flavouring, but also as a vegetable were the leaves of the dwarf willow, mountain sorrel and willow herb (which is known as fireweed on the western side of the Atlantic). These leaves were either eaten raw or added to the stews and soups of the limited 'hot cuisine' of the Inuit household.

One other plant which was used and is certainly worth a mention is the Labrador Tea Plant. Unlike the tea which is consumed in large quantities in England, this Labrador tea is not a member of the camellia family; it is a member of the rhododendron family. Although there are three types of Labrador Tea, it is Rhododendron groenlandicum which is utilised both in cooking and as a beverage by the Inuit. Like many other members of the Rhododendron family this species is known to be toxic and currently there is insufficient data to indicate what could be regarded as a safe level of consumption as the amount of toxins varies dramatically dependant on the location where the plant is found. The R.groenlandicum is the least toxic of the three found on the lands frequented by the Inuit. Although I am unaware of any fatalities related to its consumption it was recognised that over indulgence could cause diuresis, vomiting and drowsiness. Like most arctic plants it is slow growing and because of this harvesting was carried out in a careful manner to ensure that the supply was sustainable. By only harvesting one leaf from each plant a reliable supply was ensured for generations to come.

It was by adopting these sustainable methods of harvesting and hunting that the indigenous people of the Arctic were able to not just survive but to thrive in such a hostile environment. In comparison with people from other less hostile environments the people of the Arctic were in many ways ahead of the pack when it came to food security. But that was before, in the Inuit case, the arrival of the white man and his profit based society in the 18th century. Following on from this is the current issue of climate change which started in more recent times. Now what were once self sufficient hunter gatherers and subsistence fisher/farmers are facing an uncertain future where the 'food security' of bygone days has been replaced with what may rightfully be termed 'food insecurity'.

Recent climatic changes have seen the whole range of traditional Inuit and Sami way of life alter. The timing of both terrestrial and marine life migration has altered as has the routes of these migrations.

In Arctic Norway the spring thaw has been coming earlier. This in turn not only starts the snow melt swelling the rivers but necessitates the earlier movement of the Sami reindeer herds from their inland wintering grounds to the coastal grazings and offshore islands of both Troms and Finnmarken. The routine of centuries, passed down through generations of Reindeer Sami, has suddenly become a lottery of flooding rivers, exposed ground that allows overgrazing of fragile resources and dangerous swamp and thawing lakes. Swamp that, in times gone by, would have been frozen .Solid and safe for herds and herdsmen to cross. Lakes that would have had ice thick enough to take the weight of the herd and also allow the herdsmen to fish through ice holes for arctic char. Many Sami families feel that the future movements of their herds will not be the predictable time honoured way of their forefathers. If this continues and worsens many reindeer herders may be forced out of the business and this source of high quality protein will be lost.

The movement of fish stocks in the North Norwegian waters is being closely monitored but as Norway has an excellent transport infrastructure the current situation is not one of great concern. Its modern, efficient and hopefully sustainable fleet are both mobile and adaptable. So although the traditional Sami reindeer herders are having climate related problems the majority of the Sami people have currently little to worry them on the climate change front. For the Sami, food insecurity as a whole should not be a problem over the next few years.

Across the Atlantic the story is very different. Climate change is already taking a severe toll on the 'cold arctic' ecosystem. The Inuit are much more dependent on wild food. All the creatures upon which they depend to feed their families are experiencing problems. All across the North, from Alaska to Greenland, caribou numbers have, as previously mentioned, collapsed. Beluga whales are facing serious problems, including the added problem of predation from increasing numbers of orcas. Walrus hunts have failed as the walrus struggle with decreasing ice and having to travel further to find food. The narwhals are not appearing when expected in Western Greenland's fjords. Lack of stable, safe sea ice is creating difficulties in the areas where 'breathing hole' seal hunting was traditionally carried out. Increasing fresh water flowing from Greenland's glaciers and ice sheet has created problems for those shooting seals from boats. Even the collecting of berries has been affected. In the 2016 book 'The Caribou Taste Different Now', which is a collection of anecdotal evidence from Inuit leaders, the subject of berries is well stated. Taken across all four of Canada's Inuit Regions, this book takes a serious look at the effects of climate change on Canada's Inuit population.

Eiljah Panipakoochoo, an Inuit from Pond Inlet on Baffin Island, states not only the facts but also the reasons for changes in the annual berry harvest:-

" The paurngait (crowberries) don't grow as much now because they depend on sunlight, and it's never really sunny here now. --- They don't grow big. The fruits are much smaller. --- There are more blackberries and blueberries, and they grow earlier now. Blueberries used to grow in the middle of August, but now they grow earlier and there are more but they don't bloom or ripen as much as before."

The fact that he mentions the lack of sunshine indicates the tremendous knowledge and understanding that the older generations had of the natural world. He has clearly analysed the situation and come to the correct conclusion. The clouds that now prevent the berries from ripening are also the cause of rain falling on the snowfields to form ice that prevents the caribou feeding.

Another elder, Ham Annie Peterloosie, is quoted as saying:-

"When there were many caribou near Pond Inlet, they would step on the blackberries, blueberries and mountain heather. That's why there weren't any blueberries and blackberries, but now there are no caribou, there are more blueberries and blackberries."

Again this indicates the understanding of nature and also demonstrates that nature abhors a vacuum. The loss of the caribou has seen an increase in berries, but if the berries are failing to ripen they will not be the equivalent of the food lost by the collapse in caribou numbers.

The people of the Arctic have never found the procurement of food an easy task. Seldom have they found themselves in a situation of surplus. This fact of life is something that can only be described as indelibly stamped in both their culture and their DNA. However, the situation they now find themselves in is very different from anything they have experienced in the past.

Among the Sami the problem is not as acute for in the past fifty years many of their people have moved away from subsistence farming and fishing. While many are still involved in the fishing industry it is with modern boats and equipment. Others are involved in tourism or work in Scandinavia's booming manufacturing industries. Wages in Arctic Norway are high and the standard of living for the indigenous people is comparable to that of the Norwegian population. Starvation is not an issue with the Sami.

The situation in both Alaska and Canada's Inuit territories is very different.

The World Health Organisation definition of food security reads as follows:-

"When all people at all times have access to sufficient, safe, nutritious food to maintain a healthy and active life."

Canada is one of the world's wealthiest countries. Surely the WHO definition of food security would apply in such an affluent society. It may apply in the cities just north of the US border, all the way from Halifax, Nova Scotia in the East to Victoria on Vancouver Island in the West, but the situation in the frozen north Arctic wastelands of Inuit Semi Autonomous regions of Nunatsiavut, Nunavik, Nunavut and Nunatsiavut the facts and statistics tell a very different story.

In 2014 a study carried out by the Canadian Council of Academies in the Inuit Semi Autonomous Region of Nunavut revealed alarming statistics. Based in around Iqaluit, the capital of Nunavut and main settlement on Baffin Island, it revealed that the Food Insecurity Rate (FIR) was 68%. This is the highest FIR in any developed country worldwide. Many Canadians are either unaware of this or would rather be unaware of it. The breakdown of the statistics regarding the most vulnerable of the indigenous society, young children of pre-school age, is nothing short of horrifying.

Of Pre-school children included in the survey:-

25% were classified as "Severely Food Insecure"
76% had missed meals
60% had gone a day without eating.

In 2007 a survey in forty nine northern communities showed up the extreme differential in the cost of feeding a family of four people consisting of two adults and two school age children. In the southern cities of Canada a weekly food shopping that would give a balanced and nutritious for a week would have cost between C$ 195 and C$ 225. The same basket of food in the Arctic settlements would have cost between C $ 350 and C$ 450. One also has to remember that similar differentials exist in fuel and other consumer goods and this in an area where the average earnings are much lower than the national average in Canada.

As a father and grandfather I know that parents will willingly go hungry rather than see their children suffer empty stomachs. It can therefore be easily deduced that if the children had gone without food their parents would more than likely gone without food even more so! This no doubt is a contributing fact to the exceptionally high suicide rate among young Inuit males.

At the time that this study was carried out, 2014, the calculated cost of feeding a family of four in Iqaluit was $19,760 per annum. The fact that almost half of the indigenous people in Iqaluit earn less than $20,000 per annum does not bode well for the future of Canada's Inuit children.

To the west of the Canadian Inuit territory of Inuvialuit on what is known as the North Slope of Alaska the indigenous Inupiat people are also experiencing climate change related problems.

Since the first of the Inupiat's ancestors arrived on what is now called the "North Slope" of Alaska they have lived in settled communities. For millennia, before the white man even knew of their existence, they lived in communities of turf and stone houses with roof beams made from the bones of whales. Even then these people knew how to preserve food in times of plenty to tide them through the hardships of lean times and Arctic winters. These innovative people invented deep freezing.

By digging deep tunnels into the permafrost, stores of whale meat, seal and fish as well as caribou and wild fowl were able to be stored throughout the year. Even through the warm summer months this store remained deep frozen. Once the white man came and the turf dwellings were replaced by wooden houses, with such luxuries as electricity, the practice of deep freezing continued. Underneath the modern houses in settlements from Nome all the way round the North Slope to Prudoe Bay there are deep cellars penetrating down into the permafrost. This ancient system worked well right up until the twenty first century. Unfortunately in the past few years, prolonged periods of warm weather, with temperatures well above freezing, have enabled much of the frozen stores to thaw and spoil. Filmed by the people themselves to demonstrate to "climate change deniers" that climate change and global warming are real, the pictures of spoiled, hard won food are both tragic and alarming.

This problem of food insecurity is well know and acknowledged by the authorities in Alaska. In 2014 the Alaska Department of Health and Social Services in association with the Alaska Food Policy Council commissioned a study into the problem. The study, which was titled "Building Food Security in Alaska.", was carried out by two researchers from the Crossroads Resource Center in Minneapolis.

The report starts out by outlining the different perception of "food security" in Alaska to that of "food security" in the other member states of the USA which are commonly referred to as the Lower 48.

In the case of the Lower 48 the term "food security" focuses on low income families and how they can increase their own food supply by producing their own food.

In Alaska, in particular among the indigenous people, whether Inupiat, Yupik or Aleut, the meaning of food security is of even more significance. The native peoples of Alaska had well established traditions and practices long before the white man arrived and many of these were built around the sharing of food. When, for example an Inupiat hunter was fortunate enough to kill a whale it was shared among the whole community. So the traditions regarding hunting had to be passed from generation to generation. This not only fed the community it also preserved their cultural heritage. Many indigenous cultures across the world have been stripped of their heritage by the introduction of 'western ideals' and technology. Smart phones, I-pads, computers and, of course, television have led to many younger generation indigenous people being what is described as "screened out". Sadly these youngsters have lost much of the knowledge that was built up over millennia by their ancestors. The object of the "Building Food Security in Alaska" study was as much to do with preserving the cultural heritage as retaining the food supply from within the region. In rural areas, which are predominantly indigenous, the main source of the food supply is still that of the hunter gatherer. In these districts an estimated 80% of food is either caught, shot or gathered. What a family does not have someone else will have and so a form of barter trade still prevails in the outlying settlements. In the larger communities such as Anchorage the percentage of wild food is much reduced to as low as 10%. This figure is maybe somewhat misleading as the percentage of indigenous people is also much lower in these areas. From this it may be assumed that the percentage of wild food consumed by the local indigenous population will be much greater than the 10% quoted but still much less than the 80% consumed in the outlying areas. It is also well known that, as far as the indigenous people are concerned, the quality of meat and fish sold in the town shops and supermarkets is viewed as being much inferior to that hunted by the local population. A point which is causing a great deal of annoyance among Alaskans is that even if they want to buy local seafood, which is caught in abundance in local waters, this has been a round trip to Seattle in Washington State for processing and packaging. This is not a phenomenon unique to Alaska. Exactly the same thing happens to langoustine prawns caught in Scottish waters. These prawns are, in some cases, exported to the Far East for shelling as labour in places like Thailand is much cheaper. In comparison this round trip makes the journey to Seattle look like a local bus trip.

If we look at the carbon footprint of the $1.9 billion worth of food that is imported into Alaska (2014) it reveals many worrying trends.

First of all, this figure of $1.9 billion represents approximately 95% of the total of the $2billion spent by Alaskans on food. Therefore it represents an annual drain of dollars to the tune of 1.9 billion from the local economy.

Secondly it increases the 'food miles' taken to put a meal on an Alaskan table. Considering that the main sources of that imported food are places like Asia, Europe, Mexico as well as the Lower 48. Some of this will be air freight, some containerised sea freight, the rest by road and rail to ports such as Seattle for trans-shipping to its final Alaskan destination. All these long journeys not only increase the cost to the Alaskan consumer they also cost the planet dearly in greenhouse gas emissions.

The third, very worrying, point of concern is that it makes the whole issue of food security totally dependent on the cost of fossil fuel. If the price of fossil fuels, such as marine diesel, were to rise significantly it would create a further burden on the poorest sector of the Alaskan people, that sector being mainly members of the indigenous population.

Despite these concerns there has in recent years been a trend of even rural communities buying more food from stores and supermarkets.

The assessed value of local wild food has been put at approaching $1billion (2014) and yet it still remains the largest contributor to the food economy of Alaska. How long this can continue due to the pressures on the wild creatures which are the source of this food is currently unknown. If climate warming continues, caribou numbers continue to collapse and marine mammals become more difficult to hunt the days of the largely self sufficient Inupiat hunter could draw to a close. If that happens then not only would it bring increased hardship to an already heightened situation of food insecurity it could also mean the loss of cultural knowledge among the younger generations.

Far to the east where the Cold Arctic meets the Atlantic Ocean the Kaalaalit of Greenland cling on to the shoreline of the world's biggest island. (Australia being deemed a continent.) Of the 160,000 people across the four arctic counties of Russia, USA, Canada and Greenland who come under the term Inuit around 50,000 of these live in Greenland. This makes Greenland unique. If one views Greenland as an independent country, which many of its inhabitants desire, it would mean that the majority of its inhabitants would be indigenous people. However, as Greenland is still regarded as part of Denmark its indigenous people do not have what may be termed the 'controlling interest'. This is despite the fact that only one in six of its inhabitants are regarded as being 'fully Danish'. It is the 'one in six' who dominates both the administrative and business scene.

When cruise ships visit Greenland one of the first things the tourist notices is that at most ports the name "Royal Arctic" dominates the quayside. (That is if the tourists actually notice anything other than the icebergs and whales.)

"Royal Arctic" is a Greenland Government owned shipping company who operate a state run monopoly where freight shipping is concerned. Whether this is a good or bad thing is certainly open to debate.

Founded in 1993 with a staff of around eight hundred, Royal Arctic is one of Greenland's major employers. It is also noticeable that in 2011 around three quarters of its business was from government concessions. Managing thirteen harbours in Greenland and with an operational base at Aalborg in Denmark it has a virtual monopoly over both imports and exports to and from Greenland. One has to question whether this stifles business development or whether it protects the indigenous people from exploitation by foreign powers. Around 25% of the imports carried by Royal Arctic are construction materials. As timber production in Greenland is nil the timber is all supplied via Denmark. If other countries, such as Norway, could supply timber directly to Greenland it would reduce transport costs and also create healthy competition. Instead timber is sent from both Norway and Sweden to Denmark before shipping to Greenland. This sort of added cost inevitably leaves less money in household budgets for food.

Fish accounts for around half of the exports from Greenland. Within Greenland itself, the main cargoes carried by Royal Arctic's fleet of purpose built coastal vessels are fish and bottled goods such as water and beer from the capital Nuuk. Again, this monopoly may discourage competition. On the other hand, it may keep the government based company viable and ensure that less profitable sea routes and the more remote communities are guaranteed a service and access to imported food sources when local produce is scarce.

The current (2017) vessel situation is that the thirteen strong fleet of Royal Arctic ships are split into two categories. The first category being five larger container vessels which operate mainly from the capital Nuuk and either Reykjavik, in Iceland, or the Danish port of Aalborg. The second category is that of eight smaller vessels termed 'Settlement Ships' which were purpose built to enter the remotest settlement harbours under extreme conditions and either load or unload cargo. The use of deck cranes, which are absent from most modern coastal vessels globally, enable these operations in harbours where modern cranes and dockside facilities are absent. This feature may in reality help to protect remoter areas from shortages of essential goods such as food and fuel. The fact that it is a Greenlandic Government owned company does help to guarantee a service in a manner that could not be otherwise attained by private companies.

I will let the reader decide for themselves as to the benefits or detrimental effects that this state monopoly may have on the indigenous people of Greenland. The only comment that I can make with conviction is that, over the past few years, when I have visited some of the more remote settlements on Greenland's west coast, I have noticed that the local stores have been quite well stocked with both food and other more common consumer goods. I have also noted that although the prices are undoubtedly higher than in UK supermarkets they are not as expensive as in other Arctic areas I have visited.

Another name which is regularly seen in Greenland's ports is that of fishing and fish processing company "Royal Greenland". This company, which until recently was also, like "Royal Arctic", a Greenlandic Government owned company. Its origins go back almost two and a half centuries.

Back in 1774, at a time when Denmark and Norway were united under one crown the "Royal Greenland Trading Department" was founded. Its total remit was that of a state owned monopoly to administer all aspects of both trade and municipal affairs in the Danish settlements on Greenland's coast. This situation of a total state monopoly continued right through to the twentieth century ending after the Second World War. In 1950 the monopoly ceased and in 1986 the new Home Rule Government, which had emerged in 1979, renamed the company the " Kalaallit Niuerfiat". This name lasted until 1992 when this was changed to KNI.

The present name of Royal Greenland A/S was adopted when the fishing industry interests were spun off as a separate entity in 1990. This new company, which accounts for more than half of Greenland's exports, describes itself as a food cooperative. In 2012 it had a stated workforce of 1962 employees, which made it one of the biggest employers in Greenland, with a very significant influence on all aspects of the Greenlandic economy. Among its business interests and products it lists, seafood, caviar (made from lumpfish roe), commercial fishing, fish processing, smoked fish, marinated fish and dried fish. However its main product is that of both the catching and the processing of Greenland Prawns. (Pandalus borealis).

Attempts to privatise the company were initially delayed due to both negative financial results and concerns about competition.

Current activities (2017) clearly indicate the global growth in the production of seafood products with Royal Greenland now operating in a number of countries both covering both sides of the Atlantic. In Greenland it has a total of thirty eight plants and depots, spread across the west coast from Uummanaq, north of Disko Island, right down to the south west corner at Narsaq. The size of these plants and the number of people employed has a wide variance, from small plants that have maybe a couple of full time employees augmented by seasonal workers, up to large factories like the one in Sisimiut which works a 2/3 shift system and can process over a hundred tonnes of prawns plus fifteen tonnes of snow crab per day.

On the overseas front the company has considerable assets in both Canada and Europe. Its Canadian operations consist of five processing plants in Newfoundland where the main product is high value snow crab. Its sixth Canadian plant is in Matane, New Brunswick which specialises in cooked and peeled prawns for the Canadian and US market. This last plant has a staff of approximately one hundred and twenty people and can process thirty tonnes of prawns per day.

One would be justified in wondering, "Why are the detailed operations of one company being singled out as relevant to food security in Greenland?"

The answer to this question is that Royal Greenland accounts for around 50% of Greenland's GDP. So anything that has an effect on its financial viability could in turn have a catastrophic outcome for every man, woman and child across Greenland.

As the Greenland, or Cold Water Prawn, (Pandalus borealis) is the most important of Royal Greenland's products the protection of this species from over-fishing or the effects of climate change is crucial for the wellbeing of all concerned.

Prawns may be the most important species to the Greenland fishing fleet in this the second decade of the twenty first century, but this has not always been the case.

Back in the years from 1960 to 1980 it was cod that were the prime target but then during the 1980's the cod disappeared from Greenland's coast. It was at this time that many of the larger fishing vessels moved their attention from cod to prawns. What actually caused the collapse in the cod stocks has never been conclusively determined. The most likely explanation is not one individual cause but a combination of intensive fishing allied to a cooling of the marine ecosystem. This cooling may have been caused by one of the natural marine temperature oscillations which are a long time feature in the Atlantic ecosystem. This cooling drove the cod stocks further south to waters that were more in keeping with the cod's natural temperature range. Recent scientific evidence indicates that the movements of cod and prawns are interrelated and clearly indicate that climate change will have a significant influence in the future.

Although prawns are one of the cod's main prey species the prawn has a preference to colder water. When the northern limit of the cod's range became too cold it moved south while the prawns remained. This reduction in predation on the prawn stocks meant that the biomass of Pandalus borealis saw an appreciable increase in the 1980's and 1990's. Now in the second decade of the twenty first century the seas around Greenland are becoming warmer. This increase in temperature is not just due to the natural oceanic oscillation but also due to the anthropogenic effect that has created the global warming across the planet. This marine warming has seen an increase in the amount of cod returning north in Greenlandic waters.

Increased amounts of cod invariably means a decrease in the biomass of prawns and this has been observed by Greenland's marine scientists in the traditional prawn catching areas. The main area affected being the waters of the Davis Strait adjacent to South West Greenland. Studies clearly show that as cod numbers increase in prawn catching areas the biomass of prawns decline, but as the current overlap zone of the two species is not extensive it does not fully explain the overall decline of the prawns in the Davis Strait area. From the data available one has to draw the conclusion that climate change is also a major factor in the decline. Because of this Royal Greenland carried out exploration voyages to previously unfished waters further north into Baffin Bay. In October 2014 three Royal Greenland trawlers ventured as far north as Melville Bay, adjacent to the Thule Air Base at 75 degrees north. What they discovered were good numbers of prawns with a predominance of very large individuals which indicated that this was a previously unexploited stock.

Whether this stock had always been there or whether they had migrated north ahead of the warming waters would be impossible to determine. Certain challenges are however obvious. First is that of sea ice as the area is covered with ice for the majority of the year and therefore the fishing season would be curtailed to late summer and autumn. The second challenge is that of distance from current processing plants and the increased time from catching to processing and markets.

The situation further south in the Canadian waters on the Gulf of St. Lawrence is much more clear. There the prawn stocks are under severe pressure. In 2016 the Canadian Government imposed a huge 42% cut on the prawn quota. This cut was based on data collected and analysed by their fisheries scientists. This year (2017) the quota may even be further reduced. If this is the case it will bring into question the viability of Royal Greenland's prawn plant at Matane in New Brunswick.

If changes in marine temperature are causing prawn stocks to shift north they may also be changing the timing of the biological life cycle of this species.

As the larger, female prawns, prepare to breed their orange coloured roe is clearly visible through the carapace. This gives them the appearance of having orange heads. Traditionally these orange headed prawns were exported at a premium to China as a delicacy eaten at the Chinese New Year. Changes in climatic conditions are thought to have delayed the formation of the prawns roe and many are not now fully in roe until after the Chinese New Year celebrations. This undoubtedly has an effect on that particular market.

Moulting of the prawns exoskeleton, which is essential in all crustacean species, allows them to grow. The time of the year when this occurs has also changed and for this reason some of the traditional fishing grounds in the south have now been abandoned. This led to the decision to look for new fishing grounds further north.

The fact that climate change will undoubtedly create more problems for companies like Royal Greenland in future years is certain. The fact that companies like Royal Greenland are willing to listen to scientists and to give them access to the necessary facts and figures gives hope for the future of Greenland's fisheries.

As the effects of climate change take a greater hold it may be that the species that the Arctic supports will change. The Inuit have for millennia adapted to changes in their environment so that they could produce all their requirements whether food, clothing or shelter. In the past these changes took place over long periods of time, today's changes are happening over years as opposed to centuries. Hopefully these resourceful people

PROFERICROBERTMCVICARFRGS

can keep up with this new challenge.

CONCLUSION

Both the Sami and the Inuit are natural conservationists who, for millennia, lived as children of nature. Unfortunately, the attitude of the modern consumer society of the late 20th century and early 21st has changed forever the way in which indigenous people - not only of the Arctic but throughout the world - now live.

'Civilisation' has caused a culture of 'must have' greed as opposed to the 'must have' need that once prevailed. We cannot restore the pristine Arctic or enable those people who live there to return to the ways of the hunter-gatherer. Many of the species upon which they depended have been over exploited and in the case of some - like the polar bear - are now endangered. Other species have increased beyond their natural numbers due to the 'politically correct,' but thoroughly ignorant, 'good intentions' of would-be conservationists.

So does this give us the right to deny another human being an honourable and fulfilling way of life? If we must protect species - and I, for one, fully believe we must - it must be done in a manner that retains an ecological balance.

The wearing of furs and skins has gone on since not long after Homo sapiens first walked the earth. Who are we to dictate to others that they should not wear furs or skins? Who are we to tell a person whose ancestors protected the Arctic for millennia that we will no longer let them live there with their ways and beliefs? Why must we continue to pollute the Arctic seas and even the air that they breathe?

Thankfully, the Sami people need no longer deny their

PROFERICROBERTMCVICARFRGS

ancestry, which stretches further back than many other European races.

Why should young Inuit in Nunavut feel that they cannot go on or feel the need to turn to alcohol - the poison inherited from the white man?

Why should young Inuit babies be denied the comfort of a mother's breast?

Each of us must answer these questions, but only after we search our own conscience

So, before you reach into your pocket to help fund a well-meaning concept, think about whether you are helping to fund the extinction of an ancient way of life or, even worse, contributing towards the suicidal thoughts of a young Inuit.

EPILOGUE

Is there a single cause that is responsible for the problems in our two Arctics?

If so, what can we do about it?

Without a doubt, there **is** a single cause for the problems in the Arctic.

That cause is us - all of us, the human race

There are just too many of us. Too many by, in my opinion, a factor of five.

If we turn the clock back a century, the human population of our planet was about one and a half billion. Think what we would be able to do today if there was still the same number of Homo sapiens walking the Earth.

Firstly, we would not need to farm the acreage that we currently do. That would leave us room to plant trees to absorb the overspill of CO_2 that is currently acidifying our oceans, destroying corals and making life difficult for every other form of marine life.

The need for mountains of petrochemical-based agrochemicals would vanish, paving the way for more use of natural fertilisers such as seaweed.

This would open up more habitats to both flora and fauna, much of which is currently under stress.

Secondly, if there were less humans, we would not need to have millions of cattle grazing on all the grasslands - natural and man-made - creating vast tonnages of CH_4 to accelerate the problem of global warming. This would also allow the rainforests of places like the Amazon and Indonesia to recover and rebuild their natural biodiversity.

And, even if we still used the polluting invention of the internal (or is it infernal) combustion engine, the decrease in numbers would be such that the trees could, in all probability, cope with the exhaust gases. The sheer volume of things like air travel and marine freight would be at levels that nature could cope with and manage using natural biological processes.

The ever increasing plastic in our oceans, which is now present in every life form, could be stopped. Turtles and cetaceans would no longer wash up on our shores dead only to reveal that the cause of their demise is a gut full of polythene.

These are only a few examples of how our world could recover if we reduced our overall population.

So what can we do about it?

The starting point is ourselves. We must resist the desire to have large families. We must teach our younger generation that if you have one loaf, two can have a half each and neither will go hungry; but if there are a hundred, all will be hungry.

Governments must stop spending money on human fertility treatments. There are so many children needing parents to adopt and care for them. As long as there is one child awaiting adoption why produce more?

Aid to starving children in places like Africa should be given along with education and birth control in a bid to prevent another famine 15 to 20 years down the road. The education of young women and the freedom for them to decide how many children they should have should be a priority. A priority that must be freed of all religious influence.

The concept of financial growth, allied and supported by population growth, is the biggest pyramid scheme of all time. Economists and religious leaders like to appear intelligent, but don't seem to have much common sense.

It is not practical for the whole human race to become vegetarian. Greens don't grow in Greenland or bananas on Baffin Island. So why persecute the Inuit for hunting seals?

If your average American ate half the amount of beef-based products, it would not only solve the massive obesity problem in the USA but also reduce the amount of harmful methane gases, which are exacerbating the global warming problem. Leather made from seal skins could help replace the loss from cowhides. Removal of non indigenous grey seals from places like the North Sea and Gulf of St. Lawrence would help restore stocks of fish - including endangered salmon. This, in turn, could aid the removal of toxic unsustainable salmon farming - with its parasitic problems - from our coasts.

There are many ways in which we as individuals can help restore an ecological balance to our planet. Our two indigenous Arctic races lived with nature for millennia. We should learn from their wisdom, which was acquired over generations. We only have one planet and we have to share it with every other species. We have allowed our own species to expand beyond its own ecological niche to an unsustainable level.

Only we can sort this.

APPENDIX 1: ALEX RITCHIE'S STORY

Back in the 1950's Alex Ritchie's son Alex made a recording of his father telling his story of survival in the Canadian Arctic for a BBC program. His nephew, Neil Ritchie of Gourdon, wrote down verbatim his uncles words. The only difference was that, as Alex spoke the very broad Doric of Scotland's North East, Neil 'translated' this into 'English that others could understand'.(Neil's actual words.) The following is that account. The Maggie Law Museum in Gourdon has a copy of Alex Ritchie giving his rendition of that written account which can be heard by visitors to the museum, it is also available on the Maggie Law website. Neil, however, gave me permission to use his written account. But before we go on to Ritchie's story of the wrecking of the 'Snowdrop' and his subsequent journey across Baffin Island we will look at some of the events which the 'Snowdrop' and her crew encountered on previous voyages to the frozen waters of Baffin Bay.

The adventure that ensured the story of the 'Snowdrop' a place in both the history and mythology of Arctic whaling began in 1905 in a castle near Montrose on Scotland's east coast. It was here at Ecclesgreig Castle, home of the aristocratic Forsyth-Grant family, that a twenty- five year old, headstrong young man convinced his father into buying him a small whaler to go 'fishing' in the cold northern waters frequented by the Dundee whaling fleet. The fact that the Arctic whaling from Dundee had been in decline for nearly sixty years did not deter young Osbert Clare Forsyth-Grant from trying his hand in this adventurous and dangerous occupation. An adventure that would tragically end in his own early demise.

'Snowdrop', at a mere seventy feet long and a lightweight at sixty three tons, was the smallest whaler ever to set sail from Dundee but before sailing Osbert Clare carried out many alterations. He had a forty horse power engine fitted, tanks for both oil and blubber were installed and the hull was strengthened to cope with the ice of the Davis Strait and Baffin Bay. Much of the conversion work being done either by himself or under his supervision. Thus equipped he then signed on a crew and an experienced captain.

His choice of Captain was one of the oldest working ice captains with a tremendous record. Captain Ogston, at seventy-eight years of age, had captured no fewer than one hundred and three Greenland whales in his long and distinguished career. Twelve east coast fishermen made up the crew. Amongst these twelve brave men were two fishermen from the small east coast fishing village of Gourdon, five miles north of Ecclesgreig Castle. A place well known to the young Laird of Ecclesgreig, it is highly likely that he already knew the young nineteen year old Alex Ritchie and the man referred to as a 'sort of uncle' also named Alex Ritchie.

The 1905 season for 'Snowdrop' was one of success. Whereas most of the Dundee fleet came home 'clean', that is without catching a whale, 'Snowdrop' was one of the few to come home having caught a large whale. This whale, taken off Cape Hooper, was harpooned by Osbert Clair and so accurate was his aim with the harpoon gun that the whale rapidly came to the surface with rope still aboard the whaleboat. As one of the crew is said to have stated; 'She was as deid as Julius Caesar'. It was only after getting the leviathan alongside that the enormity of the task ahead was evident. Too large to bring aboard and without a winch it took the crew eight days to cut up the beast into manageable chunks and bring it aboard. On the 'normal size' Dundee whaling ships this task would have taken about eight hours. Twenty tons of blubber plus between sixteen and eighteen tons of baleen and bone were harvested. This had a value of around £2500, making the voyage very profitable.

The following year 1906 was a very different tale.

Much to the disappointment of Osbert Clair, the venerable Captain Ogston was not available to take command of 'Snowdrop' as she led the Dundee whaling fleet out of the Earl Grey Dock into the River Tay in 1906. By now the once mighty Dundee fleet were reduced to seven larger vessels, Active, Balaena, Diana, Eciipse, Morning, Scotia and Windward. All were led out, as tradition demanded, by the previous season's most successful vessel. In 1906 this was the diminutive ketch 'Snowdrop'.

This season it was under a new command, that of Captain Walter J Jackson of Dundee. Unfortunately this was not to be a good year for Dundee's dwindling fleet, for not only would the 'Windward' be lost to the icefields but the little 'Snowdrop' was to endure both mutiny and accusations of piracy. For although Jackson, now 49 years of age had first gone to the Arctic 'fishings' at the age of seventeen, his thirty two years experience were of doubtful credulity. From early on in the voyage it was clear that he did not want to go north into the icepack of Baffin Bay to hunt whales as Osbert Clair demanded. Jackson would have preferred to stay south in the Davis Strait hunting seals and walrus in the much safer waters of the West Greenland coast or in the southern inlets and sounds of Baffin Island. This caused a lot of bad feeling between captain and owner. So when the "Snowdrop" ran aground on the Knight Reefs near Holsteinborg, damaging her keel, it gave Jackson the excuse he needed to convince the already unhappy crew to follow him in leaving the ship in Holsteinborg and head home. Not all the crew deserted with Jackson and among the five that remained was the young Alex Ritchie. The older Alex Ritchie, who was referred to as 'Sandy', was one of those left with Jackson. However, before Osbert Clair sailed his crew was further reduced when two of those who initially remained decided that they would also head homeward as the damaged 'Snowdrop' was undermanned. This left just four men to sail the damaged little ketch west to Baffin Island. It was here with the aid of the Inuit crew that Forsyth-Grant took on board the unique relationship between the Inuit and the crew of the Snowdrop was forged. The Inuit who became fiercely loyal to Osbert Clare were soon to be known as "Grant's People" and from there the legend began. But disaster was on the horizon, as the story of Alex Ritchie's amazing Arctic epic tells.------

"On Saturday 9th April 1908, I sailed from Dundee in the ketch 'Snowdrop' bound for the Arctic. Our ship was in command of Captain James Brown, who had sailed in the Arctic for many years. This was my third voyage to the Arctic in this ship. We left Dundee about mid-day. I remember the weather was good, but all our crew were drunk, from the Captain to the cook. I, being a total abstainer, had to take the wheel and there I had to remain until some of the crew were sober enough to stand at the wheel.'

'We were off Aberdeen on Sunday morning. The weather changed and came on to a blow from the east, causing us to go to Aberdeen, as the gale was so heavy. We lay in port a few days, and while the two of the crew deserted the ship. We got another two men and then we sailed. Weather was good and we were off the Greenland coast in thirteen days from the time we left Aberdeen. That was not bad sailing for a small ship. This ship had a forty horsepower engine, and engines and motors were rare in those days. I remember the first year, 1905, I was in this ship, we called into Peterhead and many fishermen came aboard to see this motor engine.'

We arrived at the place we were to commence to catch walrus. This place was called Reef Coll. We could see Disco Island a few miles to the northward. We worked here a good few weeks shooting walrus. The walrus here are very large, as they are all bulls. We worked here until the ice pack got more scattered and opened, and headed for a place called Cape Haven, south side of Cumberland Gulf. The name for it (in Inuit) is 'Signia', on the west side of the Davis Straits, where the owner of the ship had an Eskimo settlement. We put ashore all our spare stores, about seven tons, to make room for skins and blubber. Then we took aboard the whole population – sixty -five men, women and children. They were to hunt for us- walrus, seals, bears and foxes. There were only ten of us white men so they helped a lot. Instead of having one boat hunting we had four boats now, besides men working singly in 'Kayaks', native canoes. The women did all the rowing in the boats and the men the shooting. Then the Eskimos would take a day or two deer hunting. They are very good shots and they wanted to get deer skins for their beds and winter clothing. These deer skins are the skins they use for all clothes in winter, including their footwear.

Well, we worked among the walrus and seals. They were smaller than the ones we got at Reef Coll, as they were mostly cows. We filled our ship. We had six hundred and fifty walrus and six hundred seals and a great many bears. We also had a great number of Arctic foxes, which the Eskimos had caught during the winter, also a great many seals. We were making everything ready for our voyage home, and we were going to land our Eskimo people back at Signia, which was ninety miles farther north.

'We were lying at anchor in Countess of Warwick Sound when the wind started to blow very heavy from the eastward.

It increased to a gale on 19th September, our anchors started to drag, and we could do nothing. We started our engine, but it was no use. We drove ashore on this barren land with no-one to help us. Sometimes the wind comes very sudden here and lasts a gale for days. The women and children were in the hold. We told them to go down there when the anchors started to drag, as we were frightened to let them on deck, as they might have been washed away as we were among the breakers. Well, after the ship struck the rocks, we knew it was going to be a bad business for us all, as it seemed we could do nothing to help ourselves. Then our Captain, (presumably he meant Brown as opposed to Forsyth-Grant, who Ritchie referred to as 'owner'.) asked if any of us could get ashore with a rope. Nobody spoke, as it seemed hopeless. Then I said that I would have a try. The Captain said if I got ashore with the rope, I had to come back on board as he wanted me on board. Well, after a struggle I got ashore and made the rope fast to a big boulder. I hauled myself back to the ship again by the rope. The Captain ordered two men ashore along the rope to haul the women and children ashore first, then the men. We got everybody, old and young, ashore, and did not lose or hurt anyone. We lost everything we had, the only things I saved being my Bible and a pair of socks and mittens. The way I saved the socks and mittens, I had them sewed in the lining of my jacket - that was the whaler's custom – my Bible was in a watertight case I had made on a previous voyage. I went below for it after I had made the rope fast ashore and took it out of the shelf of my bunk.

We were all thankful for our escape, but we had nowhere to go for shelter until some of the sails washed ashore. The first sail to be washed ashore was our spare mainsail, so the Eskimo rigged up a tent for us all. Then the next thing to worry us was that we had no food, till later some tinned food started to come ashore after our store tanks burst, for which we were very thankful. The storm died away on the fourth day during our stay ashore. After the tent was erected, the Eskimos made fires for us with pieces of blubber which came ashore when the ships tanks burst. We got all our clothes dried, and heat for ourselves. Everything that was not in tins was spoiled with the oil and blubber washing through it. The Eskimos were good at lighting a fire. They use flint and steel and dried moss. They know where to get the dried moss; mixed with a cotton-like weed one would think it shag tobacco. They make wicks for their lamps with this. We got them ashore, but they kept us alive after we were ashore. We had four whaleboats hanging in the davits when we entered the broken waters before we grounded. Every boat was washed away. Our dinghy we had to throw over the side in case it would break adrift and hurt some of us. It went ashore with many holes in it. After the storm was over, one man, an Eskimo, went up to the top of a high hill and said he saw something white under the water, out from shore where our wreck was lying. We patched the dinghy and went out to see what it was. It was one of our whaleboats which was anchored with its two davits and was not damaged. We hauled it ashore bit by bit. We fitted this boat out and four of us with a man named Nuna, and his two daughters were to go to the top of the Frobisher Straits. The Eskimos told us that the land there was narrow and we could walk to Lake Harbour on Hudson Bay. We reckoned it would be about forty miles. Well it took us about seven days to get to the top of Frobisher. We hauled up our boat and made a tent to rest until morning, as the weather was good. When morning came the snow was up to the top of the tent. It blew a gale from the North all night, with snow. Our Eskimo guide said he would not go now, as the snow was soft and someone might fall through some unseen hole, and he said it would be very dangerous.

Our intention was to intercept the Dundee whaler Active as she called at Lake Harbour in Hudson Bay, on her way home. Then we would pick up the remainder of our crew. Our Eskimo guide would not go any further, so we launched our boat and it took another seven days for our return journey. When we got back the ship had totally broken up.

We then had another try. We were to come home by the Labrador coast, all of our crew. After seven days on an island in Frobisher Straits' our Captain said he wasn't going to go as it was blowing a howling gale. He wanted taken back. So when we arrived where the wreck was, all the Eskimo had gone to walk to Signia, which was about ninety miles. Only two old Eskimo remained and we left our skipper with them. We made another try but later on we squared away for Signia, leaving our Captain with the two old Eskimo. Signia was eighty or ninety miles further north. It took us five or six days to get there. When we arrived all the Eskimo were glad to see us. This Signia had a house and a store, and before we started our hunting and fishing for walrus we had put over seven tons of stores ashore. Well, when we arrived there our owner would not give us anything, so we had to depend on what the Eskimo could give us for food. It was hard at first to get used to eating raw seal flesh. Sometimes they boiled it in a tin, but they said raw flesh was best so we just had to do as they did and be thankful. Time went on like this and every day was much the same. We were always hungry, but we always got what our Eskimo friends could give us. Sometimes I went hunting with them, but they were good hunters and very sharp shooters. They always got what they were hunting for. Hunting seals in winter is very difficult. In winter you have to find the seal hole, which is a tiny hole in the ice. They train a dog to find the seal hole, about one to two inch circle. That is the breathing hole. Under the ice there is a sort of platform where the seal lies and rests. The seal has got several holes, and you may have to stand at one of these for hours. Sometimes an Eskimo has stood as long as three days before the seal came to the hole where he was standing ready to harpoon it.

One day I said I would go hunting by myself. The Eskimo said I should not go. But I went and I was very sorry that I did not take their advice. I had no dog and I travelled a long way over the ice, looking for these small holes, but found none. My idea was to stand at the hole as the Eskimo did, but instead of a harpoon, to fire my rifle down the hole after I heard the seal breathing. But I found no hole so i returned homeward. On my way back I was walking quickly to keep warm and to try to get back to the Eskimo village before darkness, as there is no twilight there. It grows dark very quick. As I was walking along I did not notice that the iceflow had a large crack about seven feet wide and it was full of snow. I did not notice this hollow or I would certainly have kept clear. Down I went into the darkness. The snow kept me from a quick plunge but I sank into the water. Those iceflows are about eight or nine feet thick and when I was in the water I could hardly reach the top of the ice.--- Well I had to get out some way. The first thing I did was to take off my cap and throw it up. Then I took my rifle and taking it by the muzzle I pushed it up until it fell on the ice. Then I threw up my cartridge bag. I knew that if I didn't get out at the first attempt, while I was strong, I would not get out. As I thought of what I would do, I made a jump and got my right fingers on the edge of the ice. Then I gripped my right wrist with my left hand until I thought I was high enough to grasp the edge of the ice with my left fingers. After I had done that I gradually eased myself up until I got one elbow on the ice, then the other. Then I made a great effort to fall forward and there I lay, utterly exhausted, with beads of sweat all over me. I did not know how I managed to get out. Now I had to get home. My clothes were freezing and I knew if I did not get home I would freeze to death. So I walked as quickly as I could. All my clothes were well nigh frozen to me and my legs and arms were chafed with the hard frozen clothes. I had to make a big detour to get around the crack in the ice. When the Eskimo saw me and heard my story they were amazed. They took off my frozen clothes and rubbed all my body to get warmth and circulation. I never went away alone again. I always paid attention to what they told me. After that day they named me 'Kivvy Actow'. (Note 1)

Well time passed and the weather grew colder. We shifted from toopiks, or skin tents, and made snow houses to live in. They were cold at first when built, but after a few hours they grew warmer. At night we would visit one another and there was always a feast. If an Eskimo got a seal, everybody was invited to the feast. The man who owned the house who had got the seal would come outside his house and shout 'kyeat oung,' and everybody would come. Sometimes they would sing and dance.

These Eskimo people are very good natured. They always kept some food for me, although they were hungry themselves. They could stand hunger for longer than I, and could take a far bigger feed when they got the chance. They were always very well pleased with themselves, and in all journeys with them I found them very pleasant to be with.

On the 16th of December six families left Signia. They generally travel about all winter, looking for food and skins. The people I stayed with – the man's name was 'Goodilack', his wife was 'Cumni' and his mother's name was 'Luct'. She seemed to be very old. There was one of us with every family. We were to go with them to try to reach Hudson Bay with the hope of being found by the Dundee Whaler 'Active' which comes regularly to Hudson Bay each year.

Before we left Signia all the sledges were packed and the dogs harnessed. Then the owner of the ship, Captain Grant, came down and asked me not to go away. He had a bag of biscuits, some butter, tea and coffee, and a tin of marmalade, and fifty cartridges for my rifle. He said that would do me as I would soon get fed up. I told him I would not come back. Nobody else got anything from him.

Now that night, after our first day's travel was over and our snow house made, I told Goodilack to call all the natives together to get a feed of biscuits. I put all the sugar and coffee and tea in together, and we ate everything. Every biscuit was eaten – not a morsel remained. There was no use keeping a few biscuits as I was to depend on the Eskimo and live as they lived. I had stayed with those people since we lost the ship.

One day we fell behind the other sledges. We were looking for seal holes and were greatly hindered and the weather was getting bad and growing dark when we reached the shore where the people on the other five sledges went to build their snow houses. We could not land as the tide was low, the ice was all broken and twisted and the dogs would not go. So we had to go back on the flow a bit and build a snow house on the iceflow. It was a very small house. I, being tall, got the widest bit of the circle. My head touched one side of the house and my feet the other. We had to stay in that small house four days before we got out. It was a howling gale the whole time, with snow from the north. The Eskimo do not like north winds; they call them 'vagnar'. Nothing can live in the open with a north wind as the drift rises and it would choke you. Well we got out on the fourth day but we had to come out of the house through the top and we had to dig our sledges and our dogs out. We had twelve dogs. They did not seem to be any the worse after they got something to eat. An Eskimo always keeps a saw and a spade in his house. He builds the house with the saw and on some occasions needs the spade. We went into this house on Hogmanay Night, so we spent a 'Happy New Year' – I don't think. We just got out in time as the water was starting to rise and wet our bedding.

The other Eskimo were glad to see us; instead of shaking hands as we do, they rub each others' noses. We stayed here for a few days but were soon on the move again.

About the beginning of February we met some of the Eskimo who had come from Hudson Bay. None of the people we were with wanted to go any farther after they had a talk with these other Eskimo. The other five of my shipmates said they were glad they were not going further. One of our shipmates, Willie Morrison by name, got heavily frostbitten and one big toe was black, and spreading up his foot. I asked the natives what would be best to do. They said they would take it off without chloroform. They said they use a sandbag, give you a tap on the head and make you unconscious, and take off the toe. Well, Morrison would not let them touch him and this gangrene, caused by the frostbite, spread. It spread right up to both his knees before he died in June that year. I never saw Morrison again. There were four of my shipmates with Morrison, and all the Signia Eskimo, when I left them.

I left all my old friends on 6th February 1909. These Hudson Bay people asked if I would like to come with them and, as I didn't want to go back to Signia, I said I would like to go with them. There were two families of these people. The one I stayed with, the man's name was 'Sho' and his wife was 'Neevie.' They had a little son about two years old I would think, also a brother of Neevie who was crippled on one leg. The other man's name was 'Eperbeg', and his wife was 'Cumanow'. They had no family.

They were grand hunters. On our travels we met two bears. They had three cubs about the size of lambs. The Eskimo shot the male bear, but it did not roll down the cliff. The mother bear rolled down after she was shot and the three cubs came travelling down after their mother.(see note 2) The Eskimo would not eat her as she was full of milk. They would not even let their dogs eat her. The cliff was so steep to climb so the male bear had to be left. They brought the skin of the mother to the house, killed two of the cubs for food and kept one. It followed us all the time until we arrived at Hudson Bay.

We camped at the foot of the place where the glacier breaks off into the sea. (see note 3) We remained there and the three men hunted to get a stock of food before crossing the glacier. On the last day of our travel before we reached the foot of the glacier, I got very weary and tired. I don't know what happened. I could not keep up with the sledges. They told me to take hold of the back end of the sledge and hang on to the rear lashings. I had to let go. That happened a lot of times and they always had to stop. Well, day was fading, and they had to get to land before dark as the dogs would not go through the broken ice between the land and the iceflow in the dark. I tried my best to keep up, but I had to let go and they had to leave me. I lay on the ice until I grew cold, and then I would get up and walk until I would fall again. I did this many times, trying to keep to the sledge tracks. I could see them quite plainly. Then it began to blow and the snow drifted like powder, filling the sledge tracks. I lay down thinking it was all over. I thought 'what a struggle I have had, and now I am going to die or be frozen to death'. Well I prayed that I might be saved. I lay and was very cold and had given up hope when I thought I heard voices. They were two men with a small sledge and seven dogs. They put me on the sledge and took me to their home. They warmed me and treated me as no-one on earth could have treated me better. They told me they did not expect to get me alive. I did not know how I could not keep up with them that day. They had to carry the dogs down through the broken ice, also the sledge, before they could come for me after they had built their house. All the journey previous to this I was able to run alongside the sledge, the same as they were doing. We rested at the foot of the glacier a few days, then we started to climb. It was a long, hard climb. Our sledges were heavy for we had stored up extra food because we did not expect to get any food until we got to the coast. There is nothing on this glacier, just a barren waste of ice and snow. When we reached the top it was a grand sight. In the clean frosty air we could see for miles and miles all the frozen land and the sea lying away on the horizon. They told me if I could manage to stick it out I was the only white man who had ever passed over this glacier. I never fell behind again. I always managed to keep up with them and did not hinder them in any way. After we got to the top of the glacier we started to come down to the Hudson Bay coast. They unharnessed their dogs. I was placed in front, standing on the sledge runners, leaning on the built up baggage with my back. The man sat on the top, his wife and child sitting on the back end. It did not need a dog to haul the sledge for miles and miles. It ran itself at a great speed. Sometimes it would run into a snow bank and stop. Then we would have to get the sledge on the run again: sometimes we had to dig it out. We were about four days on the glacier. The side sloping down to Hudson Bay was a very long, easy slope. When we got to their village in the Saddleback Islands off the coast a bit, there was no food. Seals were very scarce. My people told their friends who I was and I shook hands with them all. I think I was a bit of a curiosity, as young and old came to see me. (See note 4) I only stayed there that night, then in the morning I was wakened early. They told me two sledges were going up to Lake Harbour and I would be best to go with them. Well, this was the hungriest time I ever had on the whole journey. I was about a hundred miles from Lake Harbour. After leaving this island I never tasted food for three whole days and nights. The first food we got was walrus skins. We cut it very thin, chewed it a bit, and swallowed it. We travelled a little over sixty miles without food. The next morning after the feed of walrus skins we were on the march again and we arrived at a few snow houses and got some seal flesh from them. That was the fourth day in Hudson Bay. The next night we arrived at Lake Harbour, and according to my book it was the first of April. Well, the next day the Eskimo in charge of the stores took me on a sledge about six miles up the fjord to where the house was. The man's name was King Agai. They took some treacle and took me back to where their houses were at the mouth of the fjord. They boiled water, and put in treacle, and I thought I never tasted anything so nice in all my life. I was to go back to the house on the morrow but I took ill. I swelled up – all my flesh grew soft. The Eskimo said that I lay twenty-one sleeps that I did not know anything. They count their time by sleeps. When I came around to know things again I was very weak and not able to walk and the igloo, or snow house was melting. They cut a hole in the side of the house, pushed in a sledge and put me on it, bedding and all. They took me to the toopik, or skin tent. I began to get stronger, and the Eskimo were on the move again to the Saddleback Islands where I had come from. They said the 'Active' of Dundee would arrive very soon, so they wanted me to come. The man I was to go with, his name was King Watchi, King Agai's son. This man was home in Dundee with the whaler 'Active' a year before we were wrecked. His wife and he were very good to me, as all of them were. The ice was melting and there was a lot of clear water.

I remember one morning I awoke early, and heard the most beautiful sound I had ever heard. It was rivers running. I thought it was the most beautiful music I had ever heard. There was plenty of food. The eider duck were in thousands.

When you went on an island you could not walk for nests and ducks sitting on their eggs. The people I stayed with collect hundreds of ducks and the boat was nearly full of eggs. We were near the islands where I came off the glacier, and one morning at the end of June there was the whaler 'Active' lying at anchor.

She had been lying there, as the ice was too heavy for her to proceed to Lake Harbour. Well, we went on board. I was so weak I could hardly climb up the side ladder. When we got on board the Eskimo shook hands with all the crew and I did the same. All the crew come up on deck and shake hands when a strange boat comes alongside. When I got on board I saw three men who were shipmates with me on 'Snowdrop' the year before, and not one recognized me. One man was standing about three feet from me—his name was Jim Scott. He was about to turn away after I had shaken his hand when I said to him, 'Jimmy, don't you know me?' He made one bound down to the cabin and brought up Captain Alex Murray saying 'There is one of the 'Snowdrop 'crew on board. Captain Murray said 'Jimmy, you have made a mistake; I don't see a white man.' So Scott pointed to me. Captain Murray came over and said 'Are you a white man?' I said yes. I always remember what he said, 'What a sight!' He lifted me on to a big steel yard hanging from the spanker boom. I weighed seven stones, skin, clothes and boots. (See note 5).   He immediately took me down to his cabin. He told the steward to make tea for me I could only take a cup of tea and a small bun. He asked me all about the loss of our ship, and where the remainder of our crew were. I told him we had tried to reach him in the fall of the year after we had lost our ship. I also let him see my diary I had kept. He also asked if he could keep it, so I let him get it. We lay here a few days until the ice opened, then we proceeded to Lake Harbour. The Captain told me I would go ashore and stay at the house. (See note 6) He also sent three men ashore as they were to work at the mica mines, a good long day's walk inland. Well I never went up to the mica mines as I was not to work. I stayed at the house. I got some clothes and I helped to make food for the miners. They always came to the house on Saturday. I was to remain there until 'Active' returned. I stayed here for a little while, then one day I saw a ship come into the harbour, so I went aboard, along with a boatload of Eskimo. The ship had a missionary on board, the Reverend Ernest Peck. I asked him when they were going home and he turned and looked at me and said he thought I was an Eskimo. There was also a doctor on board. Dr Bilby by name, also a young missionary whose name was Fleming. (See note7) I told them my story, and said I would like to go home with them. They had a house to build. It was in sections, so they soon erected it. Dr Bilby and Mrs Fleming were to remain at the house and start a mission. The ship's name was the' Lorna Doone' . The ship belonged to Dr Grenfell of Labrador. (See note 8) After the house was built the ship sailed. I had to bid farewell to all my old friends goodbye. I have never forgotten the kindness of those Eskimo people all my life.

Well, we left, and we arrived at St Antony, Newfoundland. Then Mr. Peck and I got a steamship named 'Prospero' which took us to St John's. When we arrived there, all our crew were there except Morrison. He died in June , and they told me that both his legs were eaten up to his knees with frostbite or gangrene. He must have suffered something terrible.

We were sent home in a liner belonging to the Allan Line, the 'Siberian'. We arrived in Glasgow about the middle of November, 1909.

The Eskimo used to sing hymns and Mr Peck, the missionary, translated portions of the Bible and in each portion he told where to find that passage in our English Bible. So when I was reading my Bible they often asked me and I could refer them to their Testaments. I had no other book but my Bible and I read it very much. The Eskimos used to sing hyms many of which I knew the tunes but they sang them in their own language. They also got them from the missionary. Mr. Peck told me he had been a missionary amongst the Eskimo for thirty-two years. He told me that I knew far more about them than he did."

In August 2015 I was fortunately enough to visit both St John's and St. Antony in Newfoundland. In 'The Rooms' museum in St. John's I discussed Alex Ritchie with a curator who had been to university in Dundee. She knew of Ritchie and his epic tale, -- few Dundonians have that knowledge. More recently I discussed the subject with a couple from Toronto, Canada, who were visiting the Kelvin-Grove Museum in Glasgow. This couple, who I would have judged to be around fifty years of age, knew the tale of Alex Ritchie as they had been taught it at school. It seems incredible that such an epic tale of survival in the Arctic is so little known in the country of his birth. It would almost give one the impression that failure is more worthy of fame than success. One only has to look at the tale of Scott in the Antarctic or the total loss of two Royal Navy ships, HMS Terror and HMS Eribus, complete with crew in Franklin's ill-fated expedition in the 1850's.

Notes:-

Note 1   Many remote areas across the world have myths regarding giants which vary from malevolent to benign and secretive. In the Rockies the 'Bigfoot' legend prevails. In the Himalaya it is the mythical 'Yeti' often termed the 'Abominable Snowman'.

Inuit legend is that of the mythical giant named Qivitoq. This giant lives alone in the mountains. He is reputedly immortal and only comes to the aid of the Inuit in times of extreme crisis. Alex Ritchie was taller than the average Scotsman of the time and to the much shorter Inuit would have appeared a giant. The only other man of that height these Inuit would have known was Osbert Clair Forsyth-Grant. So when Alex Ritchie rescued the Inuit men, women and children from certain death as the 'Snowdrop' started to break up their belief in the mythical Qivitoq seemed to be confirmed. By surviving falling through the ice when hunting alone all doubts that this man was the mythical giant were dispelled as only an immortal could have survived falling through the ice into the freezing water and only an immortal of super-human strength would have been strong enough to haul himself out. This only confirmed him as an immortal to these people who were superstitious. By the time he reached the Saddle Back Islands the story of him rescuing the Inuit from the Snowdrop and his subsequent survival in the icy waters had gone before him. (Note 4) Whereas he himself thought that the reason for the Inuit turning out to greet him was that they, the Inuit, had never met a white man, he was totally unaware of his celebrity, if not "mythical" status among the Inuit of Baffin Island at that time. It was only while visiting an Inuit settlement I was assured that Alex Ritchie was not referred to as "Kivvi Actow" as noted down by his nephew Neil Ritchie of Gourdon.

I was informed that he was indeed addressed as "Qivitoq", as many of those he saved firmly believed he was the mythical giant.

Note 2. It is highly unlikely that the second adult bear was a male as the two sexes only meet to mate. If a female is feeding young the male is likely to kill the cubs. The most likely explanation is that the two adults were related females with three cubs between them.

Note 3. The Grinnell Glacier in the 1970's was measured at 51 sq.miles in area and a height of 2710ft. In 1909 it would have been both larger in area and greater in height. Like all glaciers in Arctic Canada and Green land it is in retreat due to climate change.

Note 4. See introductory note.

Note 5. He was unrecognisable due to wearing Inuit clothing. The 'Spanker' is the sail set at the stern to hold the ship's head to windward when riding into a gale.

Note 6 The Kinnes Whaling Company of Dundee, owners of the 'Active' operated a number of shore bases in Arctic Canada including the one at Lake Harbour. This base was also the administration centre for Kinnes's mica mining operations which located nearby. The 'House' was a permanent building of robust construction. Kinnes were also the largest whaling company operating from Dundee at that time.

Note7 Fleming, later to be the Archbishop of the Arctic (1933-1949) was the second white man to cross the Grinnell Glacier but in a well equipped expedition. He was born in Greenock, Scotland on 8th September 1883 and died 17th May 1953. He was educated at Glasgow University and up until 1906 worked as a draughtsman in the world famous John Brown's Shipyard in Clydebank.

APPENDIX 2

The relationship between the Inuit of Eastern Canada, in the area we now term Nunavut, and the whaling fleet from Dundee is clearly highlighted in the following text. The ill-fated Franklin Expedition in which the two Royal Navy ships HMS Terror and HMS Erebus were lost with all hands had always been a mystery. The reason given to the public for the expedition was to find the North West Passage, However the letters home from Lt John Irving, third officer on the Terror give a very different reason – to find the Magnetic North. The article below shows that whereas the Inuit at the time of the missing expedition were clearly reluctant to talk to 'official' investigators they were less reluctant to talk to the Dundee whaling captains in whom they held great trust:--

The following article appeared between 17th and 25th October 1881 It is included here courtesy of the Archives of the Fraternity of Masters and Seamen of Dundee.

ARCTIC DISCOVERIES BY CAPTAIN ADAMS, DUNDEE.

Captain Adams of the Dundee whaler Arctic, who has just returned from the Davis Straits fishing (note 1) furnishes some interesting information in regard to his voyage in the Polar Seas. He states that in the course of his search for whales he went up Wellington Channel as far as that water has ever been penetrated by any expedition, and his progress was only checked by encountering heavy ice, or the Polar Barrier. This occurred in the month of August last. No whales were seen in that quarter of and the Arctic steamed up Barrow Straits till the Polar Barrier was encountered a second time. A course was then taken down Peel Sound to within a few miles of where

Erebus and Terror were lost. (note 2) Beachy Island (note 3) was visited and there Captain Adams saw the monument erected to Sir John Franklin and five of his crew. He found the house erected in the vicinity in a wretched condition, and provisions left by the former explorers not at all serviceable. Accompanied by a few of his men he made some search in the locality, and just as the party were coming away they were confronted by a polar bear, which Captain Adams shot within a few yards of the graves. The skin of the bear he intends to present to some of the relatives of Sir John Franklin.

No whales were seen in this direction and accordingly the Arctic proceeded up towards the Gulf of Boothia. An attempt was made to reach this sea earlier in the year but no advance was possible owing to the heavy ice. (note 4). In the end of August however, the ice was in a totally different condition, and the Arctic got up as far as Cape Nordenschold on the west side of Boothia. Here several whales were got. A storm coming away, the captain tried to get to the other side. A heavy fog was experienced and when it cleared away the ship was found within fifteen miles of Fury and Hecla Straits and in very shallow water.

In this district the captain got on board a very intelligent Esquimaux (note 5) from whom he obtained a good deal of valuable and interesting information. The native stated that when he was a young man in his father's hut three men came over the land towards Repulse Bay, and that one of them was a great captain. When he died the other two men were in sore distress and cried very much, stating that he was the 'Aniguk' or great captain. The other two lived some little time in his father's hut and he showed Captain Adams the spot on the chart where they were buried. The Esquimaux, continuing the narrative, said that seventeen persons started from two vessels, which had been lost far to the westward, but only three were able to survive the journey to his father's hut. From all the information furnished by the Esquimaux, Captain Adams has no doubt that the vessels referred to were those of the

Franklin expedition, and that the great captain mentioned was none other than Lieutenant Crozier. Assuming that what the Esquimaux stated was correct, it is beyond bdoubt that the members of the Franklin expedition were attempting to reach Hudson Bay territory. Judging from the present age of the native, Captain Adams is of the opinion that his allusion of having seen the men when he was a young man must refer to a period some thirty-five years ago.(note 6). It was Captain Adams intention to bring home the native, but circumstances occurred which prevented this resolution being carried out; but he is in a position to furnish information of a very detailed nature and calculated to throw light on the movements and ultimate fate of the members of the Franklin expedition. Captain Adams also brings home a few papers found in the vicinity of Fury and Hecla, and these have been forwarded to the Admiralty.

While in these high latitudes Captain Adams had the greatest possible difficulty in navigating his vessel. He was without charts and his compasses were practically of no use, (note 7) and did not indicate the course steered. He was only able to guide his ship by use of the lead the keeping of a sharp lookout; and when the fogs, which were exceedingly prevalent, cleared away, he always took the opportunity of ascertaining the position of his ship by the sun, Captain Adams has given frequent proof of his devotion to Arctic discovery, and it will be remembered that some years ago Captain Markham, of the Royal Navy, who had a command in the Sir George Nares expedition, (note 8) accompanied him to the Polar Seas. He was also fortunate in being able to render assistance to the members of the unfortunate American expedition under Captain Hall and brought to Dundee some twenty five of the Polaris Explorers. (note 9)

NOTES

Note 1) The term 'Fishing' was used to describe both the

activities of catching whales, which the whalers termed 'fish' and sealing in the Arctic waters.

Note 2) Erebus and Terror were the two Royal Naval vessels which had been converted to auxiliary steam power and strengthened to ostensibly seek the North West Passage. The expedition left England in 1852. The wreckage of the vessels has only recently been located. HMS Erebus on September 8th 2014 and of HMS Terror in September 12th 2016.

Note 3) 'Beachy Island' is now spelled 'Beechey'.

Note 4) The seas around the Gulf of Boothia are now accessible throughout the most of the year due to climate change and the North West Passage is now a reality.

Note 5) Esquimaux was the term used in the nineteenth century for what later became Eskimo and now known as Inuit. There was also a Dundee whaler named 'Esquimaux' which was active into the 20th Century. She was built by Stephens in Dundee in 1863.

Note 6) As the Franklin Expedition came to grief in 1855 this would put the age of the Inuit at around fifty to fifty-five years old, quite old for an Inuit at that time but not exceptional.

Note 7) Due to the relative vicinity to the Magnetic North Pole at that time his compasses would have been of little use and the only way Captain Adams was able to fix position was either by ' Shooting the Sun' with a sextant or by navigating by the stars. The latter being nigh impossible in the summer months due to perpetual daylight at these higher latitudes.

Note 8) The Admiral Sir George Nares Expedition to the Arctic was better known as the British Arctic Expedition of 1875-1876 as an attempt to reach the North Pole. Although it failed in its prime objective it enabled a large amount of scientific data to be gathered and charting of the coasts of Ellesmere Island and NW Greenland to be vastly improved.

Note 9) The Polaris Expedition of 1871 was led by Captain Charles Francis Hall and financed by the US Congress. Hall took ill and died a few weeks later on November 8th 1871. The expedition carried on under his friend Capt. Sidney Budington but eventually came to grief by being run ashore near Etah, NW Greenland. The crew sailed south in two of the ships boats before being rescued by Captain Adams.

APPENDIX 3: THE PEARY CARIBOU - ON THE VERGE?

The Peary Caribou (Rangifer taradus pearyi) is the smallest of the caribou sub-species and it range is almost totally confined to the Canadian Arctic Archepeligo. The females weight around 60kg and the males around 110kg. Like the Svalbard Reindeer they have adapted to suit the extreme conditions found in places like Banks Island. Their winter coat is thick and white while their summer coat is short and slate grey in colour. Unlike some of the larger caribou, the Peary do not undertake the large migrations that are normally associated with caribou and reindeer herds. In general their annual migration from summer to winter grazing is confined to around 150 kilometres. With such a limited range this makes the survival of individual groups precarious. They also differ from their larger cousins in the way form herds. Whereas the larger caribou will form herds running into thousands the tiny Peary are found in small groups. In summer the groups will consist of up to a dozen individuals but in winter the groups are much smaller, normally about four.

In 1961 it was estimated that there were around 40,000 Peary Caribou spread throughout the Canadian Arctic Archipelago. By 2009 it was stated that their number had declined to around 700. (The accuracy of the latter figure is somewhat questionable.) Facts that cannot be discounted were that their number had seriously declined and that during that period in time the number of days per annum that experienced above freezing temperatures had significantly increased. These above freezing conditions cause the formation of the ice layers which prevent the animal reaching its food.

The Inuit of Banks Island had always hunted Peary Caribou, but back in late July 2010 they failed to find any.

Even before the hunters set out from Sachs Harbour, an Inuit settlement of approximately a hundred people, they were not over optimistic. One hunter, who had grown up on the island voiced the opinion that the whole venture was "a waste of gas." He was proved right. Despite three days of searching no Peary Caribou were found.

ABOUT THE AUTHOR

Professor Eric Mcvicar

Eric McVicar was brought up in Clydebank in the wake of WW2 and the Clydebank Blitz. Although his father was an engineer in the world famous John Brown's Shipyard his family heritage was rooted in the Scottish Fishing and Whaling Industries of the East Coast. After qualifying as an engineer he spent a few years fishing on Scotland's West Coast before selling his boat and going to work in the Oil Industry. In the late 1980's, while attached to Aberdeen University, he promoted the idea of using redundant rigs as artificial reefs and advised the Thatcher Government on this. In the late 1990's he retired to Ardnamurchan on Scotland's West Coast and entered the field of sustainable ecology, working with the newly established University of the Highlands and Islands.

At this time he was a regular guest lecturer at the Scottish Association for Marine Science, the worlds oldest Marine Institute. His interest in the Arctic, fuelled by tales of elderly relatives in his childhood, led to him travelling extensively in Arctic Norway, Greenland, Canada and Spitsbergen, often lecturing to multi-national audiences. His great love and knowledge of the Arctic and its people led to the publishing of this book.

Printed in Great Britain
by Amazon

49813845R00195